The
SECRET WOMAN

The
SECRET
WOMAN

A Life of Peggy Ashcroft

Preserve me, O my integrity
Since I have diligently preserved thee.
— Plautus

Garry O'Connor

Weidenfeld & Nicolson
LONDON

First published in Great Britain in 1997 by
Weidenfeld & Nicolson

The Orion Publishing Group Ltd
Orion House,
5 Upper Saint Martin's Lane,
London, WC2H 9EA.

A catalogue reference is available
from the British Library

ISBN 0 297 81586 5

Printed in Great Britain by
Butler & Tanner Ltd,
Frome and London

For Angela Fox

CONTENTS

ILLUSTRATIONS

between pages 146 and 147

Peggy and her brother Edward as children, her mother and father[1]
Edward Ashcroft in later years[1]
Elsie Fogerty[2]
Rupert Hart-Davis[3]
Theodore Komisarjevsky[7]
Jeremy Hutchinson[4]
Peggy as Lady Teazle[7]
Peggy by Walter Sickert[6]
J B Priestley[4]
Peggy in the late 1930s[7]
With Laurence Olivier at Birmingham Rep[8]
With Paul Robeson in *Othello*
As Juliet, with Marius Goring
As the Queen in *Richard II* with Gielgud[9]
Michel Saint-Denis, a contemporary caricature
William Buchan[11]
With Burgess Meredith[12]
As Evelyn Holt in *Edward My Son*[12]
With her daughter Eliza, and the Morleys (Robert and Sheridan)
Winning her Ellen Terry Award
As Catherine Sloper in *The Heiress*[12]
As Imogen in *Cymbeline*[13]
As Shen Te in *The Good Woman of Setzuan*
Tony Britton[14]
Mark Dignam[12]
Leonard Woolf[4]
Edward Heath[4]
As Margaret of Anjou in *The Wars of the Roses*[15]
As Mrs Alving in *Rosmersholm*[12]
As Hedda Gabler with George Devine[12]
As Katherine of Aragon in *Henry VIII*[16]

ix

As Katarina in *The Taming of the Shrew* with Peter O'Toole[13]
George ('Dadie') Rylands[17]
With William Douglas-Home and Ralph Richardson
In *Happy Days*[10]
In *She's Been Away*
In *A Passage to India*
Peggy the campaigner[5]

Sources

[1] William Ashcroft
[2] Central School of Speech and Drama
[3] Sir Rupert Hart-Davis
[4] Hulton-Getty
[5] *The Times*
[6] Tate Gallery
[7] Author's collection
[8] Richard Mangan
[9] Houston Rogers
[10] Zoë Dominic
[11] Lord Tweedsmuir
[12] Mander and Mitchenson Theatre Collection
[13] Angus McBean
[14] Camera Press
[15] Shakespeare Centre Library, Stratford-upon-Avon
[16] Shakespeare Centre Library, Stratford-upon-Avon: The Tom Holte Theatre Photographic Collection
[17] King's College, Cambridge

The author and publishers apologise for any misattribution of illustrations and will
be pleased to rectify any copyright omissions in a future edition.

INTRODUCTION

In 1984 Peggy Ashcroft's screen performances as Mrs Moore in David Lean's *A Passage to India* and as Barbie Batchelor in *The Jewel in the Crown* brought her worldwide acclaim. The first won her an Oscar, the second the International TV Movies Festival USA Award. Both roles, those of elderly, lonely women, inspired a deep and lasting affection for her in the public. She had by then been a professional actress on the English stage for nearly sixty years, and, since 1956, just short of her fiftieth birthday when she was created DBE, the unrivalled actress of her generation, the only woman whose career was on a scale to match that of Laurence Olivier or of John Gielgud. The honours showered on her during her lifetime were without parallel. These included at least ten honorary degrees for someone who, to judge from her letters and her conversation, was refreshingly natural and instinctive in all departments of life and art.

Of the same epic dimension as her crowning films and greatest stage performances, notably her ferocious Margaret of Anjou in *The Wars of the Roses*, her famous Juliets and her Cleopatra, her chilling Hedda Gabler, is the full story of her life, which began in Croydon, south London, in 1907. This in time came to demonstrate powerfully an ambitious and shrewd drive. While to all intents and purposes impeccable and exemplary, her life can now be viewed in perspective as much deeper in emotional range and danger than was generally supposed. It mirrored in its suffering, dignity and moral qualities the parts she brought to perfection in her art.

For her own generation, and for all young women who aspired to a career in the theatre Peggy Ashcroft became the epitome of the great actress, for she was one of those rare performers whose power is genuinely creative and rises to genius. In her case, the genius consisted of moulding the parts she played with daring simplicity and directness from the material of her own being. In doing this her standards never faltered. As leader without peer of her profession she influenced virtually every major British actress who came after her, notably Judi Dench, Glenda Jackson, Barbara Jefford, Helen Mirren,

Vanessa Redgrave, Diana Rigg and Janet Suzman. But if for women Peggy epitomized independence and balanced assertiveness, for many male actors she also held the secret of how to deal with the feminine side of the acting personality, the interior, romantic *anima*, and nurture it into expressive life.

As such she became the treasured colleague not only of Anthony Quayle, Alec Guinness and John Gielgud, but of a whole new generation of actors including Ian Holm, Tim Pigott-Smith, and James Fox; of the playwrights Harold Pinter and Stephen Poliakoff; and the directors Peter Hall, Trevor Nunn, John Tydeman, John Barton and Christopher Morahan.

First of all this biography is an exploration of Peggy's personal life, about which she was so reticent during her lifetime. This, and the privacy with which she protected it, was the source of her power, her mystery, her ambivalence. She jealously guarded her inner creative self, offering few glimpses of her problems, or preoccupations, either to her family or to her closest friends. The death of William Ashcroft, her much loved and attractive father, in action in 1918 when she was eleven, was the formative, tragic event in her early life. Without his death she may have never discovered the drive in herself to succeed as she did, nor the way to delve into herself and express emotions that she would never have dared to show, let alone have grasped the means to do so, in real life.

Peggy Ashcroft was married three times: to Rupert Hart-Davis, the publisher; to Theodore Komisarjevsky, the director; and to Jeremy Hutchinson, the criminal barrister and judge. Just to list the names of these distinguished husbands reveals, to begin with, perhaps a naïvety – or should we call it single-mindedness? – in her which ultimately contributed to the break-up of each marriage. One elderly actress who knew Peggy well told me, 'It's very difficult being married to an actress. She never stayed in anything for longer than six months, yet six months is a long time.' There is also the important issue of her much-rumoured promiscuity.

This reputation Peggy had was general. Virtually everyone I interviewed mentioned or alluded to, in some form or other, often without my asking, her many affairs or entanglements with members of the opposite sex. I believe it was always Peggy who, as each episode or passion ended, came off the worse. She suffered in silence, only very rarely confiding her pain, like Viola in *Twelfth Night*:

... she never told her love,
But let concealment, like a worm i' th' bud
Feed on her damask cheek.

The question must be raised as to how much is revealed about the private life of Peggy. As a very private person who successfully evaded any intrusion into, and any discussion of, anything personal, her reticence also became legendary. The older Bloomsburyans she knew, such as Leonard Woolf, had a similar reticence about discussing intimate relationships and especially sexual matters. 'That's the way we were brought up and that's the way we behaved', was their attitude. But just as Lytton Strachey's *Eminent Victorians*, by hitting below its subjects' belts, transformed the public view of biography by being as alive and funny as a novel, so Michael Holroyd's *Lytton Strachey* distinctly changed the ground rules of biography. The climate today is that many people feel very different about being frank on the subject of their private lives, while reticence about the illustrious departed has long been a lost cause.

While I respect the decision of some, Peggy's family in particular and one or two of her closer, later friends, not to talk to me, I do not believe they have the right to object to the exploration of her private life. While I do not wish to make a sermon on the purpose of biography, every writer owes an allegiance to truth: 'For you shall know the truth, and the truth shall set you free'. I share the opinion of Noël Annan, who during the course of our interview on the subject of Peggy expressed the view that, after reaching a certain age, reticence about the past in today's climate was wrong: 'When you are old you should tell the truth as you see it.' Having once been against Holroyd's revelations about Strachey's sexual life, he now full-heartedly supported them.

As well as seeing a good many of her best later performances I met Peggy Ashcroft a number of times and had the good fortune to observe her in the intimate conditions of rehearsal at Stratford-upon-Avon where, just down from Cambridge, I worked on my very first assignment for John Blatchley on *Julius Caesar* and later as Michel Saint-Denis's assistant. From observation I was, even then, always conscious of how she was saving herself, 'waiting to go on', as if her real life took place on the stage. The roles she played became her family, and she would refer to them as such. I interviewed her later in the course of writing books on Ralph Richardson and Laurence

Olivier. At the end of her life I visited her when, having moved from Frognal in Hampstead, she lived alone in a rather remote flat in Belsize Park.

My last meeting with her was in 1989. On this occasion I interviewed her for a Radio 3 programme. She talked about death, about Jacques Copeau and French theatre, with which she was always closely connected. I was struck by her isolation, by a lack of any ordinary sense of domesticity around her. 'Always the juvenile', someone said of her, the 'eternal schoolgirl', and with a curious innocent streak, to the end she retained an astonishingly youthful quality.

This biography is not intended as an exhaustive account of Peggy Ashcroft's career. This has been successfully done by Michael Billington, while there have been several Festschrifts and photographic compilations, the best of which is by Eric Keown, published in 1955. I would refer the reader to these books for further illustrations of Peggy's work. As Dr Johnson wrote, 'The business of a biographer is often to pass slightly over those performances and incidents which produce vulgar greatness, to lead the thoughts into domestic privacies, and display the minute details of daily life.'

PART ONE

INNOCENCE
1907–1953

Who can give law to lovers?
Love is a greater law to itself.

Boethius

ONE

The Early Wound

What deep wounds ever
Closed without a scar?

Byron

Peggy Ashcroft was born in Croydon on 22 December 1907. This was in the days when trams, cabs and carriages were horse-drawn, and they made a clatter and roar possibly greater than the traffic of today. Everyone wore uniforms. Although her father, William Worsley Ashcroft, aged twenty-nine, a land agent who valued expensive properties, had only a modest income of £300 per year, the family had two uniformed servants – a 'cook general' and a nanny. Their house was large and unheated. Her brother Edward was only three and a half years older than Peggy, but they seldom played together. Peggy was by her own account rather a solitary child.

John Gielgud, almost an exact contemporary of Peggy, recalls a London childhood of rich characters and thick fogs: 'Maids wore caps and aprons; messenger-boys, who delivered parcels and whose arrival, with news of accidents or deaths, was always dreaded, had pill-box caps worn on one side with a strap under the chin. Then there was the muffin-man with his big dinner-bell and the tray on his head covered with a green baize cloth, and the knife-grinder with his wheel and treadle. The coalmen had grimy faces under black shiny caps, with broad flaps at the back.'

Dressing and undressing took a long time. Early in her life Peggy, whose mother, Violet Maud Bernheim, was of both German-Jewish and Danish blood, had to wrestle with a formidable set of clothes. Drawers and petticoats, hooks and eyes, corsets, camisoles, hats, veils, muffs, handbags, card-cases and umbrellas. This was just for part of the daytime. 'Teagowns or long dresses with flowing skirts,' wrote Gielgud, 'elbow-length gloves, aigrettes and fans in the evening.' Peggy at once was impatient of such finery and its accessories. She valued the natural, the spontaneous, the informal. She was at heart a girl who found 'tongues in trees, books in the running brooks, sermons in stones, and good in everything'. She saw Croydon as a market town facing the Downs, not as a south-eastern suburb of London with access to the fashionable areas of Chelsea and Mayfair.

They walked a great deal in those days. They read voraciously. They read to one another. Peggy became a great reader, both to herself and to others, and remained so all through her life. She was brought up by the nanny while her mother pursued her passion for the theatre as an amateur actress. Peggy's background was not grandly theatrical, as was Gielgud's with its mixture of sensational personalities both of stage and society, but it had its significant influences no less than his.

The greatest of these was Elsie Fogerty, or 'Fogie', as she was known, a brilliant, inscrutable woman whose influence on the theatre, and in particular on the way actors and actresses spoke on the stage, was lasting. This queen of the spoken word, as she became titled, was just past forty when Peggy was born. She was, like Peggy a south Londoner, born near the Crystal Palace. And like Peggy's mother she became especially orientated towards French-speaking culture, as Peggy was later to become. She and Violet Bernheim met and became friends and Fogie gave Violet private elocution lessons and taught her at Crystal Palace School of Drama.

Fogie encouraged her friend's daughter to take an interest in the theatre. She herself loved Shakespeare in particular. In April 1903 Fogie visited Stratford-upon-Avon, when two brief weeks of plays, staged to mark Shakespeare's birthday, were directed by Frank Benson, who later expanded his work in Stratford to an annual summer festival. Benson was the only English actor ever to be knighted in a theatre, on the stage itself. Fogie described the conditions of seeing Shakespeare in Stratford: '... in the little old theatre – a poky, uncomfortable place. The Avon was a joy in the intervals, but was to invade the dressing-rooms. None of us mourned greatly when that building was burned down in 1926.' They stayed at the Shakespeare Inn and the spring weather was perfect: 'Somehow one got to know everybody, for the visit was a pilgrimage to us all. The Procession and Ceremony of laying wreaths in the Church on 23 April took place then, as now: and there we met Benson – to whom, more than anyone else, we owe the revival of Shakespearian acting in this country.'

In 1906 in the Albert Hall, Kensington, Fogie founded the Central School of Speech and Drama, which was first and foremost aimed at training actors to speak, and set out to avoid extremes of theory or practice. She took over Frank Benson's students, to whom she had been teaching diction, while he became president and examiner. The school was lodged in a theatre over the West Porch of the Albert Hall. Fogie herself refused to take a proper salary and still paid her way by taking private pupils, while the students' fees were very low.

She was an inspired teacher, and if she spotted a glimmer of something she knew she could develop, nothing would stop her, while a pretty face that failed to respond to the first interview, had no hope of entering the school. Laurence Olivier, a pupil in 1923, wrote of Fogie: 'All her working life she preserved exactly the same appearance, that of a forceful, handsome, though smallish woman of about forty. Her past and her present seemed always to be one with her.'

Past and present ... The idyll of pre-war Croydon soon died for Peggy. During the First World War the sleepy town became one of the first targets for the Kaiser's air force, for the largest airfield in England had been built in Croydon prior to the war. Peggy had been taken on walks to view its progress. Zeppelin raids with bombs, and later bombing raids mounted from aircraft, caused nothing like the devastation of the Second World War but did none the less wreak widespread fear and panic. Belgian refugees also settled in Croydon: there was even a Catholic convent staffed entirely by Belgian nuns. One former pupil, two years older than Peggy, later recalled the strange foreignness of her education in suburban London, as well as the terror of the air-raid warnings.

Edward or Teddy, Peggy's brother, was younger than ten when the war began and so he escaped military service altogether. He was cleverer than Peggy, bookish, and all her life she was to look up to him as her intellectual older brother. But her father, now aged thirty-six, joined in the general patriotic fervour in 1915, and enlisted in the Royal Irish Rifles. He left for France in October 1915 and when the Machine Gun Corps was formed in January 1916, he joined the 8th Battalion.

From late 1915 until the final year of the war Peggy's imagination was stretched and coloured by her fear and her love for her threatened father, who came home once a year on leave. He took part in several major campaigns, while his Corps was halved in the costly actions in France and Belgium in which he fought. Peggy would daily, sometimes hourly, dread the arrival of that messenger boy with his pillbox cap worn on one side with a strap under the chin.

And then at last the messenger boy did arrive. William Ashcroft had survived unscathed until 1918. By now Major in the 25th Machine Gun Corps, he had been mentioned in dispatches. With the imminent arrival of American forces in France the Germans made a number of determined counter-offensive attacks in early 1918, only months before the Armistice.

In one of these, possibly either the last Battle of the Somme, or the Ypres attack near the River Lys, Major Ashcroft was killed. The date was 11 April, his age thirty-nine. Both his parents, William and Edith Blanche, were still living. There was no known grave, and no memorial to him. Violet, his wife, was living in the Bernheim family home in Bournemouth. Violet's German-Jewish family name had been modified by her brother to the Birnam of Macbeth's Birnam Wood. Birnam himself held the rank of a Major-General in the British Army.

Perhaps more than a tenuous connection could be drawn between the terrible news of William Ashcroft's death and Peggy's decision three years later, aged fourteen, to become an actress.

Peggy, as a child, could do nothing badly. All through her life and especially into her old age her friends and colleagues have remarked on her youthful quality, and her immediacy and passionate naïvety. But as a girl she impressed continually with her maturity and her determination. At the age of sixteen, while attending Woodford School where she had already acted Portia in *The Merchant of Venice* and Cassius in *Julius Caesar*, her grief over the death of her father made her determined to have her way. Shakespeare captured her imagination, first because of the words, while she had an 'exciting' elocutionist, Gwen Lally, who had been an actress. She had, at any rate, to earn her living, for her mother had only her war pension on which to live. But the headmistress of Woodford School was horrified that she wanted to leave just before taking School Matriculation, although Peggy was by no means an intellectual and she hated studying for exams. The headmistress promised her two roles if she stayed on: Hamlet and head girl. Peggy refused.

The Central School of Speech and Drama by now existed in an odd assortment of nine or ten rooms scattered over three floors of the Albert Hall. Lit by flaring gas jets, the corridors were always dim and malodorous. Students were alarmed by the fact that the swing doors into rooms were painted right across, just like the corridors. Suddenly, from the Great Hall itself, the organ would blast. In the theatre, as ill ventilated as most other parts of the building, the central heating would break out with 'intra-mural rumblings, knockings and hissings' so that by the end of a working day the atmosphere could be appalling. 'Small wonder that tempers flared, temperaments extruded, Fogie's hat – which, like Miss Radmer, she often wore all day – went askew, causing ill-timed mirth...'

The claustrophobia of these circumstances was dispelled once a year when the students were thrown into the aching, echoing void of the empty Albert Hall. They stood in turn on the conductor's rostrum in front of a panel of poets, while Fogie sat in the Royal Box. Each line spoken by a student floated away into the huge emptiness and came back three times.

When Peggy was first in the presence of Fogie she saw her as 'a female Napoleon, very short ... with immense power. A powerful personality.' She carried a bag with lots of things falling out. Fogie dismissed Peggy at their first interview, telling her to stay at school two more years. However, she was persuaded to change her mind by Peggy's mother. Judging from her photograph Violet Ashcroft had a strong personality: with large dark eyes, black hair and sensual mouth she may well have supplied that passionate side of Peggy's nature of which there was little indication in her father. '[Fogie] took a completely personal line because of my mother ... a debt I owed for a long time ... You became one of her children; when I began she would come round and tell you exactly what she thought. She always was a rock; all her life one of the most dedicated people one can imagine.'

The romantic Peggy of later years remembered the school as through a haze of happy memory, although she had reservations about the actual training itself: 'One early autumn,' she wrote, 'in a bygone age, when life and prospects were so fresh at the beginning of a term that the end of a year seemed like the beginning of a new one – two young people entered, separately, the Albert Hall ... Larry (Olivier) aged seventeen and myself sixteen-and-a-half.' Olivier was one of the élite – one of the five male students – she one of 'the herd' of eighty female students. She went on, 'Probably we didn't speak for many weeks – I have no recollection. But he leaves an indelible picture – dark hair standing on end, heavy eyebrows, seeming almost one rather than two, but eyes the same as now and unlike anyone else's.'

Olivier himself had no such vivid recollection of Peggy, for indeed, although attractive, she was not a striking beauty, if anything on the plain side. Her voice, her feeling for words and verse, was of quite a different order. She built myths about the five male students, one of whom was the Greek George Coulouris who was rumoured to keep a knife down his sock. But Olivier predominated in these fantasies. He was at once the born actor: 'The explosive energy, a certain eccentricity of very precise enunciation, the dynamic vigour and the fun were all there.'

Their paths crossed on two occasions. Peggy was impatient that the school never performed whole plays, only scenes, but they won a silver cup in a dialogue competition as Mr and Mrs Inkpen, heavy with jokes about Mr and Mrs Pen and Ink. It was clear to Coulouris that in Fogie's mind Olivier was the star boy, Peggy the star girl. Olivier remembered only a later triumph they shared when they played the trial scene from *The Merchant of Venice*, Larry as Shylock, Peggy as Portia, and won a gold medal (Olivier called it a 'halved' gold medal since each took away a notional half). Peggy said that Larry never received his medal, but hers remained with her all her life. They must have recognized early on that they were of equal weight, competitors rather than collaborators, cultivating for each other a healthy disregard. So Olivier came to find Peggy 'boring, a bit heavy going', while she found him 'a bit of a shit'.

When not working Peggy, like other students, would creep into the Great Hall to hear singers such as Clara Butt rehearse. She even witnessed the young Malcolm Sargent in his shirtsleeves conducting a full orchestra. His diction was impeccable. To some people Peggy much later would seem to have discounted the influence of Fogie over her development as an actress, but she undoubtedly was fascinated by the sound and rhythm of verse. As a girl she had always loved verse, wading through a volume of Browning borrowed from her parents' bedside table. At an early age she learned *The Lady of Shalott*, while her grandfather, with whom she spent much of her later childhood, was a lover of Wordsworth who fervently attended Shakespeare readings, and who gave her Palgrave's *Golden Treasury* when she was eleven. Her feeling for the music of language was not only encouraged by Fogie, but her confidence was built further by her selection as Fogie's star pupil. This confidence-building was an important factor: Fogie did the same both for Edith Evans, whose mouth she first described as looking as though it had been 'battered', and whom she taught that the only way to play a beautiful woman was to feel beautiful, and for Sybil Thorndike, who described how Fogie's personality got hold of her. Not only did Fogie teach her 'how to work through a voice worry – how to save it and increase its power while curing', but she was also, as she said, 'always "held" by a person who pursues an end regardless of human feelings and failings'. Feelings are always relative, and change with time.

TWO

Divided Duty

In their first passions women love the lover;
in the others they love love.

La Rochefoucauld

'What about the man from Boots?' asked a close theatrical colleague
when questioned about Peggy's sexual liaisons in later life. He was
referring to a well-known affair in which Peggy was linked to a local
Hampstead figure. The apparent legion of lovers had quickly grown
to become somewhat of an embarrassment to me when embarking
on this book because there had been nothing in Peggy's early, very
respectable life to suggest this unusual appetite for latter-day affairs.
Yet most of those who talked of her were enthusiastic, indeed
adamant, about her sexual appeal to men. 'When you are close to
Peggy Ashcroft,' recorded the diarist James Lees-Milne when she was
sixty-five, 'she appears beautiful', adding, 'but on the stage plain'.

Generally what made her attractive, it was agreed, was her animation, the changes of expression, her speed and her slowness, the
way she projected her personality through her face, so that you went
back to imagining how she must have been even when she was
advancing in years. For her type of woman possessed 'an incredible
power of seduction'. 'She was like quicksilver, and her moods were
like quicksilver,' Harold Pinter said of her. 'She could be very happy
one moment and very sad the next.' 'You would have thought of her
as a very Kensington lady,' said another friend. 'Yet she supported
all these alternative causes such as the Campaign for Nuclear Dis-
armament, and the Euthanasia Society. She was a rebel inside – and
this was possibly allied to sexual dynamism. She didn't seem the lady
who would – she seemed very conventional.' This was a frequent
admission from those interviewed. Had she been born thirty years
later it would have passed as unremarkable, but Ashcroft's appetite
for affairs, while she seemed an insider, put her on the outside. 'I
could understand how people could go hot for her,' was often voiced.

Here is the first paradox, or contradiction, of her biography. Peggy, for all her seeming coolness, was an extremely English lady with an extremely exotic temperament; she was serious, almost intellectual, yet she hardly ever made an original or unusual statement about anything. Her foreignness, the Danish, German-Jewish element of her background was as much played down as the military part, in the person of her uncle, General Birnam of the British Army. Apparently always in control, her passionate, emotional side was almost ungoverned. As a very tragic actress she always found a sense of the ridiculous. She was a natural-born socialist who was also a naturally born aristocrat, while as an egalitarian she was also very conscious of the status people earned.

The first man that Peggy fell in love with was Rupert Hart-Davis, who later became well-known as a belletrist and publisher. While Hart-Davis, writing in old age of his early passion for Peggy, quotes Max Beerbohm to the effect that theatrical reminiscence is the most awful weapon of old age, he does not refrain from assembling his own formidable battery of memories.

Hart-Davis was an Old Etonian, a relatively well-off young man of twenty-one when he first met Peggy. He was the tall (six foot three inches), wavy-haired, good-looking aristocratic son of a stockbroker with impeccable connections and strong literary leanings. His uncle and aunt were Duff and Diana Cooper and through them he met Hilaire Belloc, J. M. Barrie and Max Beerbohm among many other writers. He loved the theatre and aspired towards becoming an actor, while following an exhausting social round of dinner parties, country-house parties, 'the Derby, the Fourth of June at Eton, theatres (Pirandello's *Six Characters in Search of an Author*, John Van Druten's dramatization of Rebecca West's *Return of the Soldier* in which Mary Clare excelled, the Diaghilev ballet, Paul Robeson singing at Drury Lane)'.

Before meeting Peggy, Hart-Davis had been conducting a desperately fast courtship of Celia Johnson, who was appearing in *A Hundred Years Old* by the Quintero brothers at the Lyric Hammersmith. He visited her at the theatre, wrote her daily letters, escorted her to films. They would take tea together at Gunter's off Park Lane or Rumpelmayers in the Strand; they watched the boat race from A. P. Herbert's garden in Hammersmith. He brought her flowers and books, and they would read together. Celia was 'flattered by his

11

attentions, enjoyed his company but revealed no passion'.

In London Hart-Davis had acted in *The Rumour* by C. K. Munro at the Court Theatre. 'One got to know everybody', in Fogie's words, was perhaps a reflection of how easy it was in those days for a small, élite minority with the chances and the background, to make their way quickly in the theatre. Hart-Davis liked, in his 'mute and wholly inglorious theatrical career', to remember that for a moment he trod the boards with Gielgud and Olivier, as well as Sybil Thorndike. He had been playing small roles in Sunday-night productions in the West End when in May 1929 Nigel Playfair offered him the part of Hastings, Marlow's friend, on a three-week tour of Goldsmith's *She Stoops to Conquer*.

Peggy had, in the meantime, taken on some dozen or so roles in Birmingham and London. She did not deny that the atmosphere was tough, she had to steel herself to get one job after another. There were, she said, 'very few good directors'. Notably, in her first professional role, she had taken over the part of Margaret in J. M. Barrie's *Dear Brutus*, which Muriel Hewitt, who was Ralph Richardson's first wife, had left so as to be able to appear in London. Peggy's reaction to this, as to most questions put to her about acting, was characteristically simple. She felt 'absolutely hopeless' but of course she was 'absolutely fine', as she was in virtually all in which she appeared at this time.

Plays at 'straight' West End theatres, or more arty venues such as the Hampstead Everyman, were devoured with equal relish in her thirst for experience. This was more than gratified. Whether she played Joan Greenleaf in John Drinkwater's *Bird in Hand*, Anastasia in Shaw's one-act *The Fascinating Foundling*, even in *When Adam Delved* by George Paston, or in Strindberg's sombre offering, *Easter*, in which she acted the faithful young betrothed Kristina, it was clear from the other names in the cast – among them Edith Evans, Gwen Ffrangçon-Davies, Colin Keith-Johnston, Angela Baddeley – that she had joined as a promising ingénue, the most talented and active vein of the theatre of her day. In spite of her much-vaunted and professedly innocent qualities, and in spite of people at the time noticing her waif-like, orphaned air – she would make naïve statements such as 'it was very exciting to be someone else' – the hidden, granite solitariness was already, and instinctively, showing itself in her choice of roles and productions. As Peter Hall said of Peggy many years later, 'She had a tremendous nose for talent and a liking for talent as well as a fervent dislike for, and a capacity to detect, bullshit'. She was always 'where the radical thing in the theatre was happening'.

The same Lyric Hammersmith production of *A Hundred Years Old* in which Celia Johnson had appeared, adapted by Harley Granville-Barker and his wife Helen, exposed Peggy to the merciless eye of James Agate, critic for the *Sunday Times*. Agate, however, concentrated wholly on the play's projection of senility, and its easy humour and kindly glow, and ignored her smallish contribution as Eulalia. So had Hart-Davis, intent on his pursuit of Celia, who had a much larger part. Peggy was dismayed Granville-Barker took so small a hand in the direction, while apparently Nigel Playfair – according to Cavan O'Connor, who had a singing role – quarrelled with Granville-Barker. O'Connor recalls drinking cups of tea with Peggy at a café in the Hammersmith Underground station and chatting about their rows.

Hart-Davis claimed he first met Peggy at the opening rehearsal of *She Stoops to Conquer* in Playfair's touring company, noting that he liked her. But he must have met her before, as he drove Celia to and from the Lyric in his Morris two-seater. Two days after the first rehearsal he watched Peggy perform Lucy in *Requital*, a modern tragedy by Molly Kerr set in Rome and Sussex, which Hart-Davis judged ridiculous although he decided that she was the best actress he had ever seen. He at once fell romantically in love with her and declared his passion. He had lost his mother at sixteen just as Peggy had lost her father at eleven. Unlike Celia she responded with similar passion and this redoubled his ardour. Both became in love with the other's image as well as with an idealized view of themselves. Being tall and handsome, steady and aristocratic in manner, Hart-Davis's image was strongly appealing to Peggy. When his own vehicle crashed he hired a four-seater, an unwieldy Wolseley. He also drove her everywhere, as he had Celia. As well as his devoted attentions Peggy was only too happy to accept the chauffeur and the conveyance, although the latter caught fire near Bedford.

As Hart-Davis described it, his courtship of Peggy was an idyll. After the Wolseley he hired a Chrysler for a week at the cost of £20. They shared picnic lunches, explored the Cheddar Gorge, bathed at Clevedon, visited Glastonbury and watched the moon rise over the Mendips. They were always reading poetry together. Later Hart-Davis recalled his love for Peggy as 'chiefly an intellectual and spiritual passion, tied up with poetry and music, drama, youth and spring'. He went out of his way to disclaim any physical basis for it. 'Talked to Peg till 3 am,' ran an entry in his diary at Oxford: 'We love each other.'

They decided, after two days, to marry as soon as possible, a decision on Hart-Davis's part which entailed him informing Celia. Keeping to an old promise, he picked her up from Richmond and drove her to a matinee in Oxford: passing through Maidenhead he 'told her of his change of heart. She was upset.' According to him, she immediately burst into hysterical tears, 'sobbing that she had always loved me'. On arrival in Oxford Hart-Davis found Peter Fleming, his best friend, and got him to take Celia to the matinee and 'put her on the train to London'. He duly did so. Peter, the brother of Ian Fleming, the future inventor of James Bond, later married her.

Retrospective declarations of love from others in autobiographies are highly suspect. Peggy, in her more flat account of their courtship, only reported an 'instant bond ... a very idyllic marriage which was stillborn'. Her brother Edward had got married only the year before to Christine, a friend of hers to whom she had introduced him and whom, much to Peggy's disapproval, he had made pregnant. Her mother, with whom she was very close, died in 1926. She was only fifty-two and had long been suffering from kidney disease. No one had known of this, and she had suddenly collapsed, dying at her home in Bournemouth on 11 August. Both these factors might have had something to do with spurring Peggy into matrimony.

'Too rash, too unadvised, too sudden', is how Juliet's marriage in Romeo and Juliet is described. Oddly enough for someone so staid, so broad, so much in control, Juliet became Peggy's favourite role, although with a performer such as Peggy it is ill-advised to identify any role she played with her persona, for she always, and from a very early age, remained herself, growing with the complexity and challenge of the roles she played rather than becoming them.

The courtship continued to flower through the summer of 1929, when Peggy took Rupert to visit her uncle and guardian in the country, a 'little martinet of a retired brigadier and his delightful wife'. This was General Birnam, identified later by William Buchan, son of the novelist, as a 'tall, solid, soldierly man'. The discrepancy may be accounted for by the fact that Hart-Davis was well over six foot and must have looked down on the General, while Buchan was of average height. Then Hart-Davis left for a holiday on the Continent with Peter Fleming, while Peggy rehearsed for a new play, *Jew Süss* by Ashley Dukes, due to open in London that September. In this she had at last landed a leading role. She and Rupert wrote to each other frequently; her letters are lost, but in his, 'full of love and longing, intermixed with an account of all our doings' – the latter paraphrased in his autobiography – he recounted his adventures with Fleming driving through France and Spain, and then embarking at Cannes for Corsica on the *Emperor Bonaparte*. They bathed five or six times a day, lay in the hot sun and read their books. But Rupert knew of Peggy's impending first night and in Algajola he felt ridiculously nervous 'as evening approached'.

The opening was the pre-London try-out of *Jew Süss* in Blackpool. Peggy had just played the sexy young thing in short skirts in *Bees and Honey* by H. F. Maltby at the Strand Theatre, but in Ashley Dukes's successful adaptation of Lion Feuchtwanger's novel – Dukes claimed he read the book only once – she was cast as Naemi. The sexual victim of the evil Duke of Württemberg, for whom Jew Süss works as treasurer, Naemi is Süss's daughter, and his love for her is the only thing in his life stronger than his love of power. When the Duke finds her hidden away in a castle in a lonely forest, she escapes from him trying to rape her by throwing herself from a window of the keep. The melodramatic tone of the writing hardly seems promising when the Duke first advances on her. 'Why are you trembling?' he asks.

NAEMI: (*crying out*) Oh, father, father! Come to me!

DUKE: ... I only want to tell you you are beautiful! Come, call me by my name, just once...

NAEMI: Who are you? Are you Sammael, the messenger of death?

DUKE: (*as though excited by her resistance*) I know of no Sammael. I am Karl Alexander, Duke of Württemberg, and you must love me. (*brutally*) Are you your father's daughter, and so prudish? Then I must teach you! (*He covers her with kisses.*)

NAEMI: (*writhing in horror*) No—no! (*wrenching herself free*) Father! Father, where are you? Save me! (*She retreats towards the terrace.*)

DUKE: (*stumping after her*) Would you make a fool of me, hey? You shall learn obedience!

NAEMI: (*moving backward towards the battlemented terrace wall*) Save me!
Father, father!

Süss, played by Matheson Lang, whose cousin Cosmo was Arch-
bishop of Canterbury, ultimately moved to powerful grief over Naemi's
death, avenges himself with the death of Württemberg and at the
same time achieves his own ruin. But it seems that what touched
the audience, apart from the lavish spectacle, and Lang's toweringly
melodramatic style and flourish, was the exquisite, simple playing of
Peggy as the sweet shy dark girl, her untouched innocence and her
childish passion for her father. She was drawing, as Charles Morgan
said in *The Times* – he wrote without a byline – 'on an emotion not
directly of theatrical origin'. In other words, on her love for her lost
father.

Out of London *Jew Süss* played to packed houses in Birmingham
and Glasgow. Hart-Davis joined Peggy in Birmingham, where they
stayed in the same hotel. In an early taste of the theatrical gossip
that Peggy so astutely and studiously avoided all her life, a photograph
in London's *Evening Standard* of 19 September – the day of the play's
opening at the Duke of York's Theatre – showed an unusually
glamorous-looking Peggy with short, permed dark hair and glowing,
doe-like eyes below the caption '"Jew Süss" star engaged'. The
accompanying report stated that Hart-Davis had left acting to take
up an appointment with a firm of publishers.

A thirty-hour queue of first-nighters had begun at 2.30 the afternoon before. The critics were generally admiring, while the production
won great favour with the public, who flocked to see it. St John
Ervine, writing in the *Observer*, called Peggy's performance 'the most
attractive of all', acting 'with a proud innocence that was exquisitely
lovely'.

Hart-Davis and Peggy decided to get married on 23 December
1929, during *Jew Süss's* three-day Christmas break and the day after
her twenty-second birthday. The wedding took place at St Saviour's
Church, behind Hans Place in Chelsea. According to Hart-Davis,
Peggy's guardian General Birnam told them, after they had knelt for
the parson's blessing, 'You both need your shoes mending.' On the
wedding certificate Peggy's profession remained an inscrutable blank.
Arnold Haskell, a colleague of Hart-Davis's on the editorial side of

the publishers William Heinemann, lent them an Austin Seven and they spent the first night of their three-day honeymoon at the Park End Hotel in Oxford where they had first declared their love for each other, the second at an inn in the Cotswolds, and the third night with the painter William Nicholson and his family in Wiltshire.

For a virtual orphan of twenty-two from a genteel, but definitely obscure, London suburban home and with a modest background income, the visitors to Mrs Hart-Davis's first home at 213 Piccadilly signalled a definite arrival in a theatrical and social coterie or élite which she never subsequently left. However, one should not underestimate the extent to which the premature death of Peggy's father had impoverished the family. While Peggy and her mother had been very careful, Edward had been something of a spendthrift sustained by small inheritances and uncles who paid his bills. Peggy never had any trouble with, or need for, money. Indeed, one of her greatest attributes was not only an easy disposition for mixing with people of all kinds, but a capacity to attract talented creative people who reciprocated her attention with their own egocentric warmth. Thus, recorded Hart-Davis in his autobiography – with a zealous eye for such matters – the callers at 213 Piccadilly included some fifty or more current or future celebrities of the age. Included in the list were actors John Gielgud, Jack Hawkins, Laurence Olivier, Ralph Richardson, Sybil Thorndike; writers Ian Fleming, Graham Greene, Aldous Huxley, James Lees-Milne, James Stephens. This suggested that the newly-weds may not have had, or wanted to have, all that much time to spend on their own. She was performing *Jew Süss*, he was busy establishing himself as an up-and-coming publisher. Both were so ambitious that there was perhaps little hope or expectation in either of them that the marriage would deepen and that they would find lasting, common ground.

Their fourth-floor flat on the edge of the Circus looked over to the department store, Swan and Edgar, and was lit by advertisements night and day. Prostitutes lived on the floor below, and house agents and a hairdresser's operated from the flats further down in the building. What the other occupants thought of their neighbours' illustrious visitors was never recorded.

The social round, perhaps even more the nightly performance at the Duke of York's, was exhausting and towards the end of the winter Peggy found, in spite of the untaxing role she was playing (Naemi dies halfway through the play), that she was suffering from tonsillitis. She withdrew from the production, which closed in March 1930 after more than two hundred performances – a very good run for a new play at this time.

One of the callers at 213 Piccadilly was the black American Paul Robeson. His reputation as a singer and actor was almost as great in London as it was in New York: his acting in Eugene O'Neill's *The Emperor Jones* in 1925 had established him as a serious actor, while the haunting quality of his bass voice was firmly imprinted on the public's consciousness by his singing of 'Ol' Man River' in the musical *Showboat* two years before Peggy's marriage. She had been to his popular recitals of Negro spirituals, and had many of his records.

Robeson was now setting up a production of *Othello* with himself in the title role, and having with his wife Essie seen Peggy in *Jew Süss* he was determined to have her play the small but significant part of Desdemona. It was when they came out from the theatre that, or so Essie said, the 'argument' began. 'I hope you do not think what I thought.' 'I thought that Peggy Ashcroft ought to play Desdemona,' said Paul. 'That is what I thought, but I hoped you would not see it.'

But first Peggy had to audition, which terrified her because of Desdemona's long willow song: neither then nor later was she able to sing in tune. None the less she was cast as Desdemona.

Robeson, a sincere and courageous man, did much to further the interests of black people. Thirty-three years of age when he met Peggy, he had won a reputation not only as a star performer but as a brilliant football player and lawyer who graduated with distinction from the Columbia University Law School. He was a leader of whom it could be claimed that he was the first all-American black hero.

As soon as Peggy met Robeson she fell under his spell. He was a larger-than-life figure and he appealed to her first because of his engagement with the problems and sufferings of the underprivileged Negro in the United States. He talked to Peggy (and Rupert) about his concerns for his people, so that she found both rehearsals and performances an education in racism. The direction of *Othello* was in the hands of Ellen van Volkenburg, the American ex-wife of the incompetent impresario–actor Maurice Browne, who had cast himself as Iago, a part far beyond his grasp.

Both van Volkenburg and Browne were homosexual. They urged

on Robeson the theory that Iago's evil was a result of his having fallen in love with Othello. According to Essie Robeson, van Volkenburg shouted at Robeson through a megaphone from the back of the stalls, 'Mr Robeson, there are other people on the stage besides yourself!' While at another time, or so commented Essie, she talked of 'parlour junk' and 'could not get actors from one side of the stage to the other. Paul is lost.'

Peggy was horrified at this gratuitous humiliation of Robeson, and decided her director was a racist. While *Othello* was to open at the Savoy Theatre, its star, as a black man, was forbidden entry to the hotel itself. When Peggy and Robeson came to kissing in the play as husband and wife, another racial aspect of the production cropped up. They were, or so Essie said, 'skittish' during rehearsals. Peggy was often asked whether she minded being kissed by a 'coloured' man, which was the euphemism of the day for black, and responded that to her it came as a great 'privilege' to act with a 'great artist' like Paul. He and Peggy, with Sybil Thorndike, who played Emilia, and Max Montesole, as Cassio, had taken to additional rehearsals on their own in their homes.

In the meantime Peggy was growing more and more mesmerized by Robeson. As with her – and at twenty-two she was very unaware of herself – there were two sides to his character. Robeson's wife, Essie, had prepared an artless but genial panegyric to him which was due to be published in London the day after the opening of *Othello*. In it he admitted he had no fatherly instincts towards Pauli, his two-and-a-half-year son, who a few weeks later fell seriously ill with intestinal complaints and had briefly to be taken to hospital. Essie consequently wrote in a letter to Paul: 'The only times you are the least bit interested in him are the rare occasions when you deem it suitable or befitting the artist to mention such prosaic things as children and parenthood.' Robeson, on yet a third occasion, said an artist owed his wider public far more duty than he owed the narrow circle of his family. His infidelities were light-heartedly touched upon. 'She'd never believe I was unfaithful to her, even if the evidence was strong against me,' Essie reported him as saying. Her husband was also, she alleged, insensitive to racial slurs, lazy, and disloyal to his friends.

Hart-Davis, who seemed to have tagged along quite as happily as his wife during rehearsals and became equally caught up in Robeson's irresistible power, recounted a visit the three of them made to Dartington Hall in Devon to stay with Leonard Elmhirst, the founder of the famous progressive school orientated towards liberal culture. One morning he, Peggy and Robeson went for a walk after breakfast and on their return found on the hall table a roneoed sheet to the effect: (1) that Mr and Mrs Hart-Davis and Mr Paul Robeson had arrived and would leave on Monday; (2) that the recuperative power of the soya bean had now been established. Hart-Davis wrote: 'This juxtaposition made us laugh immoderately and Paul rolled on the floor with tears pouring down his cheeks. The vision of this gigantic Negro helpless with laughter on the floor of the great fourteenth-century hall will remain with me always.'

The pair of lovers rehearsed while van Volkenburg gave them idiotic directions such as: 'The trouble is that Act 3 Scene 3 slopes so'. Even then Peggy's need for privacy was so strongly developed that it became the accomplice of her other, deep-rooted need for sexual self-expression. Should she be censured or blamed even if this led her, as one suspects it did, into betrayal, however innocent of this she may have seemed? One can visualize Hart-Davis happily picking up the novels of Thomas Love Peacock, as he reports doing, in the garden while his wife was succumbing to the charms of Robeson, then retrospectively, and stoically, writing off his wife's attachments with grace and humour (and with no inclination to blame at all). But even with the undoubtedly insubstantial and superficial basis of their marriage, by the standards not only of that age Peggy would seem to have allowed her affections to wander unchecked and with little inhibition when it came to acts of infidelity. While it is not known exactly when, she and Robeson became lovers.

Othello opened at the Savoy Theatre in May 1930. First nights are crises that obliterate all other considerations, especially moral ones, but should they do so? For Peggy a production, and especially the rehearsals, were always a period of losing her identity and re-finding it again. She became insecure as at no other time. For Robeson, too, this *Othello* was an especial trial. According to Essie, despite the magnificent time he believed he would be having, he was 'wild with nerves', while her own hair 'went grey in a patch'. Even discounting the exaggeration and hysteria to which Essie was prone, Robeson's emotions and physical presence must by now have been in more senses than one overpowering to Peggy.

The sense of betrayal engendered by her falling in love with Robeson was a long way down her list of priorities. What happened between Paul and herself, she said fifty years after the event, was probably inevitable, while she quoted Shakespeare as a possible justification: 'She lov'd me for the dangers I had pass'd, And I lov'd her that she did pity them'. How could one not fall in love with such a man, Peggy commented, adding, in the cool, circumspect way that became her habit, 'my first lesson in having to distinguish between what is for real and what must be simulated'. The magnificent irony in this statement is that Desdemona's whole *raison d'être* is wifely fidelity.

This ended the marriage of Peggy and Hart-Davis in its inner core although in outward form it remained intact. In 1972 James Lees-Milne, a schoolfriend of Hart-Davis, recorded that after a concert and verse recital in which Peggy took part he sat next to her at supper in a stuffy London dining-room. Peggy, puzzled at her vague recollection of Lees-Milne, repeatedly asked him when and where they had met before. He told her that it was with Rupert Hart-Davis 'before she married him in 1928. It couldn't have been after because they were together only for a fortnight.' Facts themselves shrink or expand, relative to feelings. They were married in December 1929 and they parted in July 1931. But there was something correct in Lees-Milne's assessment of their marriage: as John Gielgud put it, Hart-Davis was 'very good looking: they walked through the fields holding hands and hadn't known what to do'. Later Peggy was to tell another lover that the marriage was not consummated.

Although it dealt a sledge-hammer blow to the continuing but insubstantial pageant of her marriage with Hart-Davis, the affair with Robeson was short-lived. Three months after the first night of *Othello* Essie found a love-letter from Peggy to Paul, and while Peggy had been such a 'lovely girl', so 'simple and appealing', as she wrote in her diary, she now became 'the little Jew bitch – not even married a year, and after somebody else's husband'. Essie's venom knew no limits: she had been aware of Paul's peccadilloes but not of their extent, while she was a jackass if ever there was one. How could she have believed his lies? 'Paul is not any different from any other Nigger man, except that he has a beautiful voice. His personality is built on lies.' When Essie discovered that Robeson had also given Peggy a piece of jewellery she went out and bought herself a far more expensive item, charging it to Robeson.

Peggy was shocked, much later, to hear of Essie's reaction. But why should she have been shocked if she felt other than vindicated? From the start she appeared to be naïvely unaware of the impact of her infidelity on others. Fortunately Hart-Davis seemed impervious and forgiving, so that whatever bitter feelings he had were generously transformed into tribute. He saw *Othello* at least six times during its six-week run and remembered Robeson as gentle, modest, affectionate and full of fun; and, further, 'one of the only four people who always call me Rupe'. Again the similarities with the play he was watching invite recall, and perhaps even more with Hamlet: '... that one may smile, and smile, and be a villain'.

The Moor being played by a black actor provoked much comment both in the press and among the public. The production was ungainly and bizarre, with enormous pluses as well as minuses. The direction was abysmal; Ralph Richardson, playing Roderigo, planted an electric torch up his sleeve in order to find his way on the underlit stage. Robeson had no experience of speaking blank verse, or wearing padded Elizabethan costume, which ill-suited him. Most of all he clearly could not rise to the heights of poetic declamation. The text was also dismally handled by the rest of the cast, with the exception of Richardson, Ashcroft and Thorndike. Maurice Browne as Iago had a motive which was reduced from the phantom that it is, 'to the shadow of a phantom', while this 'incommensurate gnat' trotted through the play 'like Jack Point in a temper'. Robeson's obvious nervousness on the first night, when he started off with his performance 'pitched higher than I wanted it to be', calmed down during the play so that he was able to relax into an impressive rage. When he threw himself on the floor in apoplexy it was, wrote the *Daily Express* critic, 'a real fall. His jealousy was terrible to see. I have not seen such rages on the stage since Grasso, the Sicilian, acted the same part to the horror of Beerbohm Tree.'

On the first night there were, to the consternation of some, as well as the Duff Cooper set and many famous players and writers, 'coloured' people dotted about the audience. One unnamed newspaper editor walked out, or so Hannen Swaffer in the *Daily Express* reported. There was much tittle-tattle about a black actor kissing a white woman: should it be allowed? The press bombardment about how the public would take to seeing them make love on stage made Robeson feel infirm in purpose. Later he recalled how every time he played a scene with Desdemona during the first fortnight of the run, 'that girl couldn't get near to me' as he was 'backin'' away from her all the time. I was like a plantation hand in the parlour, that clumsy.'

Peggy herself found the kissing – with an ambiguity of which she was perhaps unaware 'more than a theatrical experience, it put the significance of race straight in front of me, and made my choice of where I stood'.

While Ashcroft did not perhaps especially shine as Desdemona, Ivor Brown's theory and affected metaphor for her performance had a stronger erotic undercurrent than could have been intended at first sight. 'A true woman,' wrote Brown in the *Observer*, 'opening the petals of her wonder and her love to the African sunlight of her hero's triumphs.' Petals?

While James Agate commented in the *Sunday Times* that Robeson's performance had quite amazingly the quality of its defects, Robeson himself afterwards judged the experience to have been a liberating one, for playing the part had taken from him 'all kinds of fears, all sense of limitation, and all racial prejudice'. But Agnes Grant, the elderly aunt of critic Wendy Trewin, told her, 'I don't think Miss Ashcroft should have allowed herself to be handled or touched by a black man.' Goodness knows what Agnes would have thought had she known what had been happening off-stage between Othello and his Desdemona.

THREE

The Great Ambition of Woman

If you could see my legs when I take my boots off,
you'd form the idea of what unrequited affection is.

Charles Dickens

Peggy's next, most unlikely, entanglement was with the 'rebel tyke' from Bradford. Meanwhile the rest of 1930 and the first half of 1931 became a desultory, downward-spiralling period for Peggy, not only in her life but also in her work. Indefatigable diary recorder of plays witnessed and people met, Hart-Davis, drawing on these diaries for his memoir *The Power of Chance*, often projects sound judgment – sometimes ahead of his time, as when he reads Shaw's *Arms and the Man* and pronounces it, and Shaw, grossly overrated: 'always so bloody pleased with himself'. His firm, William Heinemann, American owned after the death of its founder in 1920, published the work of J. B. Priestley, whose success with *The Good Companions* had raised him to the position of the pre-eminent literary lion. Hart-Davis, his natural habitat having become that of literary lions, overheard his managing director, Charles Evans, helping the eminent philosopher George Moore, aged seventy-nine, down the firm's staircase.

> MOORE: Tell me about *The Good Companions*. It is not a very good book, people tell me.
> EVANS: Not a good book! We've already sold a hundred and fifty thousand copies.

After the short run of *Othello* Peggy appeared in six new plays before returning to Shakespeare in *Romeo and Juliet* in early 1932. In February 1931, while she was acting in Somerset Maugham's *The Breadwinner*, about a frustrated husband walking out on his wife and children, the predatory family which has sucked him dry and from which he must escape, she and Hart-Davis attended a party to celebrate Priestley's first visit to America. Maugham's play had a generally coarse and mysogynist tone. The critics, when it opened at the end of the previous September, had had mixed feelings, for while Peggy, according to the *Times* critic, was made to say things of 'fantastic callousness', her handling of a contrasting passage of great tenderness had raised the level of the whole piece. Hannen Swaffer in the *Sunday Express* roundly condemned a remark about street-walking 'put into the lips of Peggy Ashcroft, who blushed while she said it', but this was excised by the author on the second night.* Agate found *The Breadwinner* uneven and cheaply cynical.

Yet it made money. Maugham, after Shaw, was the richest author in England. Priestley, too, was making money, and at his party he was observed talking fervently to Peggy. Unbeknown to Hart-Davis his private life was also in a mess, his marriage soon to be tottering on the brink of dissolution. Although Hart-Davis noted that he was 'in wonderful form', Priestley later admitted that he was bored and lonely as hell, thinking of work and plans all the time because there was nothing else to do.

Peggy attracted him deeply. Priestley aged thirty-eight, five years older than Robeson, was at the height of his fame and his power. Forceful and strong, his heavy build made him appear solid and reassuring to women. One of his admirers described how he would take you out to lunch and talk about your problems. 'His body alone gave you reassurance ...' and there was a 'glorious commonsense to it all'. Women would feel that he was 'a kind of rock in the swirling uncertainties of life'.

Peggy, too, had a glorious common sense. But she was muddled. Hart-Davis, although he moved continually among those with rock-like reputations (the rocks themselves on closer inspection often turned out to be shifting sand), was himself no rock. Younger than those on whom he waited, more often than not he was passing round the drinks, yet astutely observing what was going on. He had allowed Maurice Browne to give Peggy an iniquitous contract by which she received sixteen pounds a week for her six weeks of Desdemona, while for the following two and a half years half of everything further she earned was to go to Browne. When she played the lovely

* The line ran 'Don't you know that since the war amateurs have entirely driven the professionals out of business? No girl can make a decent living now by prostitution.'

miniature of a novice in Edgar Wallace's adaptation of Götz's *Charles the Third* in early 1931, Wallace had intervened to cancel the contract with Browne. But neither his play, nor the over-ornate richness of James Elroy Flecker's *Hassan* in an Oxford University Dramatic Society production, nor a Dutch play by Jan Fabricius, nor *Sea Fever* by Marcel Pagnol, in spite of the most lavish West End treatment, halted her run of bad luck. Three West End failures in a row plus the Oxford *Hassan*, signalled that she must be in the wrong theatrical set. She hungered for a more solid tradition, for work of a different stature.

Priestley, Wallace, Max Beerbohm, Walter de la Mare ... the list of those visited, or invited by the young couple, continued to be heady. Wallace, when they were on a weekend trip to his house by the Thames at Bourne End, objected violently to the new panatrope, or gramophone, playing the national anthem before the curtain rose on his play and insisted on a live orchestra. In the meantime Hart-Davis left Heinemann, while Priestley promised to look out a new job for him. There was perhaps an unseen motive for this generosity.

Priestley had just found out that Jane, his wife,* had fallen in love with 'Jimmy' – whom it has been impossible to identify – who in turn was in love with her and had long been her devoted admirer. Self-pityingly, Priestley complained to Jane he had had nothing as good in his own life. He had, he said, been just a heavy, stupidish man in his wife's eyes, while he had been nothing to any other woman, and indeed had existed without an hour or two's intimate talk with another woman for years.

A couple of nights after Peggy's Dutch failure, *A Knight Passed By*, at the Ambassadors Theatre, she did find some of the inspiration in the theatre which she was now seeking. This was by attending a production of André Obey's *Noé* or *Noah*, presented in French by the Compagnie des Quinze and directed by Michel Saint-Denis. Saint-Denis was a year younger than Priestley and he, too, was destined in time to become Peggy's lover.

In the prevalent money-mad and cynical West End theatre the purity, style and dedication of Saint-Denis's company made a strong impact on Peggy with her starved aspiration for a more sublime form of theatre than that to which she had access.

---

* Jane Bannerman, divorced wife of Bevan Wyndham Lewis, married Priestley in 1926. His first wife, Pat Tempest, had died of cancer in 1925.

Noah and Saint-Denis's company owed much to Jacques Copeau, Saint-Denis's uncle. It was primarily sacred drama, going back to the well-spring of dramatic art in religious and biblical mythology, and to primitive animalism as well as stylish expressionism. John Gielgud was enormously impressed by this remarkable production. *Noé*, he wrote, was simply the story of Noah and the Ark, 'written and presented in an extremely endearing and stylized way with the animals portrayed by actors in beautifully modelled masks with the effects and sounds done by the Company'. Hart-Davis noted how, all through the play, Noah talked to God, and when the Ark had safely landed he looked up and cried '*Seigneur, es tu content?*' while as the curtain slowly fell 'a rainbow appeared in the sky'.

Two nights later he and Peggy went to see Obey's *Viol de Lucrèce* and loved this equally. Peggy was especially struck by the ensemble playing, in which everything was to a 'pattern, all orchestrated and timed to perfection. One mood holds them all. They seem unable to make a mistake.' At the interval they visited Jack Priestley in his box where he sat gloomily with Jane.

Little did Peggy know that Priestley, with his potato face, his gruff manner and brooding personality, was himself inwardly fuelling for her a romantic passion soon about to explode.

Yet Peggy must have had at this time a larger sense that all the world was in love with her. She had simply no rivals in the theatre. The night between their two visits to see the Saint-Denis productions Paul Robeson visited Peggy and Hart-Davis: he sang for them Mozart, Schubert, Quilter and Russian songs. 'Lovely,' commented Hart-Davis.

The irresistible pull of older, seemingly more stable, more worldly-wise men, perhaps for the obvious reason that she had lost her own father so early, drove Peggy into the arms of these 'mature' famous figures that pursued her. First Robeson, then Priestley, then the painter Walter Sickert, then Theodore Komisarjevsky the exiled Russian film director, then Saint-Denis . . . these were her significant lovers during the years before the Second World War. On the eve of war she reverted back to the pattern of her marriage to Rupert Hart-Davis by marrying a very English and, for her, conventional Establishment figure, the barrister Jeremy Hutchinson. But there were other lovers, too. Mark Dignam, later a distinguished Shakespearian actor, who played with her in 1935 in Glasgow when just an understudy, was one. This relationship, like many others an on–off affair, was resumed in the 1950s. Ralph Michael the actor was another of Peggy's lovers.

With Priestley, Peggy appeared to dilly-dally, half tempted, half repelled. Afterwards she would call him 'Mr Beastly', and shudder at his pursuit. During their affair, which was consummated but did not continue long, the smitten Yorkshireman (sometimes to be seen dressed in his one-piece zipper suit*), had, after seeing Peggy at the *Viol de Lucrèce*, departed with Gerald Bullett, the editor and writer, to collaborate on a novel, a fantasy called *I'll Tell You Everything*. They stayed at an inn in Broadway, Worcestershire. Priestley tried to work hard and eagerly. But he was tired out, although he stuck at the work by sheer drive. He could not sleep, wishing he had brought some adonal with him. He tried hot drinks, 'some bromide stuff' from the chemist, but all the time his mind fastened obsessionally on Peggy. She appeared to offer an escape from his hellish marriage.

One evening, on a weekend visit back to London, he went round to the Piccadilly flat and found Peggy by herself. He told her he loved her and asked her to go away with him. She at once rejected him, but he was forceful and the power of his personality could be overwhelming, according to his biographer Vincent Brome, 'once he had committed himself emotionally'. In spite of her refusal he told Jane he had fallen in love with Peggy, so the tensions in their house once again reached breaking-point.

Jane was mortified by her husband's cruelty, for he was determined to leave home and pursue Peggy. Where he followed her to is not clear, nor exactly what happened next, but as a consequence of his departure Jane fell ill and told Jack that she was dying. According to Jane, in an undated letter she wrote to Edward Davison in the summer of 1931, she telephoned Hart-Davis who knew about Peggy and Priestley, and was terribly unhappy about their liaison. When Jane and Hart-Davis subsequently met, he disclosed that Jack and Peggy were still seeing each other. Although Peggy was to claim that it was Jack who pursued her, later she admitted 'the infatuation was mutual', and that she gave in to him.

Jane and Hart-Davis agreed that they would divorce their respective

---

* An admirer said Priestley at this time 'lived' in his zipper suit. It seems unlikely.

partners if what seemed a mad infatuation turned into a serious love-affair. 'Rupert agreed that there must be no shilly-shallying,' Jane told her correspondent. Jane then met Peggy, who told her of Jack's violent infatuation with her, but that she did not know 'how she felt about it'. Peggy would seem at this moment to have been honest to the point of causing pain.

The affair then seemed to freeze. By now Priestley was deeply unhappy, too, unable to work, and constantly falling into depressions. Hugh Walpole, who chaperoned him away from Peggy on a visit to the Malvern Festival, told Jane that he wanted a temporary separation from Peggy, had stopped seeing her, and could only resolve his torment by coming home.

Priestley did not, in fact, want divorce or separation. He and Jane then had a sexual reconciliation which resulted in her becoming pregnant. But his passion for Peggy lingered on, unresolved. Why she did nothing to stop it is a mystery which seemed to bespeak an inner unkindness and disregard of feelings other than her own.

Again Priestley went away. In September he stayed in Keswick with Hugh Walpole nearby. He wrote to A. D. Peters, his literary agent, that he was the better for being away, losing his nervy feeling and fits of depression, was now sleeping quite well, and had written ten thousand words – a fairly difficult chapter – of his novel during the previous week. He had not heard from Jane, but he thought the news of the baby was doubtful 'as her doctor said she would never have another'.

He could not decide whether to press for a divorce or not. A divorce was easy, yet so was complete reconciliation, or so he thought. But anything between those two extremes needed co-operation with Jane. He did not want a divorce himself ('Unnecessary, a lot of fuss, and might be bad for the children'), but he felt it best for the time being that they had a not too obvious separation.

What a lot of heartache the slim, 23-year-old Peggy was causing the dithering literary giant. She had recently been described in *Sea Fever* as flowering the play 'with fragrant gentility, she was a middle-class violet who might have been the darling of an English tennis club'. After this failure she had rehearsed and opened in the provincial pre-London tour of a Spanish play, *Take Two From One*, by the Sierra brothers. In his next letter to Peters, Priestley states that he has not heard from Peggy since the first night, 'which suggests to me she's down in the mouth about it. It'll be the fourth flop* in succession she will have been in, if this does flop, and it's a damn shame, because she's getting a durned nice reputation. Hugh [Walpole] was saying the other day that everywhere he heard people talk of Diana Wynyard and Peggy as the two most promising of all the young actresses. I shall have to hurry up and write Peggy a play myself.'

Priestley further tells Peters that his future plans – to stay in the north – might be modified 'because of P ...' He believed he would settle in Brighton for a few months, taking a small flat. It seemed he may still have had hopes that Peggy would join him in Brighton.

In fact Priestley did write the play he had mentioned to his agent. It was called *The Roundabout*, and while he said the reactions from Peggy and Diana Wynyard were enthusiastic, no one else thought highly of it, so he put it to one side. He did move to Brighton, and while his domestic situation remained unsettled, it seemed, by November 1931, that he had not seen much more of Peggy and may even have broken with her.

'Bored and lonely as hell': Priestley was not only at the peak of his fame as an author during this highly emotional episode with Peggy; he was making more money than ever before – from *The Good Companions*, the theatrical version of which was on tour with Gielgud. He was also threatening the security of his children, creating potential new havoc by leaving it to Jane and to Peggy to sort out the mess and tell him what to do, accusing Jane at the point of leaving him of being 'frozen in a romantic attitude', and even writing to A. D. Peters asking him to find a solution which was acceptable to Jane.

Strangely enough, Priestley had continued talking to friends such as Gerald Bullett, his collaborator on *I'll Tell You Everything*, as if he intended to marry Peggy. Jane treated him like a defiant child whose self-indulgence made him ill. Yet she had tolerated his impetuous return and its result.

Tom Priestley was born in April 1932 and by the summer Jack was back with Jane, licking his wounds over what the involvement with Ashcroft had cost him in loss of royalties. *The Roundabout* was

---

* Peggy had also just appeared in a costume play, *A Knight Passed By* by Jan Fabricius: 'to see her in crinoline and pantalettes, sparkling with comedy and diamonds, and to hear her, grave and beautiful, give romance wings, is to grieve for the pretences, the reserves, the ingenuities, however pretty, that have been imposed upon her.' *The Times*, 8 June 1931.

scrapped for ever. Peggy went off to Ireland for the first time, staying with the playwright John Perry at Woodruff, his house in County Tipperary. She went fox-hunting and suffered a bad fall, but still went on hunting. She and her dog, Joey, then visited the novelist Molly Keane and her husband.

The pain of his passion left Priestley with a rosy, almost self-satisfied glow. In 1948, by which time he had fallen in love with Jacquetta Hawkes while still married to Jane, Priestley wrote to Jacquetta of a further meeting with Peggy when she had been unexpectedly thrown into his company: 'Yesterday's award business was very fatuous ... Peggy Ashcroft was the actress of the year and I found myself sitting next to her at lunch, regarding her amiably and thinking of you all the time. I feel now – what I ought to have felt before, I suppose – that you are giving me something, not only when we are together (I always felt it then) but when we are apart, the thought of you being refreshing, heartening, creative.'

Writing much later, in September 1975, of seven players who had given him 'particular pleasure', Priestley said he had seen Ashcroft in most of her roles in the 1930s, forties and fifties, and must 'make an important point very carefully. If I declare Dame Peggy is a little great actress, I shall be angrily accused of contradicting myself or attempting to insult her. But the "little" here is not pejorative.'

Not pejorative? Priestley went on, in what seemed something of a back-handed compliment, perhaps with the desire to compensate for his own painful experience with Peggy and because he was not someone to forgive a rejection, 'She tends towards contraction ... the leading actress who knows how to make use of a diminishing glass. What we see through it, in turn, on the night is usually extraordinary and memorable, a character brought to life.'

Mentioning his own intimate connection with Peggy in the early 1930s, Priestley became more generous: 'Since she played those exquisite girls in the early Thirties, she has of course acquired a tremendous technique, partly by taking thought, partly by experience enlarging instinct ... on the stage she is anybody she chooses to be.'

Peggy had a long way to go before reaching the stage described by her former lover Priestley. But there would seem to have been a very deliberate, even cold, person inside her, even in her early twenties sometimes deliberately seeking the enlarging experience. She was not to become emotionally involved with a writer again until she met Harold Pinter in the late 1960s and performed in two of his plays. By this time she was in the more secure position of an older woman with a much younger man. Her tangle with Priestley's muddle, his weakness and egocentricity, had sounded warning bells that she took very much to heart.

By now Peggy had found a new and very different lover: a Venetian-born Muscovite who, while showing the same extreme emotions and persistency as Priestley, was about as far from the dour Yorkshireman as it was possible to imagine.

FOUR

A New Contender

Marriage has many pains, but
Celibacy has no pleasure.

Dr Johnson

Not long before her death, Peggy stood impassively listening to a description of her second husband without registering any emotion, or referring to him afterwards at all. To Janet Suzman, who observed her, this – at least outward – dismissal came as somewhat of a shock and a surprise.

But Theodore Komisarjevsky's influence on the career and the being of Peggy Ashcroft must not be underestimated, nor must the colourful, larger-than-life size of this amazing character be dismissed as lightweight. 'Komis', as he was known, had an enormous impact on Peggy. As such he is worth much more than a thumbnail sketch.

Komisarjevsky was one year short of fifty when he first met Peggy. He was small and looked like a tonsured monk, but he had a mischievous smile. He was also subject to terrible rages. Born in Venice, he was the son of an actor who told him he had the choice of two things: 'Rich meals in the company of gluttons, or, as a result of sincere work, which will raise against you a host of opportunists who thrive in the stagnation of the theatrical quagmire, a solitude in which you will often go hungry, and a road which will lead along the path of unhappiness. If you feel unable to make the sacrifice you must leave the stage, or make up your mind to join the servants of Mammon.'

Komisarjevsky did not compromise. He had been born into one of Russia's most distinguished theatrical families. His sister, the actress Vera Komisarjevsky, played Nina in the first production of Chekhov's *The Seagull*, and founded her own theatre in 1904 where she invited Meyerhold to direct. Theodore, known at first as Komisarjevksy's brother, had no desire to become a stage celebrity. Although he worked for his sister, supervising the artistic side, he found theatre

33

work no more exciting than any other. 'I loved life itself,' he wrote in his autobiography, characteristically called *Myself and the Theatre*, published in London in 1929: 'That love for life gave me the energy for work and relief from it, and made it possible for me to see that which was false and poor and stale in my own work as well as in the work of others.'

He compared his sister's death, in 1910, to that of Eleonora Duse who died alone in the blackest and ugliest town in the world, Pittsburgh, USA: 'hell with one lid off'. Vera collapsed in Tashkent from smallpox having played, on the final night of her career, Rosie in Sudermann's *Battle of Butterflies*. Night after night she had acted with high temperatures until, after making her final exit, she 'fell prostrate in the wings ... she was taken to her hotel, totally unable to make the slightest movement, as her skin was coming away in large flakes from her fragile body.'

Vera's ideas on the theatre impressed her brother strongly. Although leading her company she never regarded herself as a 'star-actress', separate from the rest of the production, nor could she bear to act 'in a Theatre, the ideas of which had become alien to her'. Most of all, for her brother, she had 'a soul, which was the most beautiful and sensitive instrument imaginable'.

From 1910 onwards Komisarjevsky worked in imperial theatres and in his own studio theatre which survived the Revolution because of his dedication to art and non-commercial ideals. He had once encountered the last Tsar, Nicholas II, who on the outbreak of the Revolution in 1917 was trying to reach St Petersburg from the front. This was at a railway junction where workers had pulled up the track, so he was diverted and was waiting for another train. Komisarjevsky approached the Tsar: 'a small man in trench coat and grey astrakhan cossack cap at the far end of the empty platform'. Did he speak to him? No. 'We looked at him and he looked at us and a moment later he crossed the line to his train.' Later he was told by the stationmaster that the Tsar was drunk.

But with the success of the Revolution the working conditions in Moscow's theatres grew worse and worse, while living became hell. When they first met, Komisarjevsky would regale Peggy with almost unbelievable tales of dedication and hardship. There was no fuel for heating. Instead of tea, people drank a liquid of grilled carrot. Travelling on trains – and there were no taxis – was little better than suicide as the passengers were swarming with lice, carriers of typhus germs. Even so Komisarjevsky directed ten plays during the winter of 1918–9, having some months earlier been elected managing director and producer of the Moscow Grand State Theatre of Opera and Ballet. He never went to bed before five in the morning, and had to run from one institution to another across the enormous city, obtaining food, lodgings, travelling permits for his actors and stage-hands, even stockings for the wife of one actor and milk for the new-born baby of another. He had to join in filling and lighting the boilers in the basements, and even then iced condensation blurred the mirrors in the foyer where the pupils of his school danced bare-legged and bare-armed. The singers' breath during performances was visible 'in such clouds of vapour that they called themselves Samovars'.

One day a pianist playing in knitted gloves in the concert hall of the former Club of the Nobility had to stop as one of his fingers had frozen. Komis told of a violinist who fell off his chair because he had not eaten for days; of the women's opera choir, representing nymphs, dressed in snow boots; of an actress of his company dying of typhus alone in a freezing room, not once having mentioned she was ill; of a scenery designer arrested and shot one night by the Cheka, or secret police; of O. O. Sadovskaya, one of Russia's greatest character actresses, 'who died of vermin'.

After a terrible attack of nerves and what he called a mild form of 'mania persecutionis', Komisarjevsky left Moscow to travel to Italy. But Serge Diaghilev, the impresario, advised him to go instead to London, where he arrived two months later with ten shillings left in his pocket.

To begin with he took on quite humble productions, and established his reputation among the serious and dedicated in the theatre. In 1926 Philip Ridgeway, the impresario, 'a big coarse philistine from somewhere in the north of England', gave Komisarjevsky an oppor-tunity to direct some Russian plays at Barnes in south-west London, just over the river, in what had formerly been a cinema. Gielgud, then only twenty-two years old, had been persuaded to appear as Baron Tusenbach in the first production in English of Chekhov's *Three Sisters*, a part which Komisarjevsky persuaded him to play as a handsome young man although Chekhov called him 'ugly' in the text. Komisarjevsky's reason was that 'the English public must have a romantic hero'. It was, said Gielgud, 'a beautiful production, very simply done and with a number of very good actors in it'. This became the beginning of Komisarjevsky's success. While smart people flocked from the West End to see this production, the actors were paid £1 a week, and had to dress together in one room.

Komisarjevsky made hard work in the theatre his religion. In his next play, Andreyev's *Katerina*, Gielgud played a jealous husband of fifty whose wife dances almost naked in front of him at a party and drives off with the artist who is giving the party. On the first night Komisarjevsky and his stage manager, both almost fainting from exhaustion, had to set up the scenery and change it themselves. The sets were, said Gielgud, 'wonderfully inventive and he lit them beautifully. He really was a man of remarkable all-round talents.' During his production of *Ivanov* the set collapsed during the interval while the carpenters were putting it up, and if Komirsarjevsky had not had the strength 'to hold a couple of flats on my head and in my hand, they would have fallen into the auditorium and might have killed a couple of the spectators'.

Gielgud also praised Komisarjevsky's wonderful sense of grouping and movement. But he could be extremely 'perverse and unpredictable. Money did not seem to interest him very much, however, and he often agreed to work quite cheaply.' One of his most extravagant and bizarre productions was the first English staging of Ibsen's historical epic, *The Pretenders*, for the Welsh National Festival at Holyhead. His actors, who were teachers, parsons, clerks, postmen and miners, worked during the week and rehearsed after tea on Saturdays.

'Although the partition was blown down on the first night it was put up,' Komisarjevsky said, 'and there was no proper stage – Lord Howard de Walden had to be stage manager besides directing the music off-stage, beating the drums, and turning the wind machines – the sincerity and power of the actors were such that the applause lasted so long that we thought the audience would not leave unless we gave the whole play over again.'

But the irony of Peggy's first professional encounter with Komisarjevsky was that it was not in either Ibsen or Chekhov, as it should have been, but in the Spanish play *Take Two From One*, staged at the Haymarket Theatre and unashamedly a vehicle for Gertrude Lawrence. This farce, rehearsed swiftly on the heels of the debacle of that other, real-life farce with Priestley, was a headache for Peggy who complained later that Komis had 'torn her' apart at rehearsals. Yet after the play opened he told her she was very good. His unpredictability, and perhaps mischievousness, had presumably rammed home at once. He explained to Peggy that he had criticized her so much because he wanted to concentrate on her and 'wash his hands' of the stars, Gertrude Lawrence and Nicholas Hannen.

In the reviews one critic described her as 'unimpeachably insipid throughout, as presumably she was intended to be', and another commented that before 'she has had a chance to show her very great talents ... Miss Lawrence in savage attire and a general atmosphere of whirlwind "gives" poor Miss Ashcroft ... nothing left to do but to dissolve in tears'.

Gielgud said later that Komisarjevsky, whose nickname backstage became 'Come-and-seduce-me', had other mistresses at this time, and made Peggy's life hell, so he was 'amazed when they got married'. Indeed, not only this but all three of Peggy's marriages caused, at least in some circles, great surprise. But Peggy must have found in Komis not only an inspiring mentor, an answer to some side of herself she most wanted to develop. He also created in her, as had Priestley and Robeson, the excitement, the tension of love, either of being intensely loved, or of loving intensely. Either way a sense of drama around, or in, herself on which she thrived by continually mounting it or rising above it.

Yet it remains, as Gielgud commented, an unsolved mystery why they should have married. At the time of their first meeting Komisarjevsky was, or had already been, married – to Elena Alkopian and he had a son, Vadim, known as 'Jim', who was born in England around 1921. Vadim was a British subject, while after Elena Alkopian was divorced from Komisarjevsky she remarried and became Elena Balieva. Little is known of her otherwise except that she died in New York in 1981. Komisarjevsky mentions neither her nor his son in *Myself and the Theatre*.

In 1932 Peggy's involvement with Komisarjevsky deepened. Leaving Hart-Davis in Piccadilly Circus, she and Komisarjevsky moved into a flat together in Berkeley Gardens, Campden Hill. But not before she had scored a much-needed personal triumph as Juliet in *Romeo and Juliet* at Oxford.

John Gielgud, still acting in Priestley's *The Good Companions*, was in February 1932 persuaded by George Devine, then president of the

Oxford University Dramatic Society, to direct his first play, *Romeo and Juliet*, for Gielgud the perfect vehicle. This was the first time Peggy worked with him and they became friends. Gielgud employed the trio of professional designers known as the Motleys, one of whom, Margaret Harris, at the age of over ninety recalled Peggy as an emotional person: 'She could be moody. She was always to some extent in love with somebody.'

Gielgud believed Peggy had affairs with both George Devine* and Michel Saint-Denis. How she fitted them in and whether her affairs with several men ran together concurrently over a short or long period we shall never know. In this period the most exciting new directors became her inspiration, however, and continued to be so on and off until she married her third husband, Jeremy Hutchinson, in 1940 and for once in her life attempted to break away from the bohemian sexual mores of the theatre. As Margaret Harris succinctly expressed it – volunteering the answer to a question which I out of discretion never actually put to her, 'Peggy was promiscuous, but it was always with an open spirit. She always loved the people' (i.e., men).

It was a small family which formed the theatrical avant-garde of its time, and presumably the sexual incestuousness of some of its members did not much bother the others who did not consider it their business. The issue at stake was what Margaret Harris meant by love in the sense that she used it in terms of the real Peggy Ashcroft. Was Peggy someone with an insatiable sexual desire, like Cleopatra, the character she later came to play triumphantly at Stratford? Did her appetite border on nymphomania, as some said it did? Was she genuinely in love with all the men she slept with, temporarily infatuated, or could she simply not say no?

The fascinating contradiction, or paradox, at the centre of all these tangled affairs and her several, unlikely marriages is that Juliet should become her favourite part and remain so all through her life, so that

---

* Years before, wrote Anthony Quayle, Devine had been president of OUDS, 'an influential though slightly inflated office while it lasts; when over, one that leaves the high-flying balloon to make its own painful descent to earth ... he had persuaded John Gielgud to go there and direct PA in *Romeo and Juliet*.' Quayle further described Devine as 'portly', his voice 'harsh', while his face was 'verging on the sallow; his eyes, without his glasses, had an unfocused look; for all his virtues both as a man and as an actor he was not an heroic figure.' (*A Time to Speak*, p. 117.)

whenever she was asked which this part was, her unexpected answer would be the thirteen-year-old Veronese. Perhaps it was a strategically clever answer designed to parry any identification of the actress with the more vulnerable modern roles she played, by holding up a blank sheet of paper, so to speak, for in many ways Juliet *is* a blank. Her reply neatly sidesteps – and this is what Peggy was always clever at doing – anything that might either be complicated, or personally revealing. The tendency of plays at any rate has always been to show women as angels or devils, patient long-suffering Griseldas or temptress Eves. Webster notes this in *The White Devil* when Flamineo says, 'Woman to man is either a god or a wolf.' Juliet, unformed as she is, large of soul and universal in her appeal, falls into neither category.

But first of all Peggy did not see Juliet as a tragic character, finding in her a gaiety, a spontaneity unusual in this wooden and formal period of Shakespearian productions. This was a Juliet, the critics reported, who was passionately in love. Well, so she was: it was of great significance from Peggy's point of view to be playing in Oxford in the spring of 1932, with George Devine as Mercutio, the Motleys as her designers, and Gielgud as director, for all these figures became important. And, as if he were a leitmotif prefiguring a future major theme in her life, Jeremy Hutchinson, a PPE student and a non-acting member of OUDS, met her at a party after one performance when they stayed up till six in the morning.

Peggy had discovered that the essential thing about playing Juliet is 'youth rather than being tragic'. She saw Juliet as never changing: 'She grows but she does not change. I don't think she becomes a woman.'

Grows but does not change? Was this to be true of Peggy? Apparently now well-established was the pattern of the promiscuous actress, in keeping with earlier periods such as the Restoration but not in keeping with her own, more respectable and tight-laced age.

After playing Juliet at Oxford – a production which was seen in London for two nights – Peggy joined Komisarjevsky in a staging of Fernand Crommelynck's *Le Coçu Magnifique*, performed on a Monday afternoon at the Globe Theatre. The subject of this play was the incredible lengths to which a husband will go to torture himself over his wife's infidelity. Bruno, the husband in question, forces his wife Stella, played by Peggy, to sleep with everyone in the village in the hope of finding her true lover. But, of course, like Chaucer's Griselda, she loves Bruno and never yields to another. Bruno then disguises himself as someone else to test her fidelity. The piece reaches its ultimate 'catastrophe' when Stella sees in the romantically disguised Bruno the projection of his early, untormented self. Of course she then yields, while Bruno cannot tell whether she recognized him or not.

'He made me realize that to be an actor is to be a perfectionist,' Peggy said of Komisarjevsky later. Note how, in the egalitarian spirit of the 1980s, she calls herself 'actor' not 'actress'. She learned dedication from him at a time when dedication was a rare quality in the English theatre. But it was not a dedication which was puritanical, remorseless, or spiritually deadening. All of Komisarjevsky's productions, indeed his whole attitude to the theatre, was leavened by wit and by irreverence, above all by delightful, childlike imagination. Thus in *Le Coçu Magnifique* when Crommelynck called Bruno a writer, Komisarjevsky made him mount a pylon 'like an exalted contraption used for mending overhead tram-lines and then dip an outsize goose feather into some monstrous, inky carboy'. Komisarjevsky would seize such opportunities to endow an everyday action with absurdity.

Peggy found later his 'funny, sharp fox-face with a little pointed nose and a sly humorous look' accorded with something in her which was very un-English. In fact his manner on the whole – there are stories of him throwing temperamental fits and dashing actresses' photographs to the ground – was 'very quiet, [he] never shouted, just waddled about with his feet turned out'. His dress was always the same: brown tweed jacket and grey flannel trousers. Peggy saw in him the deromanticizer of the English theatre: everything was to do with 'reality and the truth of human relationships'.

Clearly Komisarjevsky could be different things to different people. Who was he to himself? It is difficult to tell from *Myself and the Theatre*. Here, for the most part, we see the measured sage at work, attempting, without success, to produce something of the weight of Stanislavsky's *My Life in Art*, but nowhere near as well-ordered, as consistent, as systematically secure as that handbook of enormous influence.

Instead we have a weave of vivid anecdote, heartfelt conviction, the revelation of a spontaneous and giving personality who was in essence impish and mecurial. For example, at the first rehearsal

Komisarjevsky ever took and which he wrote about in the book, he underlines the value of patience and presence of mind. He described how he was polite to the actors who greeted him, as an inexperienced young man, very stiffly, naturally thinking he had a lot of foolish, new-fangled notions in his head. So they made no effort to act. After an hour his patience wore very thin. Blowing out the candle on the producer's desk he said something rude and left the theatre without his hat and coat. He regretted this later, but went on to account for his nervousness by virtue of having fallen in love with one girl at the same time as being pursued by another. That same night, leaving the house of the girl he loved (she had a lovely round face, eyes like a young calf, and very fair hair), he was stopped by the other girl, who was spying on him. This one swore she would throw herself into the River Neva and 'actually flung fifty roubles that she had borrowed from me a month before into the snow'. To pacify her Komisarjevsky had to take her home, and talk to her till three o'clock. Ringing his previous and truly loved one next morning he was horrified when she told him she had seen him through the window leaving the house with another woman. She said he had ruined her life for ever, that she was through with him and intended to kill herself.

Next day he was, he said, in hourly expectation of something terrible happening to them – neither girl would speak to him – and it was against this background of a complicated love-life, which made him feel 'like a criminal ... and the most wretched man on earth', that he was taking his first rehearsal.

From his book Peggy, or Peggy in essence – as archetype of the dedicated, sensitive actress – shines as an exemplar. When working on opera – he produced sixteen in France, England, and Italy between 1919 and 1928 Komisarjevsky found selfishness on all sides ruining the quality of the work, especially on the part of the conductor, the 'worst enemy' of the producer. In the commercial theatre it was the leading actors and actresses who took unwarranted liberties with the plays, adapting them to their egotism and vanity. 'Selfishness' was 'a contagious disease'. Above all he hated the motivation of practically all actors and actresses, namely the desire to become rich and famous. As this is virtually taken for granted in our own, self-centred epoch, it is perhaps worth being reminded that both Peggy, who undoubtedly became the greatest actress of her generation, and, surprisingly enough, Laurence Olivier, had at the centre of their being the ideal of service to the theatre.

For Peggy this sense of the ideal comes from Komisarjevsky. He mercilessly revealed the petty vanities of actors who saw in acting the chance of becoming important and unique people surrounded by crowds of admirers. He believed, also, that some kind of sexual and psychological perversity – 'the desire to exhibit themselves bodily and a neurotic desire to put "le coeur à nu" ' – often had something to do with the longing to go on the stage. 'We have with us a young actress, the shyest and most prudish creature in ordinary life, but on the stage she has no objection to showing her legs as far up as where they begin, and she can act the most passionate scenes in the most realistic seductive way.'

Komisarjevsky's description of good quality in acting is both lyrical and moving. It is worth summarizing for it has had little attention, much overshadowed as Komisarjevsky was by Stanislavsky. Its appeal to Peggy was such that it became her artistic credo, followed with all the rigour of deep observance. There was, also, in her Jewish side, something which appealed to her deeply in Komisarjevsky's profound and soulful intellectuality.

First of all Komisarjevsky believed the actor must free himself from all stereotypes and become him – or herself. The body was of pre-eminent importance as the actor's prime instrument; Komisarjevsky quoted Kaintz the German philosopher:

The movements of the actor's body are the expression of the *Psyche*, the external signs of what is happening within. As the sea moves slightly even in calm weather and affords us but an inkling of the coming storm, so the actor's body reacts all the time to what is passing in his mind. But as passions have thoughts behind them, and every reaction has its limitations, an actor, during the stress of emotion as well as when calm or ecstatic, must always remain a thinking human being (immer Mensch bleiben) ... His acting must always be music ... He must become neither a restrained God from Olympus nor a mere beast who surrenders himself to his instincts ... He must know the limits of the scale of his instrument.

But, body apart, the main quality an actor should show was one of soul.

The 'inside' of an actor – call it 'soul', 'consciousness', or whatever you like – with which the producer has to deal, is a very complicated and delicate instrument. That instrument is what matters most on the stage and only an extremely sensitive and careful producer can play on it without hurting the freshness of the actor's conception of the part and his own creation of it. Of course, what I am telling now about a theatrical producer only concerns the Theatre of art, where plays have some inner meaning to them which is to be interpreted scenically. The commercial Theatre needs no producing nor does the Theatre of the 'stars'.

I quote at length from *Myself and the Theatre* because it was Peggy who, as a zealous acolyte of Komisarjevsky, took such advice deeply into her being. Such teaching remained with her all her life, deepening and broadening her acting. Komisarjevsky's strictures, too, on Stanislavsky, remain convincing and persuasive. He was not to know the effect which Stanislavksy's teaching was to have on the American theatre of the 1960s and seventies, or on film-acting, for he was to die in 1954. But he rightly described the system of Stanislavsky as 'by no means new', pointing out that certain French theorists, notably André Antoine, of the 'classic' theatre, founded their system of acting on the same outlook.

Peggy's next play, *The Secret Woman* by Eden Phillpotts, was not with Komisarjevsky. This, at the Duchess Theatre, was her last West End performance unattached to what Komisarjevsky unashamedly called uncommercial 'highbrow' values: a pretty piece of acting, 'like a Dresden china dairymaid contemplating Gilbert's silver chord'. *The Secret Woman* had been banned in 1912 and had caused a stir in Parliament because it dared to treat of adultery: Phillpotts refused to delete certain lines and expressions. In 1932 it seemed 'no more poisonous than a pint of cider'. The critics approved, especially the vengeful wife and the 'Secret Woman' herself, the farmer's bit of fluff on the side, played by Peggy and applauded by the *Daily Sketch* as 'one of the finest pieces of acting to be seen in London just now'.

One critic reminded his readers that the mainspring of the young farmer's unfaithfulness was that he had married a woman older than himself, quoting Shakespeare's admonition that it was the woman who should always take an older man: 'So wears she to him, / So sways she level in her husband's heart'.

But Peggy, already now living with Komisarjevsky and persistently bidden by him to marry him – she gave in to his repeated demands in the autumn of 1933 – still found and needed additional security from the company of much older men. In the autumn of 1932 she was engaged by the Old Vic Company to play Cleopatra in Shaw's *Caesar and Cleopatra*, Imogen in *Cymbeline*, and Rosalind in *As You Like It*. Still only twenty-five, she had definitely arrived at the top of the ladder. Years later she would comment, 'It's tough at the top. I started terribly early as a leading actress and that does make very heavy demands, but then how lucky I was!'

So her new and slightly more permanent theatrical home was now the dusty stronghold of Shakespeare over the river, more often than not immersed in the smoky sunshine of the Waterloo Road – when it wasn't raining. Its atmosphere, although it had been a theatre since 1818, was not unlike that of a mission hall, while the missionary mother was Lilian Baylis, a plump figure in pince-nez invariably carrying a sable tippet which she wore over a nondescript black dress.

In spite of the earnest, do-gooding intentions of 'L.B.', this was contemporary theatre at its most romantic extreme of dedication. The actors were paid little – the highest wage was £20 per week.

The conditions were perfect for dedication. Actors breathed in the Vic's unmistakable, glorious stink of the stage, the predominant note of which always seemed to be tomcat. This was really the smell of fireproofing intermingled with the boneyard, cow-heel smell of distempered paint. As everyone in those far-off days seemed to smoke cigarettes, the stage and empty auditorium was also as heavy with stale tobacco smoke as with the black overwhelming dust of the theatre.

Ashcroft played Shaw's Cleopatra as a heavenly minx and in a beautiful rapid voice.* (She called Shaw 'the person who taught me to think ... who was my hero'.) Harcourt Williams the director was her influence in rapid delivery, especially of Shakespeare. She was plunged into a work mill such as she had never known before. Every production played at the Old Vic for an average total of three weeks

---

* Anthony Quayle also appeared in this. He took his grandfather to meet PA backstage after the performance: as a result, grandfather laid to rest all doubt he had about becoming an actor. 'If this lovely intelligent young woman was the sort of actress he would be working with – then the boy had chosen the right profession.' (*A Time to Speak*, p. 167.)

and at the Sadler's Wells Theatre for one week. In the course of nine months Peggy acted ten exacting parts and while there was little time for detailed preparation or character development, there was no other chance in England for actors to stretch themselves in Shakespeare and other classic roles, however much they might feel under-rehearsed and overworked.

She thought the whole nine months 'a killing venture, quite beyond my scope at the time and I knew it'. In the Campden Hill flat she shared with Komisarjevsky she would rise early and take a bus across London to reach the theatre at ten. She felt constantly unwell. When she was playing in the evening she would arrive home at ten-thirty at night. Komisarjevsky gave her wise advice, telling her to regard her performances only as studies for what she might in time have the chance to play. Her director for nine out of the ten plays was Harcourt Williams, who wrote in his subsequent memoir of these Old Vic days over which he presided, 'Her insight and clear-headedness, and her own particular technique which demands absolute honesty in method and is free from any suspicion of false sentiment, was a joy to work with and observe. She does not know what it means to use a "trick" ... and as an artist instinctively rejects the commonplace.'

One relaxation during this intense time was a relationship she began with Walter Sickert, the artist. He was no longer in his prime, but still a very good-looking man loved and admired by many women. He was even, in fact, considerably older than Komisarjevsky. But he was, Peggy said of him later, both youthful and very old. He had 'terrific gusto and vitality', and was always 'absolutely himself', without any sort of shyness. Unlike Komisarjevsky, who was forever restless and involved in many projects with mercurial lightness of touch, he accepted his personality and 'one felt completely at ease with him. One could feel the same except one hardly got a word in edgeways.'

FIVE

Heart Lines

My Lords, if you would hear a high tale
of love and death...

Joseph Bédier

Even now Peggy's base in terms of contacts outside the family was broad, and with time it was to broaden still more. Her brother Edward was close to her, and from the time of his first marriage, in 1928, she shared in his family life right up to and beyond the year of his death in 1983. He was a 'walking literary genius', the 'brains' of the family. With his first wife, Christine, Edward had three daughters, Margaret, who became an actress, Sophie, who died, and Gabriel. But he was a philanderer and left Christine for Katie, with whom he ran off. Peggy, who was furious when he divorced and remarried, remained supportive towards Christine and disapproving of Katie, even though divorced herself. The difference, she felt, was that no children were at stake. Edward had two further children, William (born 1937) and Chloë. Peggy's part Danish, part German-Jewish blood often asserted itself by hankering after a life outside the theatre, and while she had this intense succession of demanding parts, while she also had her theatrical Svengali genius to give her advice and further her career, she also sought, or if not sought, accepted, life as it came to her from outside. She had the breadth not to turn anything away.

It is hard when writing about Ashcroft not to slip into the 'Higher Gush', as so many others have done. In my attempt to delineate the early, perhaps harder, self-seeking qualities that went towards her making, I have of necessity to write frankly of her sexuality. English actresses, from the first moment when, roughly eighty in number, they were bribed and seduced on to the London stage at the Restoration, have never been noted for their chastity or fidelity in marriage. The greatest of those first English actresses was 'trained' by Lord Rochester, the notorious rake and poet. Elizabeth Barry played opposite Thomas Betterton and made her reputation as an outstanding tragedienne, but she would still receive a horse-laugh from the audience when, as Cordelia in Nicholas Tate's contemporary adaptation of *Lear*, she spoke the line, 'Arm'd in my Virgin Innocence I'll Fly'. They knew what she had been doing before she achieved fame and respectability.

Nell Gwynn, painted enticingly in the nude by Sir Peter Lely for Charles II's own private pleasure, owed her early chances to being the mistress of Charles Hart, who acted the first Manly in Wycherley's *The Plain Dealer*. Later Peggy was to stay in one home built for Nell Gwynn by Charles II near Tring. Gwynn's histrionic powers, unlike Peggy's, were in short supply, but like Peggy she was much ogled in 'breech' roles such as Florimel in Dryden's *Secret Love*, and she achieved celebrity as the King's mistress. In the narrow circles of the theatre Peggy already had this dual reputation, adding to the excitement of those who gossiped about her. She may not have been as extreme as another early actress, Elizabeth Boutell, who played Manly's mistress and was venomously described in the off-stage dispensation of her favours as 'the chestnut-maned Boutell whom all the town f****', but that smouldering fire-in-ice quality of virginal beauty had the substantial shadow of the libertine actress expected of women who acted for their living.

Changing backstage in these early days, actresses had no privacy: witness Pepys, who discovered Nell Gwynn in her dressing-room in a delightful state of undress. But even in the 1920s, as in the 1680s, young women were first and foremost sex objects on the stage and still displayed in a spiralling number of rape scenes with clothes torn, breasts exposed, or enticingly laid out in 'couch' scenes – on a chaise-longue, a bed or a grassy bank. After the deprivation and grief of the First World War a desire for frivolity, even for coarse depravity, took hold. In some ways the 'entre deux guerres' period in which Peggy made her reputation was similar to the Restoration and, although less publicly, a spirit of licence flourished after the dark puritan interregnum. The poor actress, like the hungry, beautiful Charlotte Butler of the Restoration, might become the target of the satirist who wrote: 'I must be blunt / She'll for a Dish of Cutlets shew her C***.' Bodily presence was, and has remained, the foremost attribute of the actress struggling to establish herself even though she might have, like Peggy, a strong expressive voice, a mind of her own, and stubborn determination. But freedom to act on stage often amounted in popular belief to little more than 'freedom to play the whore'.

Like Sir Peter Lely, Walter Sickert painted Peggy, while she, in the new identification of that period of actresses with aristocratic women – perhaps an attempt on the part of the aristocracy itself to revitalize its blood and genes – slipped easily into the aristocratic mould. Her inner feelings, especially her political, left-wing aspirations first stimulated by Paul Robeson, moved at the same time in a very different direction.

Sickert was a great supporter of Sadler's Wells. He lived in Islington, and he would often go along to matinees, accompanied by a photographer, preferring at that stage not to paint from life. He was 'bored', as Peggy said much later, 'by working from life, while he did not want to paint the detail and intimacy of a person's face'. When interviewed, Peggy talked of Sickert a little coyly, but with a certain pride. She recalled 'the loud gusts of laughter from a solitary person' as he reacted to her playing a line of Rosalind's. As Kate Hardcastle in *She Stoops to Conquer*, she delivered the line, 'Would it were bedtime and all were well' at the back of the stage ascending a staircase. Sickert painted 'an enormous picture of backcloth and tiny figure going upstairs'.* As Lady Teazle he painted her as 'this figure in the footlights, a complete distortion. I'm almost blank.'

It seemed a strange marginalization, or minimalization, of the actress from this larger-than-life figure who had begun life as an actor himself and who invariably wore a huge tweed tailcoat, sea boots and a chauffeur's cap. He loved dressing up, but he was naturally punctilious, and with exquisite manners. Like Peggy he couldn't sing in tune.

Sickert had just acquired a new studio in Canonbury, some distance away from his home. Circular, 70 foot high, it was a disused bus station. An iron ladder rested against the wall, and Sickert would climb it to the roof, and make his friends do the same. 'Why do you want to go on the roof?' a friend's wife, who was frightened for him, asked. 'To see the little servant girls undressing,' he answered.

He wrote to Peggy and asked her to lunch with him and his wife

---

* He also painted, in 1934–5, a picture of PA in Venice which she bequeathed to the Tate Gallery on her death in 1991. It was she who said she did not sit for him at this time.

Thérèse. 'I went to his house, and he came to mine; we met often.' But he did not paint from life and Peggy did not sit for him. She gave him a more privileged role.

Not much of Peggy's deeper personality, as it was to emerge, was engaged in her acting at this time. Gielgud said in 1961, emphasizing the self-consuming, victim side of the actor, 'You have to spin it all out of yourself, like a spider. It is the only way,' while Olivier echoed him in 1969, 'Great parts are cannibals. It's a dangerous game.' These were the heroic, self-dramatizing statements which Peggy would never ascribe to, for the whole drift of her developing personality went against exaggeration. 'I always see the part as outside myself,' she said, 'and hope it'll be unrecognizable as me,' and, further, 'The aim of an actor should not be the part, but the whole.'

The second of the four productions she did with Komisarjevsky was as the title role in *Fräulein Elsa*, which her husband adapted from a story by Arthur Schnitzler, the author of *La Ronde*. With the minimum of settings, this was performed as a club production at the Kingsway Theatre to avoid the Lord Chamberlain's censorship. Elsa was a very long part, entirely a monologue and once again a challenge to Peggy. As she described it herself, Elsa wanted to save her father becoming bankrupt and so she approaches on his behalf a supposed philanthropist who is 'just a dirty old man'. He offers money if she will meet him in a wood and take off all her clothes. Instead of this she swallows laudanum, and then, appearing in the hotel lounge where he is waiting for her, removes her cloak. Under this she is naked. She falls to the ground and never recovers consciousness.

This was the scene for which the Lord Chamberlain banned the play. Alec Guinness, in the audience, noticed the sudden intake of breath at the sight of Peggy's naked back. (Not very daringly she was, as she said, 'suitably covered in front for the near-onlookers'.) No less remarkable was her revelation, said Guinness, of the mental anguish she went through.

But were these occasional studies of the morbid, sandwiched between, for good measure, the great, outgoing Shakespearian heroines, really advancing her career, or merely adding to a burgeoning reputation which was by now slightly stereotyped? After Elsa, Peggy continued her run of Shakespeare with Portia in *The Merchant of*

Venice, praised by J. C. Trewin for her natural, very human delivery of the courtroom speech, but criticized by some as lacking stature and grandeur; then as Perdita in *The Winter's Tale*; as Kate in *She Stoops to Conquer*; as Juliet, again; as Lady Teazle in *The School for Scandal*; as Miranda in *The Tempest*.

The only modern play in which she appeared at the Old Vic was John Drinkwater's *Mary Stuart* which opened on 13 February 1933, and which R. B. Marriott praised as showing the lonely, unappeased soul of the woman: '... a rare delight to see the mind behind the words which came with half-concealing gravity from her lips. Regal, sensitive, feminine, Miss Ashcroft fills out the part to admiration.'

I suspect we would have found Ashcroft's performances in the early 1930s very insipid and dated by the standards of today: gutless is perhaps too strong a word, but certainly they were lacking in passion and any deeper sense of being a woman. She was very constrained and inhibited. Her 'soul' as defined by Komisarjevsky was extremely delicate and still limited, which is to say it was hidden. Perhaps it came out more in her private relationships, but even here there was a stormy, unrevealed side to her character which, later in life, would show itself by swearing or growing angry on occasions and surprising everyone.

If so, there was no sign of it at that time. She was the perfect head girl of that very respectable girls' grammar school of the highbrow English theatre. She was in the 'can-do-no-wrong-club'. Undoubtedly it was not her fault if she came to represent the ideal, for she had no part in the formation of society in the dream roles that society wanted her to play. Even when she came to play Ibsen a little later Michael Meyer, Ibsen's biographer and translator, remained very unsatisfied with the lack of passion and the sexlessness of some of her great roles. The truth, perhaps, is that many Englishmen, and by extension English audiences, always were and still are rather frightened of the full-blooded display of women's feelings. Every generation would seem to need one actress who, in an odd way, could be sanctified. Perhaps this was because people had an atavistic suspicion of actresses in the first place, a half-buried puritan unease not without sexual connotations. So, periodically, they made use of stars whom they perceived to be 'respectable' or 'safe'.

Certainly in this period Peggy benefited from the English preference for actresses who were asexual in performance and not in competition, off-stage, with the predominantly homosexual set-up of managers and leading male actors. An actress, if she were to succeed, had to be perceived as offering no threat to the male actors who dominated the stage. Again, Peggy was a master of the art of mixing socially, helping and generally nurturing her male colleagues, especially the ones whom she perceived as talented. Continually we must return to Peter Hall's assessment of Peggy as having a brilliant eye for talent in others. For instance, Michael Redgrave, in his book *In My Mind's Eye*, records how it was Peggy (then only twenty-six, for this was in 1934) who suggested him to Gielgud for Macheath in *The Beggar's Opera*. His wife Rachel (Kempson) and he 'used to sing at Peggy's house in Campden Hill Road ... and hearing that John was thinking of an actor–singer for the lead in the Glyndebourne production she said, "Why don't you have Michael? He sings." ' She was quite without jealousy, for she was tone-deaf.

But how would she break out of the mould in which she was set? How would she raise herself out of the antiseptic ranks of asexual English actresses so admired at the time, typified by Beatrix Lehmann, Madge Titheradge, or Wendy Hiller?

Some believed that the turning-point was her third production of *Romeo and Juliet* in 1935, directed by Gielgud, in which Gielgud and Olivier alternated as Romeo and Mercutio. Before then she had had a desultory year during which she made her first appearance on the screen, in *The Wandering Jew*, with Conrad Veidt. Fortunately from the theatre's point of view, she was not considered photogenic, while she herself disliked acting in film studios. She was not asked to play Naemi again in *Jew Süss* when it was filmed in 1934, and she was to make only six film performances in the next thirty years.

It is curious that what was Shakespeare's most religious play should have turned out to be the favourite play of Peggy, who throughout her life subscribed to no religious values and was quite sure that she did not believe in God or an afterlife. Yet she had what may broadly be called sound humanistic beliefs about morals and behaviour. But of course the deeply religious feeling in *Romeo and Juliet* is disguised, so one may take it to be a celebration first and foremost of earthly love. Yet no other play of Shakespeare has a sense of providence so deeply rooted in it. Also no other play embodies, with its continual invocation of love in spiritual terms, with its broad Italian feeling and its explosive emotions which must be expressed and atoned for, such a catholicism of feeling which revealed the power of faith over Shakespeare's imagination.

Peggy still had no doubt that it was her favourite. But, as she said many times, her job was to act plays and 'not to talk about them', so she would not analyse her reasons for liking it beyond saying that *Romeo and Juliet*, as 'a golden tragedy', was in her 'top four' plays. She saw the characters as not following Meredith's dictum, 'We are betrayed by what is false within us', but being 'betrayed by what is false without'. As such, the main pair were victims of a series of fatal accidents in what was an 'intensely human domestic drama'. It was fate rather than any individual flair which enabled Shakespeare to bring about the death of the lovers.

For Shakespeare was dramatizing a story which, as myth, incorporated a permanent truth about the human condition. Romeo and Juliet symbolized the power of Eros – 'It is too rash, too unadvised, too sudden'; the opposite of Christian love, in which the pair would have accepted their limitations. They symbolized the abandonment to passion to which lovers who love love and being in love ultimately succumb. Psychologically Romeo and Juliet are hardly people of any individual soul or quality; their most lively encounter – in terms of crisp dialogue which reveals character and contact – is their first. Passion has not yet geared itself; so Juliet pushes her would-be lover around like a precocious fifth-former. Had they ever settled down to married life, Juliet would have become a frightful, egging-on shrew.

But from the moment their love catches fire they lose touch with reality. Romeo never comes to know who Juliet is, nor does she see in him more than an excuse for a rising inner intensity. Their love is not a love for one another as they really are: their love is based on a false reciprocity, which conceals a twin narcissism. They love in each other the reflections of themselves. Their passion is blind and undifferentiating, and therefore has to lead to mistakes, to mutual blindness and ultimately to the fate of any love that is based on egocentric passion: to death. It could be argued that their love contains a great yearning for death, for, not able to know one another, each wants self-obliteration in a glorious form of sacrifice that would transcend life and raise them to a permanent, eternal plane of love. By their martyrdom to love they give love immortal power.

But are we to view Peggy's identification with Juliet as disguised self-biography on her part? No. She saw it entirely as romantic fiction. Reality would have killed the lovers' passion and made them ordinarily happy. Happy love has little to attract its representation on stage.

Peggy's attachment to the play, and especially to the part of Juliet – although she agreed that it contained two of Shakespeare's other greatest characters – bordered on the unusual belief that it was the biggest challenge an actress could meet. To begin with, she pointed out, no other character has such a long part.

'My first attempt at Juliet was agonising,' she said. 'I learned when I played the part at the Old Vic that the essential is to be a child of fourteen, if that is credible. Then her awakening, her passion, her refusal to compromise and finally her tragedy, will take care of themselves.' On her second attempt, at the Old Vic, Komisarjevsky had kept her up all night after the performance telling her how awful she was.

In fact, it was in not attempting to be a child of fourteen that Peggy's third attempt at Juliet was so successful: many have called it the turning-point of her early career. It seems she could combine realism – the sense of Juliet's right age – with a flawless technical control which was far from realistic. Juliet has to speak conceits and puns at intense moments, while most of her utterances contain complicated verbal fireworks. Paradoxically, it was Peggy's control of complexity, together with her simple heartfelt projection of passion, which made the part seem so challenging to her.

Also she was acting in Gielgud's company which had a very solid centre 'with two sides round us', as Gielgud described it, 'very enthusiastic young people' (Glen Byam Shaw, George Devine, Alec Guinness), and the other side made up of experienced people (Edith Evans, Leon Quartermaine, Leslie Banks). 'The young people matched with their youthful enthusiasm what the old ones had in experience – an ideal situation, it seemed to me.'

Edith Evans played the nurse. Peggy admired her and learned from her. Gielgud thought her the finest actress of his time, and considered that he was privileged to have known her and worked so often with her. But she was not always easy to work with because there was something aloof about her: she was by no means a cosy person, 'except when you could get her alone occasionally'. Nor was she gregarious and she found it difficult to open out to people. Like Ellen Terry and Peggy Ashcroft, 'she longed to be an ordinary woman, to have a home, husband, children'. But she never had them. 'At different times she tried to take up dancing, farming, attempted to drive a car or skate, to do the everyday things that an ordinary woman does. But she was always driven back to the theatre just as Ellen Terry was.'

Edith Evans, unlike Peggy, was considered plain and leading ladies were expected to be beautiful. Gielgud described her as no beauty, although her face had 'an enigmatic originality'. She could paint on this any character she chose, so that Gielgud could say of her that he never knew what she looked like because she always looked the part. As Peggy grew older we see how she, too, almost cultivated her face into an impersonal canvas. Pretty to begin with, she became plainer as the years went by, but not the less rich for this.

Such was the birth of what was generally thought of as 'the finest as well as the sweetest Juliet of our time', as W. A. Darlington called her. Technically, wrote Peter Fleming, Rupert Hart-Davis's old friend and now the husband of Celia Johnson, 'her performance is perfection: there is no one like her for conveying the sense of a difficult passage without, so to speak, being caught in the act.' She made Shakespeare's expression of Juliet's thoughts seem entirely natural.

Romeo and Juliet ran for eighty-nine performances at the New Theatre (now the Albery) and, with Olivier and Gielgud alternating as Romeo and Mercutio, broke box-office records. Not all critics loved it: A. E. Wilson, for instance, found it fast and furious. Olivier's Romeo was resonant rather than melodious, while Peggy was touching and gentle rather than distinguished. Twenty-eight years old when it opened, Peggy once again found herself without a husband. She and Komisarjevsky had parted after their lightning, year-long marriage.

Their married life had been happy till August 1935, ran a newspaper report, when Komis went away for a three-week holiday. After his return Peggy found a letter from which she learned that he had spent this time with Ernestine Deroch, a young American dancer. Technically they stayed married until June 1937 when she was granted a decree citing adultery at a West End hotel with Miss Deroch. Evidence was given by a chambermaid.

Peggy claimed in retrospect that she had been unwilling to enter into a second marriage so soon after the break-up of her first. She could never work out whether the number of wives before her was three or four. At any rate she did not want to take much responsibility for the marriage. Yet she had wanted to marry in church. As she told James Fox many years later, during the filming of *A Passage to India*, she had gone to a vicar to arrange a church wedding and the vicar had refused on the grounds that she was divorced. This had turned her for ever against the Church.

Gielgud commented that Komisarjevsky had a very emotional love-life and was always changing partners. Once he had met him at the country house of Constance Spry, the well-known florist, where he observed him very 'taken' by a lady novelist. The ladies decked themselves up in a lot of costume jewellery designed by Spry, and they dined on an alabaster table lit from beneath.

After dinner Gielgud played the piano. When it was time to go home he could find Komisarjevsky nowhere but finally discovered him sitting under the piano with the lady he fancied, 'telling her fortune in a pudding-basin filled with candle grease'.

Riots were unusual in the London theatre in 1933, or at any other time, but when Werner Krauss, the famous German actor, appeared in *Before Sunset*, written by Gerhardt Hauptmann and directed by Komisarjevsky at the Shaftesbury Theatre, the anti-Nazi spirit of the audience erupted in demonstration. Or was it deliberate, as some have suggested, the action of a claque 'developed by that awful old rotter, Ivor Montagu' as William Buchan called him?

Krauss, playing the elderly widowed publisher Clausen who falls for the village schoolmistress and who wants to leave her all his money – to the fury of his children, who wish him locked up as insane – was horrified at the unseemly disorders on the first night, which took the form of ironical applause, abuse (naming Hitler), and stink bombs. Suspicions that he was a Nazi sympathizer ran deep: they were later proved not altogether unfounded.

According to Fabia Drake, another actress in *Before Sunset*, Peggy watched the disturbance from the wings and after the curtain had come down twice during the play she appeared on the stage in a frenzy of rage, telling the audience to either respect Krauss or go home. Peggy herself later recalled how ridiculous it was that she should have gone out in front of the curtain to make a speech wearing white cotton gloves. She was by then a master of playing down the emotions she felt, for the *Daily Mail* at the time wrote that she was 'deathly white and obviously on the verge of tears' as she made this appeal. But she saved the play, as Krauss's obituary in *The Times* attested some thirty-three years later.

It was only afterwards that Peggy found out about Krauss's Nazi connections. She was sent a cutting from a German newspaper headed 'England's Nazi actress defends Werner Krauss', which horrified her. After this she became more wary of impetuous gestures of sympathy which might give the wrong impression. When she and Komisarjevsky had travelled to Berlin at the end of 1934 to see Krauss as Lear, and he offered to introduce them to Hitler, she wisely declined, or her face would have been all over the papers.

Before Sunset was poorly received in spite of the favourable attention given to Krauss (and Peggy's defence of him). In spite of Miles Malleson's skilful adaptation and production it was heavy going on the whole, or such is the impression one gains from reading the notices today – humourless, and on the morbid side, like *King Lear* without the poetry. James Agate noted that Krauss had the power to impose himself on his audience, while Peggy was full of 'spirit, fire, and dew'. Generally, though, everyone found it too theatrical and over the top for English tastes.

Before Sunset did not foretoken a new sunrise, however, but another bad run of continental, or international, luck. A Pirandello part at the Little Theatre; a Hindu role at the Coliseum in a spectacular called *The Golden Toy* which featured a live elephant; a partnership with Oscar Homolka, the Austrian actor, as the blind mesmerized girl in a Glasgow, pre-London try-out of *Mesmer*, by Beverly Nichols, which flopped: these disasters were only eclipsed by Komisarjevsky having by now deserted Peggy for his young American dancer. Permanence or continuity was not Komisarjevsky's forte in marriage. His was the mercurial spirit, just as Mercury himself was the god of fiction and fabrications of trickery and sleight of hand.

She must have thought back more than once, as her second marriage foundered, to the tall, handsome physical presence of Hart-

Davis. Their divorce had only come through in the early summer of 1933, just before she married Komis, while at this time, less than a month after her second divorce, Hart-Davis also remarried. His second wife's name was Comfort and within a few months they were expecting a child, who was born in early 1935. The desire was strengthened in Peggy to raise her own family, but in the meantime she had joined a theatrical family in embryo which was to bring her more professional satisfaction than she had experienced up to now.

It was the collapse of Gielgud's plan to stage his own adaptation (with Terence Rattigan) of *A Tale of Two Cities* that had led him to stage *Romeo and Juliet*. At first he wanted Robert Donat to play Romeo and Mercutio, but Donat declined, so Olivier was approached instead. After the success of the production Gielgud asked Peggy and Edith Evans to appear with him again, this time in Chekhov's *The Seagull*. Gielgud wanted Komisarjevsky to direct, which posed a problem because he had only just left Peggy. There was also the knowledge that Vera Komisarjevsky had played the original Nina in 1896, an ideal which Peggy felt she would never be able to match in her own performance.

This was the first Chekhov play ever performed in the West End. Komisarjevsky designed a beautiful scene for the first act and boasted to Gielgud that the trees were all made of real silk and that the set would cost at least £1,000, 'an enormous sum in those days', as Gielgud recollected. 'Of course,' he remarked to Gielgud, 'Albery is just a tradesman.' Bronson Albery was the distinguished London theatre manager.

At the first reading of the play Komisarjevsky, perhaps discomfited by the presence of his ex-wife, delivered a terrible harangue on the dreadful state of the English theatre, with its wretched actors, completely lacking in style. Edith Evans (Arkadina) sat listening and looked very cross, so Gielgud worried over whether she and Komis would ever get on together. They started rehearsing. In the middle of the first act, when Arkadina stops to listen to the voices of the choir singing on the other side of the lake, Komis said 'his favourite word "powse" (pause), Edith "powsed". She "powsed" for five minutes, the longest "powse" I have ever heard, and from that moment she and Komis were delighted with each other.'

No one has recorded the undercurrents of feeling that must have existed between Komisarjevsky and his Nina. But Komis was a master of directing Chekhov, and this production set a standard and became historic, as well as proving an inspiration for all those involved in it.

Stanislavsky, when working on Chekhov's plays of inaction, 'discovered' his 'method' which was, as Komisarjevsky described it, a form of 'psychic naturalism', enabling the actor to look beneath the lines of the play and find what feelings had prompted the author to write them, then recall his own feelings in similar circumstances and substitute them for those of the author. Stanislavsky, said Komisarjevsky, had found that Chekhov intentionally *concealed* the feelings of the characters in the words they were saying, and the silences and pauses were more important than any of their speeches:

> The plays lacked action as understood by the old dramatists and had no obviously effective theatrical situations. 'The significance of a human being and his life-drama are within him' – was a saying of Chekhov. In all his plays we are shown a more or less schematic picture of life, which is drawn merely to express certain emotions and their rhythm. Chekhov's characters never utter any 'beautiful' speeches, which are theatrically 'actable'. At the vital moments they are very often silent, they repeat themselves and talk quite a lot of trivialities. It is easy to turn Chekhov's plays into skits by accentuating certain points, and thus make the most tragic 'inner' situation humorous.

The 'inner' life was intimately connected with the life of things and different sounds in the external world and these needed to be made to live. The actor had to – and such was Stanislavsky's experience of directing *The Seagull* at the Alexandinsky Theatre in St Petersburg in 1896 – act 'from within', and the ensemble on the stage should be based on the 'inner contacts' between the actors.

But later – and here Komisarjevsky's own genius and intuition comes into play – when Stanislavksy tried to systematize and analyze what he discovered intuitively, he 'misinterpreted' himself. Speaking in his 'system' about the reproduction of 'feelings experienced in the past', Stanislavsky forgot that pure recollections of feelings were strong enough for the purposes of acting. It would be completely impossible for an actor to make use of them; the associations of such feelings would be so strong, they would carry with them past representations and would 'dictate actions which would have nothing to do with the play'. Komisarjevsky continued with a passage which deserves wider attention because it is common sense and shows how the 'method' has distorted, or falsified, the whole basis of actors' real feelings so that many, such as Olivier, have ended up by pursuing naturalism to its limit, never knowing if they were acting or if they were not. You cannot lose touch, Komisarjevsky was saying, with your real feelings:

If I love a woman, that emotion is inseparably connected in my mind with the image of *that* woman, and I do not want to make any declaration of that love to some lady provided for me by the management whose image would simply hinder the production of my emotion. If the management were to go to the expense or inconvenience of engaging the woman I loved to act with me I should certainly be ashamed to express my sentiments to her in public. If, by any chance, I succeeded in being so shameless as to forget the audience, I should certainly forget also the fact that I was on the stage, and probably act in a manner far from that conceived by the author, and my performance would develop on lines most undesirable for everyone present.

Komisarjevsky wrote this before he directed Peggy in *The Seagull*, but in Peggy's head there must have been some sense of Trigorin's betrayal of Nina that hurt her in the way Komisarjevsky's unfaithfulness had done. In any case she found the telescoped sense of renewal which Nina had to play in the last act before Constantine's suicide very demanding, for she had to convey two years of professional and personal failure, and then recovery, in the space of ten minutes.

Gielgud, in his memoir *Early Stages*, portrays Peggy off-stage just before her entry in that final act sitting alone in a corner with a shawl over her head, working herself up to her big entrance 'while the rain and wind effects whistled all around'. She herself told Michael Billington that at first she never had the confidence to play the last act as she wanted. 'I used to have a tiny sip of brandy before I went on to take off the edge of terror.' Jacques Copeau came to see the performance, when the play opened in May 1936, and the comment he made to Peggy was, 'You are very good in the last act but you don't yet trust yourself. You have to know what you are doing and then do it.'

The poor playwriting in the last act apart, it seemed that during this production, for reasons that were entirely clear, Peggy felt vulnerable and unsure of herself and transferred on to her part all her existential concerns, her loneliness, and her fear of failure. This is the first time we can identify how a part became for her not a challenge as such but specifically the focus of a nervous crisis. As this ultimately drew forth greatness from her as an actress it could be no bad thing. But it was uncomfortable and demanding, and did indeed show a very different Peggy from the cool image of herself which she so successfully cultivated, and the calm, balanced image of maturity which she was to attain. Although this, thankfully, was the Peggy Ashcroft whom everyone in time came to love and revere, as well as the Peggy Ashcroft who used her life and background as raw material both for her acting and for her personal sense of fulfilment, it was by no means the whole story. Nor can it be with any person, however remarkable.

Komisarjevsky was bored and grumpy after this production. By all accounts it was, as James Agate called it, 'endlessly beautiful', although Gielgud's Trigorin ('an exquisite exhibition of sensitive Gielgudry') was a 'shade too young and not raffish enough'. Edith Evans played Arkadina exactly right, while the five-minute 'powse', reduced in Alec Guinness's memoir *Blessings in Disguise* to four minutes when she supposedly missed a cue (an account wildly at variance with Gielgud's), became legendary. Martita Hunt played Masha, radiating glumness. But Agate judged that Peggy, when it came to the end of the play, could not quite yet deliver the goods, although he modified his view slightly in another review. While he found her performance of the earlier part of the play 'heart-rending; she sparkenbroke all hearts', when she came to the last scene 'there was not enough power in her to carry it through'. I suspect Agate was right for she was, while an actress of truth and sincerity, not yet one of power.

So ended Peggy's short and stormy life with Komisarjevsky, who had, as Janet Suzman reported Peggy telling her, 'wanted to Pygmalion her' like a forced flower; it had 'burst her out of any artistic reticence'. But if it did so, the process in her case was a very slow and gradual one. She was still too ladylike on stage. 'Not quite naked enough, not passionate enough', as the critic and novelist Francis King commented nearly sixty years later. He preferred Wendy Hiller as being 'much more earthy'*.

As for Komisarjevsky, we leave the final word to Gielgud: 'Komisarjevsky was always moving from one country to another, adopting the new one for a few years and then becoming disillusioned. Finally, he went off to America, married a new wife and started an acting school.'

The last time Gielgud saw Komisarjevsky was in New York in 1947 when he directed *Crime and Punishment* for him. He was rude to any foreigner in the huge crowd who came to the auditions in the blizzard conditions, turning his back whenever a German or Jew came on to read. 'You never knew when he would be difficult.' He had once thrown to the ground and stamped on a photograph of an actress he thought no good, who failed to turn up to rehearsal. Yet Gielgud also found him modest and disarming. In the week before Gielgud opened in *Musical Chairs* by Ronald Mackenzie at the Arts Theatre in 1931 Komisarjevsky had gone around smiling and joking with the stage staff and putting up fly-papers to combat an invasion of flies. He died in April 1954 at the age of seventy-one.

---

* Francis King never felt Peggy had genius, 'much preferring Edith Evans, Beatrix Lehmann, Pamela Brown, Diana Wynyard and Jessica Tandy' (letter to the author, 8 February 1995).

SIX

More Schools for Scandal

When love is satisfied all its charm is removed.

Corneille

Perhaps Agate was also saying of Peggy's performance in *The Seagull* that she had not released her darker feelings into it. She undoubtedly had been, or was now, experiencing these in her own life. Especially, during this time, she experienced the feeling of jealousy and a desire for revenge against the inspired yet torturing genius of Komisarjevsky, and while she was continuing to have other affairs she simmered with a sense of betrayal.

During the run of *Romeo and Juliet* she played the young Scottish crofter's wife in the film of John Buchan's *The Thirty-Nine Steps*, directed by Alfred Hitchcock. Everyone remarked on her perfect Scots accent, which she copied from Mary Muir, her Scottish dresser.

In the early part of 1937, according to Margaret Harris of Motley, she began a serious love-affair with John Buchan's 21-year-old son, Billy ('he followed Komis'), but there were other passing ships in the night for, as Angela Fox said, there was still always the 'avidly sexual woman'. Michel Saint-Denis in 1937 was also Peggy's lover – if he had not been so before – and deepening this liaison with the French director brought Peggy into lively conflict and competition with Vera Lindsay, one of the most powerful and self-dramatic society ladies in London, a pure Arkadina if ever there was one.

It says something for the lack of a strong sense of her own identity at this time that Peggy set out for New York in 1937 to appear in a play whose script she had not even read beforehand.

Rumour glues itself to the single celebrity. At this time it was rumoured that John Gielgud and Peggy were going to marry. Although it was well-known privately that Gielgud was more attached to John Perry, his companion, Master of the Tipperary hunt, this rumour even surfaced in the newspapers. 'I could not be more surprised,' declared Lilian Baylis, 'if Oxford won the boat race' (in those days they were always losing).

Gielgud had left the cast of *The Seagull* early. Nineteen thirty-six had been a taxing year for him and he was, as he wrote to a friend, 'dreadfully tired with double job and all the elaboration of plans for following Hamlet to America' (he opened as Hamlet at the St James's, New York, in October). But he was profoundly pleased *The Seagull* had worked, especially with Edith Evans's performance, for he had been so worried that she and Komisarjevsky would not click.

Recovering energy from his New York season as Hamlet, Gielgud had time to spend with Peggy in New York and to see her play the part of a three-hundred-year-old Dutch ghost called Lise in Maxwell Anderson's verse-play, *High Tor*. Lise engages in a 'somewhat tenuous love-affair' with a young landowner on a rock above the Hudson River. Behind the scenes Peggy herself engaged in a more concrete, although short-lived, relationship with Burgess Meredith, her lead actor.

'She came from England, fresh and beautiful and saved the show,' Meredith wrote later. He started to fall in love, but then they 'kept it cool'. If he had married, and gone back to England, 'Might I have become Sir Burgess?' asked the actor who at one time was married to Paulette Goddard. Although Peggy disliked the play, it ran for six months and won the New York Drama Critics' Prize for the best new American play of 1937. During this period Peggy lived on her own in a flat overlooking Washington Square. She hated it. In New York you 'either sink or swim and I sank'. But the address, Washington Square, the title of one of Henry James's best novellas, was to become of great significance some ten years later when, in an adaptation of that story retitled *The Heiress*, she truly and perhaps for the first time found her own measure of greatness as Catherine Sloper.

She could not wait for *High Tor* to come off and returned to London with relief. Newly divorced, she was considerably better off, for her life with the extravagant Komisarjevsky had reduced them to near penury. Gielgud once again asked her to join him in a season at the Queen's Theatre, this time more lengthy and ambitious than any previous attachment of hers to a Gielgud company.

Peggy's hate for New York was expressed much later. In fact the trip had ended on a high note. New York became the location for her intense and passionate affair with William Buchan, whose father's fame as a novelist gave an enhanced glow to his high position as British Governor-General of Canada.

Buchan was the handsomely blond, blue-eyed, and gifted second son; ultimately he became heir to his father's title of Lord Tweedsmuir. At this time Billy – as he was generally known lived with his parents in Government House, Ottawa. He was unsure as to what he wanted to be; Peggy was the well-established leading lady, twenty-nine years old.

The irony of their meeting was Billy's introduction to her through Michel Saint-Denis, who visited Ottawa in the spring of 1937 to be a judge at the Canadian National Drama Festival. Billy, who entertained Saint-Denis, became an enthusiastic supporter of the director. On a trip Billy had planned to New York to look for work, Saint-Denis insisted that he should visit Peggy. Armed with a box of stephanotis which shared his diplomatic immunity through US Customs, Billy arrived at the Martin Beck Theater stage door to see Peggy after her performance in *High Tor* which had raised his feelings 'to the highest pitch'.

'She was older than me; I was fairly scatter-brained. Friends and relations raised their eyebrows.' Thus began a genuine passion for both of them which swept Buchan off his feet. It lasted, as Buchan wrote in his autobiography, for two years, with one interruption. His attachment to Peggy, whom he did not name, would 'completely absorb my emotional existence to the almost entire exclusion of everything and everybody else'. They lived, so he told me, 'completely in one another's pockets'.

On Peggy's return to London the lovers spent much time together. Billy took a flat in Gloucester Walk, near where Peggy still lived. He enrolled at Saint-Denis's theatre studio. Billy still idolized Peggy and they talked often of marriage. One day towards the end of 1937 the interruption came. Peggy told Billy that Saint-Denis had asked her to marry him and she had accepted. Billy was, as he told me, 'congédié' – given his leave or, in other words, put to one side.

It shattered him. The relationship and the hope it created for the future had 'filled my world'. Hurt, Billy retired for several months to Florence, where, by letter, their love for each other revived. Meanwhile the intended marriage to Saint-Denis fell through. On Billy's return to London they tried to start all over again. In the end Billy met someone else and went off and married her in 1939. Peggy took it very badly. She wanted a lasting relationship outside the theatre and once again it had eluded her. She turned back to the theatre, and to Michel. 'She was in the swim. For a while I swam with her,' commented Billy.

Fired by enthusiasm for the Compagnie des Quinze, which Peggy had first seen when married to Hart-Davis, Gielgud planned a new season of four plays over a nine-month period under the financial aegis of that 'tradesman', Bronson Albery. Peggy was cast as the Queen in *Richard II*, due to open in September 1937; then as Lady Teazle in Tyrone Guthrie's production of *The School for Scandal* in November; as Irina in Michel Saint-Denis's production of *Three Sisters* in January 1938; finally, as Portia in *The Merchant of Venice* in April.

What of the 'interruption' in Buchan's youthful passion? Monogamy, conventional faithfulness, was not, it seemed, Peggy's style. Michel Saint-Denis was now forty. A stocky, earthy character both in appearance and flavour, he had a broad Burgundian accent when he spoke English, smoked a pipe, and often had a merry twinkle in his eye, especially when talking. His shrewd eyes would miss nothing. He was interested, as Abdel El Kader Farrah, the Algerian designer, said, 'in the roots of life: wine, women, trees, cheese ... an extraordinary mixture of the chairman type, who could also put his finger on the weak point. For instance he would never accept "grey" as a description, he would want to know precisely what kind of grey.'

In England Saint-Denis always gave the impression of being French; in France he would seem very English. He belonged – and this magnified his appeal for Peggy – to the world rather than to a particular country. According to Farrah, he hated prejudices and always spoke what he thought was the truth. In the very artificial and insecure world of the theatre, this made him both feared and respected. 'If someone said to him English women are ugly, he would say "Fuck off!"'

Saint-Denis, unusually for the avant-garde directors of that day, had been an actor but given it up. William Buchan described his face as that of a true actor, 'its components capable of being assembled at will to suit a turn of thought, a reaction or an emotion'. Actors as directors understand the technical problems of their casts, and do not 'marshal' them as production numbers in the way that more eye-catching directors tend to do. So runs the argument. Saint-Denis's method was extremely careful and methodical: he had a meticulous eye for detail and he insisted on a long period of rehearsal. In the case of *Three Sisters* this was seven weeks.

Not many people at this time could make a distinction between feelings and emotions, either off the stage or on. Komisarjevsky could and did:

> You can always get things out of English actors ... not through their emotions, but through their feelings. I make a distinction. The French actor acts on his emotions. You ask him to do something, and he makes a great scene, with explosions, and sweeps the floor of the stage with his emotions. The Englishman does it in a subtler way, with his feelings.

By now Peggy was identified primarily as an actress of feeling, not emotion, and as such was especially suited to being Gielgud's leading lady. As such she posed no threat to him, while the scale of her performances matched and suited his own. But when it came to being directed, by Tyrone Guthrie, with Gielgud as the Teazles in *The School for Scandal* the result was disastrous. Guthrie was what can only be described as a 'breathless' director. He was against stars, while Peggy, for all her later modesty, was now just that, or, at any rate, perceived as such by Guthrie. While Guthrie could nurture and support the anti-star nature of young actors such as Alec Guinness, in this production of *The School for Scandal* he could find no way into Peggy's soul. She, for her part, seemed to baulk at the exaggerated quality of display expected of the actress in this largely artificial role. 'Peggy,' Gielgud cried out at a dress rehearsal, 'I can't see your eyes – you look as if you haven't got any make-up on at all.'

During the dress rehearsals of *The School for Scandal* Saint-Denis was also struggling to direct *Macbeth* at the Old Vic. Oddly enough Saint-Denis's style, the opposite of natural, seemed to suit Olivier, who played Macbeth, about as much as Guthrie suited Ashcroft as a director. As Olivier put it, registering his own failure in the role, he had to 'share the pie' with Michel:

> We arty lot were at this time going through a phase of avid pre-
> occupation with size; everything had to suggest godlike proportions,
> and the results could be pretty extraordinary. The audience was given

some sort of warning by one's appearance with deliberately mask-like make-up, but appearances, sets, costumes and props were none of them whole-heartedly abstract: it was 'stylised.' I need hardly add that Noël [Coward] nearly died laughing when he came to see it.

This compares admirably with Charles Morgan's description of *The School for Scandal*, as directed by Guthrie, in *The Times* as 'elaborately stylised musical comedy' with the emphasis 'neither on the dialogue nor the characters nor Sheridan but on pattern-making and elegant diversions'.

In fact Saint-Denis lacked just what Guthrie had in plenty: a heightened sense of selectivity, an eye for editing and consolidating a performance for the public's benefit. In Chekhov this is not altogether necessary as the playwright has done the work so well to begin with. The main effect is towards bringing the characters to life – and at this Saint-Denis excelled.

His approach was immediately attractive to Peggy who still yearned for a teacher, a mentor (and perhaps was to continue all her life to do so). For nearly a week before he began rehearsals he made the company read the play every day. He inspired above all confidence in Peggy who believed that acting was at base 'a question of confidence'.*

Everyone was happy and confident in this production, which approached perfection, and whose lightness and gaiety, and yet poignant nostalgia, were somehow all the more heartening but also sad because of the darkening clouds of war: 'The last evening of tranquil beauty that the British theatre was to know for many years.' All who took part attested to the rich influence it had over their work and their lives. Peggy called it, 'the particular triumph of the season ... I think the company, under his influence, reached its climax as a wonderfully welded ensemble.' Alec Guinness, who played Fedotik, said, 'Lots of people flowered in *Three Sisters*: it was like going to some delightful and sad party: we couldn't wait to get back to the place every night.'

During the run of *Three Sisters*, and while rehearsing the next play

---

* This was not true of everyone. Ralph Richardson described how in *Oedipus* at the Old Vic in 1946 he gave the chorus but two notes: 'Perhaps today zere vas not enough emotion. Go away and rehearse,' or 'Perhaps today zere vas too much emotion.' Once he told them, 'You look like a lot of dirty old men pissing against a wall.'

at the Queen's, *The Merchant of Venice*, Alec Guinness became engaged. His fiancée Merula Salaman, the actress, came from a family known to Peggy. When married to Komisarjevsky, she had often visited Merula's family, while Merula's father, Michel Salaman, was also a friend and admirer of Saint-Denis. After their wedding in June 1938 the Guinnesses stayed with Peggy at 92 Campden Hill Road when they were in London. Peggy loved Guinness for his unfailing courtesy and consideration, pleasure and sense of fun. She called him 'a raconteur of fantastic range'. Their paths would next cross on the eve of war.

When Peggy played Portia in *The Merchant of Venice*, one of the handmaidens in attendance on her was played by Vera Lindsay, née Poliakoff. They were soon to be rivals. For three years Vera had been Michel Saint-Denis's mistress. Vera, on whose projected biography at various times both Francis King and the critic John Russell Taylor worked, was an extraordinary figure of her times. The power behind the throne of Saint-Denis, whom she met when he came to London in 1931 with *Noah*, she had married in 1932 a millionaire (and also a communist) named Burton, and subsequently still carried on an affair with Saint-Denis in an open way. They had a son, named Richard, who took the millionaire's name.

Vera was a great mythomane. Her uncle was Anna Pavlova's lover. Born in Russia, she claimed she escaped the Revolution by travelling over the Baltic ice-floes. Whenever a new book by an emigré from Russia was published, she added to her story, elaborating how she had survived greater dangers. If challenged that her own account – never published – resembled that of the latest book, she claimed this had stimulated her memory. According to her, she was also a key figure in the art world. Later in her life, when engaged as a war correspondent sent to cover the liberation of Paris by the Allies in 1944, Vera was asked why she failed to produce more than a few dilatory reports. It was, she said, because Picasso was painting her portrait, but it could never be proved that she was Picasso's model, for nothing could be found except a drawing of a hand or foot to substantiate it. When, after the war, she married Gerald Barry, director of the 1951 Festival of Britain, she claimed responsibility for the whole Festival.

Yet, because even her most flagrant lies contained at least a grain of truth, she could not be dismissed. She had the most dangerous, wounding tongue and no one could surpass her in the art of spreading malice. But when she was good, as Yolanda Sonnabend, painter and designer, pointed out, she could be powerfully so. She was unafraid: later she became 'a sacred monster', but she did love artists and she loved their work, finding ways, as Sonnabend said, 'to make them grow'. She had many friends/enemies whom she loved and denounced equally.

Vera was tall, handsome, voluptuous, a master plotter and manipulator, streets ahead of most other women in terms of sexual allure and sharp and clever in artistic judgment. She gravitated naturally towards the theatre. She changed her name from Poliakoff to Lindsay after the name of a stream near where she was staying in Scotland on holiday. She could be immensely flattering and she managed to land some leading roles in the Compagnie des Quinze. Lots of men found her appearance devastating, but, while looking marvellous on stage, she was a terrible actress. This did not stop her from being employed in distinguished companies.

But she did not get the breaks. In her mind, appearing in *The Merchant of Venice*, she and Peggy were rivals, but when she was with Peggy, Vera treated her as an old friend. Socially they were equals.

What had happened with Paul Robeson earlier in Peggy's career now happened again with Michel. 'This does often happen with vivid plays,' Janet Suzman had commented of the Robeson affair: 'you're inevitably taken up with your opposite number because you're working towards the same thing.' Or the director, she might have added. 'She respected him so much. She had a great respect for those she respected.' Respect, in her case, quickly turned to love.

When the Queen's season ended Peggy followed those members of the company who joined Saint-Denis at the Phoenix Theatre, where he tried to continue his experiment of a permanent company with a wide repertoire.

The omens seemed good, especially with *The White Guard* which centred on a party of old-school Russians stranded in Kiev in 1918, and double-crossed by everyone. A Soviet play, first produced by Stanislavsky, it was free from revolutionary tendentiousness in Mikhail Bulgakov's sympathetic treatment of the characters, and it blended sadness and gaiety in the true Chekhovian spirit. Peggy played the pivotal Yeliena, on whom all the others relied. Her radiance and strength provoked an enthusiastic reception from both audiences and critics alike.

There is no instance of Peggy declaring any feeling for Michel beyond the generalized admiration and love that everyone felt for this great director who was also a warm and humane teacher and human being. Love of their mutual aims and company work threw them together. They toured in *The White Guard* and in the subsequent production of *Twelfth Night*, but Vera hovered in the background, in her capriciousness, her love of power and her wit a more tantalizing off-stage companion than Peggy, whose presence more often than not was plain, zestfully ordinary and down-to-earth.

Although she loved working again with Michael Redgrave, Glen Byam Shaw, George Devine and Marius Goring, there was now also the stirring of a deeper self in Peggy which was even more heavily activated by the impending war. The Munich crisis fell a few days after the opening of *The White Guard* in October 1938. It was a depressing time for everyone, but in that darkness, by some profound instinct by which life is sought in its fullest possible reassuring power in the gravest moments of time, Peggy aspired to a lasting marriage based on love and the desire to raise a family. In December 1937 she had passed the age of thirty and perhaps the rumblings of a second world war – not forgetting that her father had died at the very end of the 1914–8 war, when his chances of survival were high – were like the bell 'Forlorn' in Keats's ode which tolled her back to her true self. For she always needed a life outside her career and her love-affairs in the world of the theatre, however intense they might be, now more and more seemed to be of a temporary nature.

As regards Peggy, Michel Saint-Denis's ultimate failing was that he had no feeling for Shakespeare. Although French by nationality, English by adoption, his artistic soul was deeply Russian, to which he brought all the calm, ordered intelligence of French culture, all the clarity and lucidity of a certain pessimism, or if not that entirely, an irony bordering on cynicism. His ordering of the unformed chaos of emotions, of soulfulness, was quite extraordinary. I once assisted him on a production of Chekhov's *On the High Road* at Stratford-upon-Avon, where he brought this sensitive classical severity to the environmental storm of Chekhov's melodramatic atmosphere and the inner turmoil of all the misfit characters in the play. He was an ideal man in a crisis, but while the condition of all theatre is continual creative crisis, he needed passion, jealousy, a high temperature off-stage. Peggy, calm and thoughtful herself except during her peaks of rehearsal anxiety, was the very antithesis of these emotions. Vera was his cauldron of passion, deceit, his necessary volcano on the edge of which he could sit and reflectively pull on his pipe.

A question frequently asked of Saint Denis's production of *Three Sisters* was how it could be so brilliant, while his *Macbeth* was the worst most people had ever seen.

His *Twelfth Night* was not deemed much better, and was certainly against the expectations of the English audience for he removed the bitter quality from the sweet, prettified Illyria in fancy-dress-ball manner and 'dangerously forced the fooling on Feste'. Peggy's Viola was judged by Herbert Farjeon 'too nice'. while Saint-Denis 'seems to approach Shakespeare as an outsider. How could he so perfectly understand the mind of Chekhov and fail so dismally to understand the mind of Shakespeare?' *Touché*!

Twelfth Night was televised by the BBC as only the second play ever to be so transmitted in full from a theatre (the first had been Priestley's *When We Are Married*). One reporter wrote at this time that a dreadful but true rumour had reached him that Redgrave, who played Aguecheek to universal acclaim, had been signed up by a film company. 'I hope sincerely there is no truth in it. What business has an actor of quality with film studios?' One might well imagine Peggy enthusiastically nodding in approval. But, with the impending isolation of England in its lonely stand against Germany, Peggy had perforce to shed her continental ideal of an ensemble company and that part of her spirit which was European in its romantic attachment. Saint-Denis returned to Paris to join the French army, then came back to London during the fall of France to head Gaullist radio broadcasts under the pseudonym Jacques Duchêne. Later he was joined by Peggy's brother Edward, who much later wrote a biography of de Gaulle.

Although he proposed to her probably more than once, Peggy's second thoughts about marrying another director remained firm. Saint-Denis would never have been the right husband for Peggy now that she was in the mood for permanence. This earthy character already had three children born outside marriage, two sons and a daughter. One son, Jérome, was killed in the advance into Germany before the end of the war. Earlier Saint-Denis's name had been linked with Valentine Tessier, the famous French actress with Russian blood. In due course he met, through Darius Milhaud, a Romanian–French dancer at the Paris Opéra called Suria Magito whom he later married. Although he set a standard in the English theatre, his didactic, authoritarian manner was much criticized. He did not, some claimed, allow for moments of inspiration. When Saint-Denis directed *The Cherry Orchard* at Stratford in 1961 with Peggy and Judi Dench, the latter, who played Anya, complained that he spent all of one day making her come in and clap her hands because it had been done forty years before in Stanislavsky's production. She was reduced to tears.

SEVEN

Reason and Impulse

Whatsoever therefore you do you will be the object
of observation upon a great stage.

Ovid

On the eve of her third marriage, her final and most important one,
we are sufficiently into Peggy's life to reflect upon her nature in love,
which as a subject for biography is undoubtedly her most intriguing
side, and that which she was able, with considerable skill and
cunning, to conceal from public attention. Vera Lindsay, with whom
she had a daggers-drawn relationship, called her a nymphomaniac.
Others referred, more tactfully, to the fact that she could not help
falling in love over and over again. It has been said that she could
not resist any handsome man in the cast, although some of those
handsome men, whose names may be easily deduced from the record
of those she acted with, have been understandably reluctant to
declare that they had relationships with her.

There was, in the immediate post-war period at least and as Michael
Caine reveals in his autobiography *What's It All About?*, an almost
obligatory bedding order in theatrical companies.

As to the men Peggy chose as marriage partners: what do they
reveal about her? For all three would seem to have been her considered
choice, although to Komisarjevsky she claimed she 'gave in'. 'The
type of human being we prefer reveals the contours of our heart,'
wrote Ortega Y Gasset.

The first man Peggy chose, Rupert Hart-Davis, was a romantic
stereotype, tall, handsome, from the kind of background that would
be likely to appeal to a girl from the London suburbs. Both had lost
the opposite parent and felt very hurt, and to some extent sought an
escapist form of relationship that would compensate for this. Both
chose also a narcissistic image. What causes the rush of good feeling
we call romantic love? Psychopharmacologists, if one is inclined to
listen to the biochemical cant of the 1990s, say that lovers are

literally high on drugs – natural hormones and chemicals that flood their bodies with a sense of well-being.

'Talked to Peg till 3am. We love each other.' During the attraction phase of a relationship the brain releases dopamine and norepinephrine, two of the body's many neuro-transmitters. These neuro-transmitters help contribute to a rosy outlook on life, a rapid pulse, increased energy, and a sense of heightened perception. During this stage, when lovers want to be together every moment of the day, the brain increases its production of endorphins and enkephalins, natural narcotics, enhancing a person's sense of security and comfort.

Here we have, in soulless vein, the essential attraction of Romeo and Juliet. Dr Michael R. Liebowitz, associate professor of clinical psychiatry at Columbia University, takes this idea one step further and suggests that the mystical experience of oneness that lovers undergo may be caused by an increase in the production of the neuro-transmitter serotonin.

The fact remains that Hart-Davis might have had this romantic love triggered off in him by Peggy, but scientists cannot explain what exactly causes the release of these potent chemicals or what especially causes them to diminish. It is also likely that Peggy, who had severed her bond from her first husband in a quick decisive way when she felt her sexual appetite awakened by Robeson, at the same time stimulated in Hart-Davis a lifelong desire to 'keep' his Peggy as a romantic image, with the even stronger social intention of preserving her as an ex-wife of extraordinary status value.

With Komisarjevsky, it seemed clear that most of the chemical production was on his side – Peggy inspired him; she was the watching, observing, analytical person who saw in him her mentor. As her teacher he was able to reinvent the world for her. At that time, in the exciting modern fashion of the emancipated woman, she was out to see how she could profit from her mentor, in one sense perhaps steal from him everything that was useful to her. And why not?

With Peggy, Komisarjevsky had gone through, in broken English and strong Slav accent, the four basic approaches of romantic love: (1) 'I know we've just met, but somehow I feel as if I already know you.' They felt at ease with each other, a comfortable resonance, the phenomenon of recognition. (2) 'This is peculiar, but even though we have only been seeing each other for a short while I can't remember when I didn't know you.' Their relationship had no temporal or rational boundaries. (3) 'When I'm with you I no longer feel alone. I feel whole, complete.' This was definitive Komisarjevsky. He could experience this feeling with a multiplicity of different partners, and at one and the same time. He was perpetually in love. This sense of being reunified, and made whole, goes back to the Greek myth of one larger hermaphrodite being split in half and described in Plato's *Symposium*. (4) 'I love you so much I can't live without you.' In other words, Komisarjevsky had to have Peggy with a burning necessity which had no limits. But, of course, when he met the next woman he straight away transferred to her all the feelings that he had had for Peggy, leaving her furious and hurt. What he had failed to discover in Peggy was her uniqueness.

What of Jeremy Hutchinson, called to the Bar in 1939? As Rupert Hart-Davis and William Buchan had been, he was the embodiment of myth, the perfect attractive Englishman from both an Establishment and culturally attractive background. He repeated the pattern of older woman–younger man relationship. 'To the unconscious, being in an intimate love relationship is very much like being an infant in the arms of your mother.' There is the same illusion of safety and security, the same total absorption.

But was it not a curious time to be setting out to build a family? Perhaps not. Through a grim and devastating war, Peggy's hunger for a normal home life, the sense of reality as yet undeveloped in her acting, a yearning for expression in everyday life, completely took her over. As she later told one of her close Bloomsbury friends, Trekkie Parsons, the painter, 'I longed to feel a child breast-feeding.' She had a very strong maternal instinct which as yet had no full expression.

At the age of thirty-three her trust and her desire to settle down was complete. Yet she was a divided soul. She was old, especially in that period, to be embarking on motherhood. How could she be both a leading English actress, and settle down to calm domestic life, and feel that she was giving of her best?

When Peggy started going out with Jeremy Hutchinson in 1940 he was twenty-five while she was thirty-three. The age-gap was exactly that of Anne Hathaway and William Shakespeare, although they had married when he was eighteen. Shakespeare wrote later, in the lines already quoted, that the woman should take an older man:

'So wears she to him, / So sways she level in her husband's heart.' Anne Hathaway may well have been Shakespeare's childhood sweetheart; Hutchinson and Peggy had moved in much the same circles.

Hutchinson had attended Stowe School. At Oxford, where he had taken a degree in PPE at Magdalen College, they had met when Peggy played Juliet in Gielgud's production for OUDS at the New Theatre. Hutchinson was a non-acting member of the dramatic society. Michael Meyer recalled Peggy in this production as being 'all arms and legs'. Although only seventeen at the time, his background was colourful and complex. He shared rooms in Magdalen with Ben Nicolson, art historian brother of Nigel Nicolson the publisher and author, both sons of Vita Sackville-West and the politician and diarist, Harold Nicolson.

Jeremy's father was St John Hutchinson, KC, a famous criminal lawyer. His mother, Mary Hutchinson, was a grand hostess in what was known as the 'smart art set', the original Mrs Dalloway, or so it has been claimed, of Virginia Woolf's novel. A friend of Lytton Strachey, the well-known Bloomsburyite, Mary had a celebrated, open affair with Clive Bell, the art critic and post-Impressionist apologist.

In the first five years of Jeremy's life she was a particularly close friend of T. S. Eliot, who sent her copies of poems such as 'Gerontian' before he revised them. Eliot took a house near her in the Chichester area, and even on one occasion went dancing with her in a dance hall near Baker Street. Able to confide easily in Mary, he accused himself in one letter of 'suspiciousness and pusillanimity in human relationships', while she remained a close correspondent well into his later life.

Jeremy's sister, Barbara, was the first wife of Victor Rothschild. George Rylands, who did not get to know Peggy until the beginning of the war and who was also at Cambridge at this time, knew Mary Hutchinson and had first met her in Bloomsbury in 1924. He recalled buying Jeremy, aged eight, an ice-cream at the Café de Paris in Piccadilly.

Peggy may have felt she shared some traits with Jeremy's mother, above all that great capacity for falling in love, for if there was one principle of the Bloomsbury ethos known generally to the world it was the *Romeo and Juliet* spirit of being carried away by feeling, by impulse, of responding to the 'holiness of the heart's affections'. Also, like Juliet, the Bloomsburyite in his or her passionate feelings had an immense ability to extend into self-consciousness and destructive self-analysis, although Peggy was little aware of this at that time. In addition, as the designer Jocelyn Herbert said of Peggy, Mary shared with her a great sense of humour (Lindsay Anderson, the director, always wanted Peggy to play in comedy but never managed to organize this for her).

Hutchinson was aware of Peggy all through the 1930s, for they met quite often, at weekends, or in London at parties. It must have been a very romantic image of her that he received, yet one of strength and feminine capability. Peggy was, as Jocelyn Herbert said of her, 'in everything'. She commented further, 'She was always very nervous.'

In 1939 while Jeremy was called to the Bar (the Middle Temple), Peggy followed *Twelfth Night* with a tour of *Weep for the Spring* by Stephen Haggard, another good friend, and then, just before the declaration of war, she played Cecily Cardew in *The Importance of Being Earnest* at the Globe, directed by Gielgud, which opened in August. She had just begun rehearsing Anya in *The Cherry Orchard*, with Saint-Denis directing, when, as she recalled later in a broadcast, Britain declared war on Germany.

3 September was a Sunday and Peggy had gone to stay in Huntingdon with friends who had an evacuee centre for children. She had been driven down in the afternoon, and she was taken to the tennis court which had loose red sand, and which was 'packed with toddlers' who had been sitting there for a long time, 'who all had wet bottoms and runny noses, which I had to blow for them'. This was before, she went on, the birth of her own children, and she found herself changing nappies for the first time in her life, and putting children on potties. 'Butterflies don't have potties, do they?' asked one little boy. This story hid a hard grief for Peggy to swallow. The previous morning, 2 September, Binkie Beaumont, of H. M. Tennent, had assembled the cast of *The Cherry Orchard* and told them he had to cancel the production.

There's an overtone of the patronizing, theatrical dame in this account, which we have to discount if we want to keep to the idea of the unassuming, modest, down-to-earth Peggy. But of course she had acquired the attitude, common most likely to almost every theatrical star at the time, that children were a distraction, even an issue of conflict, in their careers. And so, now, was war. 'I can't act with bombs falling: what am I to do?' declared Edith Evans in the grand, entirely selfish manner.

Now there was a war on, the theatre became very much put to one side, in Peggy's mind at least. It deepened her hunger for children of her own. Although *The Cherry Orchard* had been called off, when the expected Blitz failed to materialize, Peggy, in the same family of actors, found herself as the young feminine lead in *Cousin Muriel* by Clemence Dane, again with Edith Evans as the middle-aged *éminence*. She was still very nervous during rehearsals. In a much repeated anecdote, Edith Evans gave way to a temptation to hysteria because she thought Alec Guinness, who played her son and defended his playing of a line she disliked, didn't love her any more. 'He hates me!' screamed Evans, and threw herself down on stage, drumming with her feet, seizing and tearing the corner of the Persian rug between her teeth. What raconteurs of this amazing episode, notably Guinness, failed to add was that Peggy was so distressed by the hysteria that she followed suit by throwing herself down on stage wailing and screaming.

Cousin Muriel revealed to Gielgud another, very different side of Peggy, namely that she would give way sometimes to 'sudden spates of bad language'. At one point during what Gielgud called this 'dreadful play' she trod on her dress and tore it – and said 'Shit!' So striking the way she did it,' said Gielgud, 'so striking!'

In the meantime Jeremy Hutchinson, newly qualified as a barrister, joined the RNVR at the shore training base of HMS *King Alfred* in Hove, where he was shortly to pass his selection board to become an officer. But in February 1940, when *Cousin Muriel* was on its pre-London tour and playing Brighton, he went backstage and visited Peggy's dressing-room. 'I simply went and saw her,' he said later, 'that was when our romance developed, it was pure chance. We went out and so on.'

It was a whirlwind romance, in the style of those times, for after their courtship in Brighton (lasting not quite a week) Hutchinson joined Louis Mountbatten's destroyer fleet in Plymouth and was appointed to HMS *Kolvin* as a junior officer. In the summer when on leave he met Peggy again and they decided to marry.

Mary and St John Hutchinson were living in Prince Albert Road,

Regent's Park. Peggy was still on Campden Hill. She had written, on 4 April 1940, to Gabrielle Enthoven, a friend with whom she communicated for years and who gave her name to the Victoria and Albert Museum's theatre collection, that she was back in her house again after 'many vicissitudes'. Alec Guinness and his wife had been living at her house but they were about to leave and then she would have a spring clean – 'war or no war' – and a new maid. Guinness was extremely keen to join up, and Peggy, he reported later in his most Evelyn Waughesque style, 'knew' a colonel, her 'uncle' to whom she sent Guinness. He was very small, 'wore a hairy tweed suit and while trying to look helpful was in fact very cross'.

This may have been Peggy's guardian and true uncle, General Birnam, now retired and living in Addison Road, Kensington. Yet Hutchinson said he found him – if it was the same man – 'terribly proud and awfully sweet'. He added, not clear as to which side of the family was which, 'I think her father must have been a wonderful chap.'

Barrage balloons were now swaying over Hyde Park. The Battle of Britain had been in progress for some weeks. 14 September 1940, Peggy and Hutchinson's wedding day, was the day of the first big air raid on London. They got married from the house in Prince Albert Road, driving down to the Register Office in Marylebone. Victor Rothschild and St John Hutchinson were the witnesses. Jeremy wore the uniform of a sub-lieutenant.

Despite Peggy's fame as an actress and as the former wife of Komisarjevsky, there were no photographs in the papers, for larger events occupied the press. Back in Regent's Park they ate their reception lunch while the sirens wailed endlessly. They must – certainly Peggy must – have had certain premonitions, for the shade of Major Worsley Ashcroft of the Machine Gun Corps could not have been far from the wedding party. As Mary's friend T. S. Eliot wrote, life was peculiar; it was a 'changing and bewildered world'. Eliot was to serve as an air-raid warden during the December blitz.

The couple then drove to Dorset down the Great West Road which was 'absolutely quiet and deserted'. They had their honeymoon in a little mill at Burton Bradstock where Peggy had by chance made friends with Stanley Robinson, 'a wonderful man with a club foot, who had a family of five'.

EIGHT

Made of Glass

Behaviour is a mirror in which
everyone shows his image

Goethe

Peggy admired Jeremy's parents, especially, according to Gielgud, 'his bohemian mother'. Parents-in-law are always important role models, especially for someone who was and who remained throughout her life so continually sensitive and responsive to others. Mary was, like Peggy, a great Francophile; as Noël Annan said, she was the 'very appealing, slightly fluttery, wounded bird' type of woman. Although destined for the law like his father, Jeremy was brought up very much under the aegis of Bloomsbury. Yet St John Hutchinson was highly correct in the conduct of his own life, as people at the Bar at that time had to be, and especially about their sex-life.

As a cross-examiner, Hutchinson fell into the 'bullying advocate' type. Annan recounted an anecdote of Hutchinson's which showed his method: it concerned a homosexual Fellow of Clare College, Cambridge, Manny Forbes, who lived in a house called Finella and who was arrested for holding male orgies. 'I'm not defending,' said Hutchinson, 'but call in Henry Curtiss Bennett. Don't let it go to the High Court.' Hutchinson did cross-examine the policeman who alleged the offence. It went something like this. The officer said he had seen all sorts of dreadful goings-on through a gap in the curtain. 'Officer, how long have you been in the police force?' Hutchinson asked. 'Twenty-three years.' 'You saw these disgusting acts through a chink in the curtain? How long did they go on for?' Answer: 'Four to five minutes.' 'How long is four to five minutes?' Long pause. 'Why don't you answer?' 'I was counting four to five minutes, sir!' 'Were you counting when you observed these disgusting acts?' And so on.

Mary Hutchinson's public affair with Clive Bell, propagandist for Roger Fry's theories of art, enhanced the appeal of this liberal-minded and brilliant cross-examiner. Bloomsbury was very choosy. Its cliquish spirit made it hard to accept anyone from outside. But 'they' – Vanessa and Clive Bell, Duncan Grant and the Woolfs – 'tolerated' Mary although Virginia, who must have picked up some of her sister Vanessa's, woundedness, 'never took' to her personally. Briefly, the Bloomsbury group believed that 'ranking' was rubbish, in both art and literature, attaching greater importance to what the artist or writer was trying to say. Clive and Vanessa Bell were the fountain-head of Bloomsbury lore. The critics, writers and artists who shared their values defended and practised modernism, their creed being that generalized critical judgments and broad moral assessments could not be passed on art or literature (or indeed on people's sexual behaviour, although their political behaviour came in for much puritan assessment). Ranged against them was Dr F. R. Leavis, fellow of Downing College, Cambridge, who believed passionately that what a work was trying to say deserved moral evaluation; and later T. S. Eliot, who emphasized tradition and was prepared to judge that Dante was greater than Shakespeare, or that *Hamlet* was an immature play.

It is easy to fault members of the Bloomsbury group on their sexual behaviour, and point to the hypocrisy and high-minded treachery in their often incestuous relationships. Their humanistic approach ('Man is the measure of all things'), stripped of its style and standards, could make them seem both selfish and decadent. They taught 'our age ... that the conquest of jealousy was the mark of civilized behaviour'. Sexual fidelity was not highly prized but sex was often disguised from being seen as an end in itself; more often than not if you liked someone you had to fall in love with them, for this was the necessary self-deception that enabled you to go to bed with them.

So what were they? In love with love? Or in love with themselves in a narcissistic way? Subjectivity was certainly the name of many of the Bloomsbury games. They liked to alarm. As Lord David Cecil said of Virginia Woolf: 'She used to ask questions designed to embarrass you. But they were all rather shy and gauche, except with one another. And they all thought that their attitudes were the only attitudes.' Their preoccupation with immature love brings us back to Juliet (or rather to Peggy's fascination with her as a very young woman).

Victor Rothschild, who married Jeremy's older sister Barbara*,

* Annan mentions her in *Our Age*, p. 3, together with Ann Fleming, Pamela Berry and

ended up hating the whole family spirit which Peggy was now embracing. On their honeymoon Barbara went to bed with a waiter. While Victor was away on war assignments, she threw wild parties at Merton Hall, the Rothschild home near Cambridge, and had an affair with a 'dashing' RAF commander named Mole. This was while Peggy, with her very young family, was staying on the other Rothschild estate, near Tring, in a three-bedroomed 'folly' built by Charles II for his mistress Nell Gwynn. Finding his carefully husbanded French wine disappearing at an appalling rate Victor locked the cellar door, which was considered great treachery by Barbara and her friends, one of whom, Robert Boothby, MP and lover of Harold Macmillan's wife Dorothy, took an axe and broke down the cellar door. Barbara was incensed when she heard that Victor had fallen in love – with Tessa Mayer the actress, daughter of a fellow of King's College, Cambridge. The tragedy was, by the end, that each wanted to wound or *épater* the other. When Victor, on the morning of Barbara's birthday, gave her a treasured edition of Pope's *Essay on Man* she just dropped it on the floor by the bed. When her friend Rosamond Lehmann was having an affair with Cecil Day-Lewis the poet, Barbara was heard to remark, 'She's got a great literary figure, why shouldn't I have one?' (It echoed Vivien Leigh's 'All great actresses have lovers. Why shouldn't I?') Barbara then ran off with Rex Warner the poet. Rothschild, who later divorced her and remarried, became very bitter about the female side of the Hutchinson family, saying that Mary would go to bed with a donkey if required, and that she had been a bad role model for her daughter, who took after her.

What of her son Jeremy? He was a most amusing young man, and masterful, which women liked. He was a different kettle of fish from the older, parental figures of the lovers Peggy had taken earlier. Socially, he was a big 'catch'. But was Peggy someone who would ever have stayed with one man? Perhaps the deeper question ought to be asked, as it was put to me by Noël Annan ('purely a subjective judgment'): Was Peggy really interested in sex? Annan suspected the answer may have been in the negative. I can only add that sexuality, in its outward form, was to become an important weapon in an

Joan Eyres-Mansell, as examples of 'certain women who never went to university ... life-enhancers'.

armoury by which she kept the allegiance of younger men as she grew older.

For the moment Peggy was newly wed and extremely happy. Her husband, like many hundreds of thousands of young men at the time (he was twenty-six in May 1941) was away on active service. In the autumn following her wedding she had taken over from Jessica Tandy the role of Miranda in an Old Vic production of *The Tempest*. With her husband absent for long periods, she was settled into what some would consider the ideal form of matrimony, and was now pregnant with her first child. But there was still the shadow of her father's death falling over her – as the shadow of death fell over everyone in some form or other. Indeed, she shared the dread of Lewis Casson and Sybil Thorndike whose son John, during a performance of *The Tempest*, was reported missing, shot down over the North Sea. Casson, playing Gonzalo, wept on stage. Much later John was found to be safe in a POW camp. Yet for the most part in early 1941, during the darkest days of the war, Peggy was comfortably pregnant, warm with the sensation of new life growing inside her; she went on tour playing Mrs de Winter in Daphne du Maurier's *Rebecca*, but for the last months of her pregnancy she withdrew to Barbara and Victor's house in Tring. And then for fifteen months she gave up the theatre.

Happy families, as Tolstoy wrote, have no history. This was not to be so in Peggy's case. Even in the month before her baby was born she had a terrible fright. Jeremy was with Mountbatten's destroyer flotilla at Malta serving on board his flagship, HMS *Kelly*. When the Germans invaded Crete the flotilla was sent to intercept them. *Kelly* and her sister ship were separated from their escort and had to come out at dawn alone, and without cover. Both ships were sunk by German planes.

'I was one of the lucky ones,' said Hutchinson. He spent three or four hours in the water. The planes were machine-gunning everyone, and there was 'an awful lot of oil; I was thinking about myself I'm afraid,' Hutchinson told me. 'A third ship came along and some of us were picked up.' The family kept the news about the sinking from Peggy for a whole week and pretended that everything was all right until they heard Jeremy was safe. On 14 June their daughter was born and christened Eliza, but Jeremy was unable to return from the Mediterranean until August.

He was then given a shore posting at Devonport. 'Didn't tell you,'

Michael Redgrave, a naval rating of thirty-three, wrote to his wife Rachel, 'of my interview with the Divisional Commander, Jeremy Hutchinson, Peggy Ashcroft's husband.' Hutchinson told him he was to be relieved of being class leader 'because Menzies had to be tried. He said, "I'm thoroughly satisfied with your performance, and have put you down as commission-worthy. It's just that Menzies, do you see, is secretary to the Duke of Atholl and we have had a little pressure!" ' To Redgrave it smacked of a snobbery of which he disapproved.

Was Peggy deeply into being a mother? She told Pauline Jameson, the actress, who appeared with her in *The Heiress* in 1949, 'Feeding my children was the most magical thing in the world.' Magical? The word is perhaps not the first that might spring to mind today, but she clearly derived great satisfaction from breast-feeding. She had a maternal nature, although she quickly shared care of her child with a nanny, a rather old, straight-laced and grumpy one, and later engaged a younger one, Euphemia, who stayed for the rest of her life. 'Sad and disappointed,' Tamsin Day-Lewis, a childhood friend of Eliza, called the nanny, 'always a mother, never a wife.' Yet having permanent help freed Peggy from the exhaustion of motherhood. 'She was always doing things for people,' remarked Jameson of Peggy. 'She was so generous with her time; she was very spontaneous. She did things and did not let people know she was doing them.' This perhaps flowed from her becoming a mother. Margaret Harris also noted the maturing process brought about by Peggy having and caring for children: 'After the war she became a great woman without sacrificing any of her charm.' But possibly the conflict and guilt over leaving her children to be looked after by others also contributed to this maturity. Most mothers of her class had no qualms at all about leaving their children with the nanny. Later Peggy would not talk about her children, or, as Janet Suzman disclosed, 'only in blits and blabs': it was to her 'a wonder how Peggy could have loved him [Jeremy] so much, as they were such different types. But she did.'

In late 1942 Hutchinson joined Mountbatten on the aircraft carrier *Illustrious*, for Mountbatten took back with him the officers and men who had survived *Kelly*'s sinking. One night, when he was on watch during a zigzag across the Atlantic, he 'biffed the back' of another carrier. He went on leave in Liverpool. Peggy had her nanny, 'because she was working', and she came to Southport where they spent

Christmas together. Eliza was by now one and a half. Subsequently, in February 1943, Jeremy was posted to a signals school in East Meon, Sussex, where they saw more of each other, then he was sent in the fleet to take Madagascar with Ceylon as his main station. He stayed in the Indian Ocean for eighteen months.

'What a man is at twelve years old,' wrote Alain, the French philosopher, 'so will he be all through his life.' If this statement is to be applied to Peggy (and like all generalizations it may never be wholly true but can be taken as a useful pointer to the truth) then she must have been, since the age of eleven, the grieving daughter. Grief is a many-mooded animal, expressive of a whole range of conflicting states and emotions through which the bereaved person must pass. To begin with, there can be the terrible, physical pain of loss which is like an amputated limb; then there is numbness, deadness, depression, perhaps with corresponding lapses into anxiety: the sense that one is alone, and abandoned by all. After this there may be a terrible rage at the infliction of this blow, by someone or something, on one's life.

The rage against fate might be superseded by a false dawn; or a real dawn of hope, as yet a small and distant glimmer of light but gradually increasing, and, while beckoning, also widening. This may be the reality of coming to terms with the loss of a loved one, but it can be a slow and painful process, and it can take a long time. Light hurts. Reality is painful. Escape is a more comfortable way out, whether it is escape through acting many romantic roles, or escape through many different forms of relationships which may either comfort or console. There are no simple answers. What might offer an excruciatingly tough possibility of growth for one person might, for another, be a flight into blind reassurance, or an intolerable hell.

For Peggy, with her powerful inborn talent as an actress, the years of her twenties and most of her thirties had been years of escape, escape into roles, both off-stage and on, which gave her great power and recognition, but were not great tests of whether she had survived and come to terms with the great grief of loss she had suffered when a child. Neither were these years a test of her capability to develop and deepen her art. She had not been pushed to her limits by any means and while, in retrospect, she might be seen to have greater potential than other actresses of her age and background, such as

Diana Wynyard or Celia Johnson, there was as yet little to distinguish her from them.

She was like the 'chrysoberyl' to which *The Times* had likened her in her eve-of-war *Importance of Being Earnest*. In this she had played Cecily Cardew for eight matinee charity performances, lined up by Gielgud alongside Edith Evans, Margaret Rutherford, Jack Hawkins and Gwen Ffrangçon-Davies. The Motleys had decorated this production and Peggy, as the 'chrysoberyl', had been just as she had in almost all the parts she had played up to now, changing colour with the light, reflecting back to others what they wanted to see, 'now innocently olive-green, now an audacious pink'. But her love-affairs, especially with older, famous men, her marriages, her searchings for contacts, showed that something deeper still had to be worked out. Peggy had yet to shape that grievous void, that depression probably not even raised into her conscious mind, which acted like a weight, a spring, a source of energy because it was dark, unexplained and sometimes frightening, into an emotional force on which she could draw.

War was also a formative experience while she herself, towards the end of it, was reaching the difficult age of forty. War released that 'so clear, bell-like voice', as Noël Annan called it, into a new realm of endeavour – that of the poetry-reading – which brought audiences and performers even closer together than before. The formation of the Apollo Society was Peggy's idea, as was its name; she also produced medallions of Apollo which were used as the society's letterheads. She described to the pianist Natasha Litvin, who was married to the poet Stephen Spender, how she and Edith Evans had done poetry-readings at the Globe Theatre and wanted to expand this activity, including music on an equal footing.

The founder members of the society included George Rylands, Cecil Day-Lewis, his wife Jill Balcon, Stephen Spender, Natasha Litvin, John Laurie the actor and Maynard Keynes the economist, who was chairman of the Council for the Encouragement of Music and the Arts. The Apollo Society was launched at the Arts Theatre, Cambridge, with a poetry-reading given by John Laurie, Robert Harris, and Peggy. John Masefield, the poet laureate, introduced the programme in somewhat condescending style, describing the beautiful Litvin as 'winsome'.

Later they would meet and plan meetings at the Spenders' home in St John's Wood, or at the Troika restaurant off Shaftesbury Avenue. They would match or interleave poems with music, as when Dylan Thomas came to a meeting to suggest they read Walter de la Mare's *The Feckless Dinner Party*, giving a brilliant virtuoso performance and Edith Sitwell suggested the right macabre music, Prokoviev's *Suggéstion Diabolique*, to go with it. They performed everywhere; for example, when Peggy was pregnant with her second child in 1946 the Apollo Society did a tour of mining towns in Northumberland and Durham where Peggy found audiences were more responsive and intelligent than those in the south. She always had an arrangement whereby she never appeared in a play during the summer holidays, which left her free to appear in recitals.

Later Rylands was to read in his flamboyant, booming voice,

> 'I feed a flame within that so torments me,
> That it both pains my heart and yet contents me'

—perhaps the perfect motto for Bloomsbury.

Nobody read as musically as Peggy, although she would 'boom' at the beginning before settling down. She insisted on understanding completely what she read and could not perform unless she had.

The outward expression of the many worries, toils, and griefs which Peggy saw all around her found an inner response of identification through what she herself had suffered in the First World War. Her response was positive, outward-going. She would use her gift to alleviate the sorrow and suffering of others.

NINE

A House Pulled Down

'For myself,' said Lopez, 'I can conceive no vainer object of ambition than a seat in the British parliament.'

Anthony Trollope, *Phineas Finn*

While the currents were moving at unseen depths, the war itself produced no extraordinary or even outstanding work from Peggy. She made a few minor films, one for the Ministry of Information called *Channel Incident*, another, *A New Lot*, directed by Carol Reed, in which she played an insubordinate ATS girl. In January 1943 she was starting to rehearse *A Month in the Country* to open at the St James's Theatre, where it subsequently ran for more than a year, when she broke her ankle as she jumped into a taxi; as a result, she had to withdraw from the production. Soon afterwards she visited Rachel Kempson, Michael Redgrave's wife, while, as Rachel reported, she herself was breast-feeding her daughter Lynn. 'Oh God, why do we go on acting when there's all this?' Peggy burst out. But she found Eliza a difficult child to manage, as a mother often does who has had a long career previous to the birth of her first child. Later, according to Hutchinson, Peggy always found it hard to 'balance the demands of the family with the pursuance of her career'. That she managed ultimately to do both was attested to by Jocelyn Herbert, who said that Peggy was two people: the marvellous actress, 'totally dedicated,' and the 'warm, loving, mother, friend'.

In October 1943 Peggy appeared in Rodney Ackland's *The Dark River*, which Ackland himself directed. While some have seen in Peggy's depiction of Catherine Lisle, in what Eric Keown in his monograph of Peggy called 'a rather depressingly nostalgic play – apart from one character who lived for the future, and not very sympathetically at that' – a new dimension of emotional truth in the unhappy ballet dancer who is always harking back to past success, the role was, at bottom, tiresome. It was an unhappy work by an unhappy writer, whom Francis King called 'a very tragic figure' suffering from the literary equivalent of stage fright. Ackland was terrified of being put to the test. *The Dark River* did not last long.

George Rylands, fellow of King's College, Cambridge, since 1927, had first acted in Cambridge in 1920; his first part was Electra in *The Oresteia*, directed by J. T. Sheppard who later became Provost. He made a great early impact in female roles, including the Duchess of Malfi, which he was shortly to direct with Peggy in the title role, but he later played Othello, Macbeth, Lear and 'the part which I think suited me best', Angelo in *Measure for Measure*. Through the formation of the Apollo Society in 1943 he and Peggy had begun a strong and lasting friendship.

The artist Dora Carrington described Rylands in the 1920s with 'hair the colour of a canary bird, and the most heavenly blue eyes'. A college guest of Maynard Keynes witnessed him as an undergraduate reading grace in Hall with 'incredible panache and virtuosity', wearing a bright blue suit with an equally bright blue tie. He apparently elicited a suppressed cry of 'blasphemous' from Dr Clapham, the Senior Tutor. Since Keynes had started financing the Arts Theatre, Cambridge, with Rylands as the main director, amateur drama had begun to thrive in Cambridge, attracting enthusiastic notices from the London press and ultimately producing directors of the calibre of Peter Hall and Trevor Nunn, and actors such as Daniel Massey and Derek Jacobi. Noël Annan recalls in *Our Age* how Rylands 'drilled his undergraduate actors to think while they were speaking, what the Elizabethan and Jacobean blank verses meant instead of ranting or throwing away the lines. They learned how to respect the interplay of rhythm and metre of the lines – a discipline that after the war was to transform for three decades the speaking of verse at Stratford and on the London stage.'

Throughout the war Gielgud had not stopped acting: by 1944 on his own admission he was exhausted, especially as a director, and when that year Binkie Beaumont persuaded him once again into management he chose to do five plays in repertory, with Peggy as his leading lady in three: *Hamlet, A Midsummer Night's Dream* and *The Duchess of Malfi*. Leading lady in the two Shakespeare plays meant, quite bizarrely, Ophelia and Titania. Ophelia would seem to be somewhat of a pushover for a 36-year-old actress of Peggy's power and experience. But she was extremely keen to return to the classical stage, and Gielgud saw her still as the 1930s ingénue, himself caught perhaps by the stultifying effect of war on the theatre. The production of *Hamlet*, according to Kenneth Tynan in his book *He Who Plays the King*, was 'snail-paced'.

'All in all it was a somewhat tricky company, and at that stage in the war we were all feeling rather middle-aged and found that changing the bill and playing different parts was a strain.' So Gielgud pronounced his verdict later. Rylands was directing *Hamlet* and Nevill Coghill, of Oxford, *A Midsummer Night's Dream*. Gielgud thought it would be interesting to have these distinguished professors to work with, 'but I found that they did not get on very well with the actors and found it hard to understand their problems'.

When Peggy was rehearsing Ophelia and had just left Piccadilly Underground station she was injured by a V-2 rocket bomb which landed on the Regent Palace Hotel nearby, one of the first to descend on London in the summer of 1944. She was propelled by the impact into a barber's shop and into the 'unresisting arms of a fat man who had asked only for a shave'. The glass that lodged in her knee kept her off the stage only for a week or two of the pre-London tour, but it affected her for the rest of her life.

This production of *Hamlet*, and the subsequent *A Midsummer Night's Dream* (and *The Duchess of Malfi*) were very much marginalized as old-fashioned and backward – by comparison with the Richardson and Olivier Old Vic seasons of 1944–5 and 1945–6. 'I would have loved to have been part of that company', commented Gielgud, who decried the attempts of his 'end-of-war middle-aged company trying to be spirited'. He would have been, he went on, 'if Ralph Richardson had had his way. But it was Olivier who fucked it up.'

Ever since they had acted together in the Albert Hall, briefly at Birmingham, and with the one exception of alternating the role of Romeo with Gielgud, Olivier had steered clear of Peggy. No one has ever elicited the reason why, and of course professional good manners during the lives of this pair would not allow anything other than expressions of the deepest mutual respect. Yet Olivier had, as far as we know, never asked Peggy to be in the Old Vic seasons, nor did he later, when he began running the National Theatre in 1962. But those facts do make nonsense of the claim that Peggy had been at the forefront of every theatrical movement of her times.

She was now at rather an awkward age as an actress and a woman. Approaching forty, she was caught uneasily between the desire to preserve her ability still to play younger roles and her emergence into the Edith Evans category. For all her much-lauded sexiness, which she developed distinctively later as a middle-aged woman – the change in social attitudes encouraging her to do so – she had no means by which she could compete with the stunning Margaret Leighton, who played the Green Woman in *Peer Gynt* to Richardson and Roxanne in *Cyrano de Bergerac*. Nor could she rival Celia Johnson* in soulful, wifely or mistress roles in films, the hallmark of which was the Captain's wife in Coward's *In Which We Serve*, David Lean's film about Mountbatten and the sinking of HMS *Kelly*. Vivien Leigh also out-rivalled her in this period, both in films (*Fire Over England*, *Lady Hamilton*, and *Anna Karenina*) and on stage at the Old Vic later (in *Skin of Our Teeth*, *The School for Scandal*, and *Richard III*).

Gielgud's three plays seem in retrospect very much second-eleven stuff. There was nothing very spectacular about Peggy's Ophelia, which was praised for its simplicity and sincerity, so much so in fact that one might question the value, at that particular moment, of such a quality. After five years of war, people needed waking up. The supreme merit of Rylands's direction, wrote the *Times* critic, was that it passed unnoticed. Peggy's Titania in *A Midsummer Night's Dream* was by all accounts more impressive, and especially powerful in its word music. But one has the feeling that she was otherwise disengaged in this dull and routine production in which Gielgud was grim as Oberon.

The Duchess of Malfi gave Peggy more scope for some acting in depth but I am not convinced she was that good, or that it developed her acting at all. Gielgud said Rylands knew the play too well, and 'he sat with his nose in the book'. Leon Quartermaine, playing the Cardinal, took exception to Rylands and tried to get him sacked during rehearsal: he went to Gielgud, said Rylands, because he didn't want him to risk his reputation: 'He did all he could to undermine confidence.'

---

* See p. 198. Apart from the early rivalry they had in love it is hard to understand why Peggy disliked Johnson so much. But the latter had a successful film career and stable family life, such as Peggy may have desired.

But the leading lady loved her director. She sent him a piece of doggerel, which had the refrain

Darling Dadie don't be sad!

and listed the actors and their shortcomings, even suggesting that she herself might lack the necessary grandeur for the Duchess. As it was, Gielgud seemed not to have much confidence in it himself: his Duke Ferdinand was described by *The Times* as a 'petulant pervert', while the production was faintly cheered by 'the respectful curiosity' of the audience which never once 'descended to misplaced tittering'.

Tepid praise indeed. But the review that really wounded Peggy was James Agate's. 'Miss Ashcroft's Duchess?' he wrote interrogatively in his most amusing yet damaging way. 'Walkley [the critic] once divided leading ladies into "mousey-pouseys" and "roguey-pogueys". With this example I venture to coin "teeny-weenies" as a designation for exquisite, sensitive, delicate actresses whom Nature has cast out of the tragic mould. The Duchess is a part for a Titan not for Titania.'

In her hurt, Peggy, as always, felt defiant and challenged. Actors might dismiss Agate's harsh words but critics, in the case of many great actors of that time, provoked and stimulated the best because they had a power of learning and authority. Most of all Agate complained that Peggy's performance lacked size:

I say, with respect, that in the part of Webster's Duchess nothing but the grand manner will do. A contemporary critic wrote of Mrs Siddons in Franklin's tragedy *The Earl of Warwick* that she made her entry through a large archway, 'which she really seemed to fill'. Any actress who is to present Webster's heroine must fill, and fill completely, the archway of the spectator's mind. And to do this she must have the tragic quality of voice. Something more than plaintiveness, however touching, is wanted if 'I am Duchess of Malfi still!' is not to sound like 'I am still Little Miss Muffet!'

Even Gielgud subsequently, and somewhat grudgingly, agreed: 'I think it should have been Pamela Brown – more sinister!' 'At least Lewis [Casson] liked it,' said Binkie Beaumont. 'He'll probably want to take it round the Welsh mining villages. Can you *imagine?*' To those who were not greatly impressed Kenneth Tynan also added his voice. He felt that Margaret Rawlings, who played Vittoria in *The White Devil* in 1947, gave a much greater performance.

Peggy's protective and indeed motherly warmth towards Rylands was very different in form to the way in which she might have expressed it to Devine, Saint-Denis or Guthrie. She could see he was a denizen of another world, but a world which attracted her as much as the theatre, the more academic world, with its Bloomsbury flavour, of the poetry recital. Dadie was a great friend of Leonard and Virginia Woolf and of the Hutchinson family, and in her way Peggy felt 'responsible' for him. But she was never again to be directed by him on the professional stage.

In the meantime Peggy paid homage to Gielgud's great-aunt, Ellen Terry, in whose direct line of theatrical dames she was now securely planted. A centenary service was held for Ellen Terry in St Paul's Church, Covent Garden, on 27 February 1947. She had maintained freshness and vitality throughout her long career, and she had been an inspiration to all those who had played with her. Like Peggy she was a great lover of Shakespeare; she gave readings and lectured on him. He was, she once said, the only man she had ever really loved.

The day of the service was cold and yellow, 'in which no woman looked her best', according to James Lees-Milne. The church was packed, the Sadler's Wells Choir sang anthems. Edith Evans, Sybil Thorndike and Peggy Ashcroft read Shakespeare sonnets, while the lessons were read by Ralph Richardson, Leon Quartermaine and Harcourt Williams. 'With the exception of the last, who is a handsome elderly man, all the others looked remarkably plain, Richardson a flunkey, Quartermaine a Glasgow thug masquerading as an undertaker, E. Evans as a painted clown (male), and Thorndike as a downtrodden school-teacher.'

Jeremy Hutchinson had been in England on D-Day – 6 June 1944 – but shortly afterwards he was posted again, this time to the headquarters of the Commander-in-Chief, Mediterranean, at Caserta, where he remained until early 1945. Coming as he did from a liberal legal family he had always aspired towards a political career. Peggy supported this. From the time she had played Desdemona with Robeson, and passionately embraced his attitudes towards racial injustice, her leaning had always been to the left. Priestley, too, had been a committed socialist.

It was a very upper-class, English form of socialism which Peggy now pursued through Jeremy. Philip Noel-Baker, a junior minister in the Coalition War Cabinet, had long been a Hutchinson family friend. Fifty-six years of age, he was keen to recruit new blood for the Labour Party, while Hutchinson, as a barrister, with his excellent war record, his youthful and engaging manner, and his famous wife, was an ideal choice as a Labour candidate for the first post-war election in 1945. Noel-Baker himself had read history at King's College, Cambridge, and had a distinguished record in the First World War, surviving Mons and winning the *Croce de Guerra* as commander of an ambulance unit on the Italian front. In the short-lived Labour government of 1929–31 he had been a junior foreign minister.

King's College, Cambridge, was predominantly Labour in spirit. Maynard Keynes, the most influential economist of the war and immediate post-war period, was a fellow and bursar of the college. Rylands was a fellow of King's. The Rothschilds, too, were sympathetic to Labour policies: it is not surprising, therefore, that Peggy and Noel-Baker became friends and that she should have encouraged Jeremy's adoption as Labour candidate for the Abbey Division of Westminster. Although a safe Tory seat, with a majority of 12,000 in the previous election, it was an achievement for this young naval officer to be selected.

Hutchinson called it later 'another wheeze' to be at home. He and Peggy canvassed the staff of 10 Downing Street, who lined up in uniform. Hutchinson commented that all Peggy's political passions were awoken, and connections made, during this period. One of these was Michael Foot, who wrote for the *Evening Standard* and who edited *Tribune*, the left-wing weekly, but was not to become a Labour MP until 1945. As a schoolboy he had seen and greatly admired her performances as Juliet and Desdemona.

Hutchinson's driver during the 1945 general election was a man of nineteen in RAF uniform: Tony Wedgwood Benn, son of Lord Stansgate. With the business vote more or less wiped out, Hutchinson believed he stood a good chance of being elected, but unfortunately the Communist candidate, G. Garritt, polled 2,964 votes: 'If his vote and my vote had been put together we would have won,' said Hutchinson to me. This was not strictly true: Lieutenant Hutchinson polled 4,408 votes and Sir Harold Webbe 9,160, leaving a comfortable margin for the Conservatives over the other two. None the less, it was a glorious moment when Labour got in as the next government. Noel-Baker was elected for Derby and later became Commonwealth Minister and Minister of Fuel and Power.

Jeremy then returned to his headquarters in Malta and waited eagerly to be demobbed. This happened early in 1946. Peggy was by now pregnant with her second child and living at 4 Hampstead Hill Mansions, a flat in Downshire Hill; their son, Nicholas St John, was born on 3 May in a Welbeck Street nursing home, named after a former Hutchinson (Nicolas) who had been a doctor in Newark and Nottingham and Jeremy's father. Later in 1946 Peggy and Jeremy bought Manor Lodge, an imposing house in Frognal, Hampstead, where they also installed Euphemia, known as Nan, their family nanny who was to remain Peggy's faithful retainer and housekeeper long after the children had grown up and left home.

Peggy's most recent performance on the London stage had been in *The Duchess of Malfi* during Gielgud's somewhat backward-looking season at the Haymarket Theatre. Her next play was Robert Morley and Noel Langley's *Edward My Son* in which she played Evelyn Holt, the neglected wife of a self-made figure who ultimately ruins his son by over-protecting him in the most extreme ways. Peggy was not happy as Evelyn, at least during the rehearsals, when her own role and those of others were being constantly readjusted, a practice she found both upsetting and distasteful. *Edward My Son* was an unashamed vehicle for Robert Morley,* who played Holt, and he obviously felt it incumbent on him to keep the leading actress happy. As rehearsals advanced he worried that Peggy was deeply unsettled in her part and had got herself into a state 'because of her capacity for self-criticism'. She would stop in rehearsals and stare blankly in despair, which Morley could not understand as he himself had never taken acting that seriously. Even so, affected by her mood towards the play he went back to the Ritz, where he was staying, and wrote

---

* 'You can't argue with the system,' said Alan Ayckbourn of having Robert Morley play the lead in *How the Other Half Loves*: 'He's an actor who rapidly gets very bored, and in order to refresh himself and to engage himself he always treats the theatre as one huge game organized by himself ... Unfortunately the people who suffer are the people who are on stage with him, or who are attempting to get on stage with him.'

in a scene at the end of the play where Evelyn, drunk, stumbles up the stairs, counting them as she goes.

Leeds was the try-out town for *Edward My Son*. But before the play opened Peggy suggested it might be best if she dropped out: Morley went to Manor Lodge in Hampstead clutching 'an enormous and highly unsuitable' plant. He had another actress in reserve.

Peggy was at the crossroads. She had been breast-feeding Nick, and she was at that moment ready to give up the stage for her greater passion: domestic life, her children – and her husband. Morley recalled dramatically telling her that if she gave up the part then, she would give up such opportunities for ever after. This was patently not true. But in any case, while Morley waited, she went upstairs and consulted with Jeremy. He advised her to take the part, in other words, to put her career before her family.

What if she had obeyed her feminine instinct, and not been overruled or persuaded by the two men involved? Clearly the masculine side of her responded, squashing her more sensitive appraisal of the situation. There are many ways in which an actress can put her career before her family. The way Peggy chose was eloquently summarized by Audrey Williamson in *Theatre of Two Decades*: 'Its special quality is the manner in which, without over-emphasis, it [Peggy's performance as Evelyn Holt] revealed the woman's habits before even the text had drawn our attention to them.' Gielgud reinforced this observation as to how Peggy brought the interior life of the character into play, taken from her own life, saying that at one moment she had so evidently been interrupted in giving her baby a bath 'that the child seemed more real than if it had actually appeared on the stage'. At another time Gielgud picked up how, in looking at a butler bringing in a tray of drinks, 'you could see at once by her glance and her stance that she was on the way to becoming an alcoholic' and had 'a slightly vicious streak, which was amazingly vivid just for a moment'.

It seemed as if her own holding back, her all too real sense of divided commitment, nurtured the very centre of her performance, for it was this vulnerability on which she ultimately drew.

Accounts are legion of Peggy's utter truthfulness in the part and the impact made by Evelyn Holt's descent into alcoholism, especially in the final scene which Morley had penned for her in haste. However, in the long run, and it ran for 787 performances during 1947 and

1948, *Edward My Son* probably owed more to Morley's flamboyant showmanship than to Peggy's unfortunate progress from bright suburban mother to broken-hearted soak, a twenty-two-year span. Eric Keown criticized the play as episodic, while also noting that at any point Edward could have thrown himself 'into the Serpentine and we shouldn't have cared'. Some critics were wildly enthusiastic over Peggy's playing, but strangely enough Harold Hobson, who had taken over from James Agate on the *Sunday Times*, only praised her perfunctorily, which suggests that her performance was not all that extraordinary. If anyone could have gone out of his way to be enthusiastic, this would have been Hobson. Instead he wrily noted how much the play owed to Victor Hugo, who wrote 'a long novel to show that a good many may be ruined for life by stealing a loaf of bread to feed his family'. It romanticized, its political allusions were surprisingly maladroit, and it was 'intensely theatrical'. He might have added, what was an actress of Peggy's calibre doing in it?

But Peggy went on to play in New York with *Edward My Son*. She appeared for six weeks of the run at the Martin Beck Theater, which was the longest time she would allow herself to be away from Nick and Eliza. In New York she saw Komisarjevsky again – he was directing Gielgud in *Crime and Punishment*. She spent one weekend in the countryside with Gielgud at a fairly grand house to which they had been invited. Arriving back at one in the morning, they put their car away and let themselves into the house. 'We were greeted,' Gielgud said, 'by three or four dogs who'd left steaming heaps all round the room.' They had to get down on their knees, 'clearing up the dog shit'. Gielgud added further about New York, 'Peggy didn't like all that razzmatazz.'

One completely unexplained mystery of this year, 1948, was the death of a London man, Harold Roose, a wine-shipper who in his will of £71,389 left to Peggy £4,000 in trust. This yielded an annual income of £120 for the rest of her life. What relationship he had with her is unknown.

Could it be that Peggy was, even now, becoming disillusioned with her marriage to Hutchinson, finding she had little in common with him? It would seem possible, even likely, although completely unsubstantiated (most of those close to both have remarked how little Peggy ever talked about her marriages). He, a rising barrister, worked long hours while she, now in her forty-second year, must have felt, with all the wealth of her past attachments, and the fascination she had exerted over some of the greatest personalities of her time, that her capacity for short-term passionate attachments was sorely under the strain of temptation. How and when she began to stray again is impossible to determine but she did remark later that the last fifteen years of her twenty-five-year marriage were 'fifteen years of attrition', although she wanted the marriage to last until the children had grown up. If Hutchinson's six years of war service are deducted from them, this leaves only a few years when she felt truly happy with him.

Yet she was bound perhaps, by the very nature of the volatile art she practised, to be pushed out on emotionally choppy seas. Conflict is one *sine qua non* of artistic creation, especially perhaps in the actor whose identity is continually fragmented or dissolved between roles, then re-forged into new ones. Peggy was no exception to this, although she had hoped for, and committed herself entirely to, a domestic role, believing that it would both provide and demand a deeper security and a base from which to develop.

This deepening process, into the darker side, was much in evidence in her next role, that of Catherine Sloper in the play by Ruth and Augustus Goetz adapted from Henry James's *Washington Square*. Peggy took the script of *The Heiress* with her to read on her trip to New York: she had been discountenanced by Robert Morley's cavalier method of throwing together *Edward My Son* by writing scenes or new lines at the last moment, and she had a semi-religious attitude to the art of acting. As Sheridan Morley, Robert's son, pointed out in his biography of his father, Peggy somewhat disapproved of the theatre being 'fun'.

The seriousness of the role of Catherine impressed her. When she saw Beatrice Straight play the part on Broadway her beauty struck her as false: it didn't make sense, she felt, unless Catherine was a plain girl. She would make her plain, or, rather, define or render her soul as a separate form of truth from that of attractive looks. James himself saw Catherine as unalluring to the opposite sex: it was necessary for her to be so, for it had to be clear to everyone but herself that her appeal to Morris Townsend, her suitor, did not stem from the way she looked.

Off-stage motherhood brought to Peggy something not previously evident to those in the same acting company. Donald Sinden, later to play York to her Margaret of Anjou in *The Wars of the Roses*, had a small part in the production. Sinden found her enchanting, but also recalled that she became the mother-figure of the company, 'like the Queen Mother'. He found her 'electric' in the way she built up the character, progressing from the trusting, father-respecting virginal figure of the early part of the play to the embittered old maid at the end, the love in whose heart had been murdered by her father, described by Ibsen once as 'the ultimate crime'.

Ralph Richardson played the father; recently knighted, he was aloof during rehearsals, and very much the older actor. As Sinden said, it was still a time when actors wore their best suits to rehearsals. Richardson employed, if that is the right word, John Burrell as director, but while this crippled ex-BBC director had functioned adequately for Laurence Olivier's *Richard III* and for *Henry IV, Parts One and Two* – two of the landmark productions by the Old Vic Company in 1945 in its temporary home at the New Theatre – with *The Heiress*, perhaps because Olivier was a much better director, or self-editor of performance, than Richardson, the rehearsals were not happy, to say the least. As Sinden aptly put it, 'Ralph and Larry at the Old Vic would direct each other and John Burrell's job was to make sure the extras didn't get in the way.'

Burrell was, according to Gielgud, 'an also-ran'. He didn't make much impression on *The Heiress*, lacking confidence and energy. One day he dragged himself into rehearsal on his calipers saying he had an announcement to make – 'I'm leaving. John Gielgud is taking over.' Without apparent premeditation or explanation, and with only five days to go to the opening, Richardson had suddenly sacked him. He told Gielgud gloomily, 'We have today assisted at the murder of Caesar.'

Gielgud said, 'I don't know what I'm going to do. I don't want to change anything.' When I was writing Richardson's biography, Gielgud described the first run-through played for his benefit. The 'blocking was appalling – they were strung out from side to side like a football team'. Later, in 1993, he told me it was 'like a railway station, it never stopped milling around'. Both similes are apt. Richardson, he said, was always going to the door and looking out, as if to see whether the police were coming.

Gielgud stilled the *mise en scène*. The production needed both playing and listening to. He had the cream set repainted green and hung different pictures on the walls. 'A weight was lifted,' said Peggy. Sinden recalled her arriving joyful but late at the theatre one afternoon for a run-through in a new small Standard car, 'called Bluey or Bluskie', of which she was inordinately fond. She drove up Sussex Street and dropped the keys with Sinden, asking him to go and park it for her. Sinden, who had not yet passed his driving test, was embarrassed at having to refuse.

The Heiress had already been made into a film with Richardson as Sloper, but his acting needed freeing and amplifying from the constraints of the film set. Gielgud said he adapted very quickly. Harold Hobson in the *Sunday Times* did more than mellifluous justice to the power of his acting: 'a cruel relentless figure whose cruelty and restlessness were due to a great grief within; and I can hear his voice ring out, "That is no consolation!"' Peggy's performance, on the other hand, obtained its power by diminution of effect and inner truth. She was, attested Gielgud, awfully good from the beginning: from her first entrance down the stairs in a heavy red dress – 'loud and inappropriate' – her performance grew and grew, not in histrionic display but in verisimilitude. When she was waiting for Morris Townsend to come back, and he failed to return, the young Sinden found her so moving that it was all he could do 'to stop myself going on stage, saying "Peggy, it's only a job."' The vulnerability she showed on stage was terrifying. But when that face tightened with pain – 'I have been taught by masters' – it was an inner glow. She didn't use even any plain make-up; only a wig. Of course the progress into dowdiness suited Peggy. Or so Gielgud thought. 'She would never take any trouble with her clothes,' he declared almost with disdain, 'and offstage was bohemian. She hated going to the hairdresser and once borrowed a dress from Diana Wynyard to go to a party.'*

After six months she and Richardson left *The Heiress*, which had opened in the spring of 1949. Before this Gielgud told Pauline Jameson, who was playing Maria and due to take over Catherine, 'Now don't watch Peggy!' But she did. 'I stood in the wings and I was overcome by the subtlety, the depth that had developed since

---

* Yet curiously enough she insisted on designer clothes for a television verse programme in the 1980s; and on keeping them afterwards.

the rehearsal ... John was right. My performance wasn't at all what you might have hoped.'

'All superlatives are pale and feeble things,' wrote Hobson of Peggy as Catherine. But enough of the Higher Gush. Greatness in acting is 'an elusive personal quality that makes you speculate about the private character of the person on stage' – at least according to Henry James. Peggy followed Catherine with Beatrice and Cordelia in 1950, at Stratford-upon-Avon, and with Viola, Sophocles's Electra and Mistress Page at the Old Vic in 1950–1. She was now well established as England's finest classical actress of her generation.

TEN

Via Dolorosa

A person grows as he is set higher goals.

Schiller

As always in the genre of theatrical biography there is little of direct personal recollection from the early years, extraordinary testimony from several long-lived witnesses whose versions of past events go uncontested, and then, at the middle point, there is suddenly too much, most of it tending with forceful repetition to reinforce a point already made. When I interviewed Donald Sinden about Peggy he sat, dressed wholly in red (as Polonius in *Hamlet*). 'The moment I die I go home. As long as I'm working it keeps me happy.' This applied very much to Peggy. She was a solid trooper. She had arrived. From henceforth nothing would stand in her way. Peggy's world was very different from that of Edith Evans; her range of acquaintances was, according to Sinden, 'absolutely astonishing'. Nobody knew Edith: she was 'nobody's friend. Sybil [Thorndike] had this intellectual world. She felt safe.' But Peggy was 'very like Ellen Terry, totally molly-coddled'.

There is, as many have pointed out, a great burden in being idolized. After playing Catherine Sloper at the Haymarket Peggy became such an idol and did not cease to be so for the following forty-one years, until she died in 1991. How does one explain this unique phenomenon?

To begin with the negatives. A similar idol, or a pair of similar idols, Laurence Olivier and Vivien Leigh, courted and offered to the public, were cannibalized by that public in their lust for human sacrifice. Even in biography, the practice of sacrificing one's idols to the primitive instincts of society has increased with time, and especially since the end of the Second World War. The noble idea of the artist's anonymity, and with it the principle of service, the dedication to a higher ideal, has completely vanished.

Perhaps, and very unlike Olivier and Leigh – the former enjoying the limelight, the latter sensitive and destroyed by it, as well as by the competition it entailed with Olivier – Peggy knew this instinctively. Her early grief, possibly, had distanced her from identifying with the fame engendered by her talent and her beauty, enabling her to keep her feet firmly on the ground. It was grief that gave her acting weight, rooted or earthed her in a form of human suffering common to all.

Yet paradoxically she also had to live on the rich nourishment of continual and never-ceasing admiration, take encouragement from it, receive strength and renewed inspiration to make ever more effort. Peggy's extraordinary balancing act was that she could remain at the pinnacle of her ability, the focus of complete admiration as she had now become, but also stay continually productive, self-challenging, and self-renewing. There is a lesson in her, then, for all of us, for like the Shakespeare she most admired, she had universality.

How did she not, as so many actresses and creative artists or people in other fields, become *passé* at forty-two, having already enjoyed nearly twenty years as an actress and increasingly at the forefront of her public's attention?

First and foremost this continuing productivity is explicable in terms of her restlessness. The descriptions of Peggy's endless affairs, her second and third marriages, might seem intrusive and 'vulgar' in so far as they have broken down the very carefully contrived, protective barriers that she herself had cunningly built to keep the larger, baying public from invading her inner citadel of privacy. As Pauline Jameson said of her, 'She was the most discreet person I've ever known. She never said anything without reflecting first. Everything she said was of interest. She was as natural off-stage as on.' In Peggy's case it was this privacy, no longer necessary in a proper celebration of her power and personality, which kept her restlessness in check, and contributed to her balance.

The happily gifted child is the restless one in the family. Of course it can go too far, become wildly out of hand, arrive at great unhappiness, or illness. But restlessness in the fecund or pregnant sense, the restlessness of the sea, the originality which stirs the waters with spirited life, and with healing or stimulating power, restlessness of such an elemental kind as Peggy possessed, signified her genius because it became a spirit of continual tirelessness, an inexhaustible playfulness. It meant, in her case, that she was able to reach down and draw on it endlessly. It is in this context that one has to look at her private life and her family life.

Above all Peggy was an exuberant performer who, once she became sure of her performance, existed on stage and in the eyes of the audience as having the right rapport with the necessary terms of the stage. The ability to act may be a gift but creating a structure of soul and of emotion to support and deliver that gift is a lifetime's work, changing from day to day, and never slacking in its demands. In fact it was Peggy's exuberance, her playfulness, her 'enthusiasm' which gave her the sense of trustworthiness everyone found in her, the security that everyone clove to, the rich power to soothe and give enjoyment, both off-stage and on.

That is why, in a sense, people shy away from embracing her too warmly-expressed promiscuity as an elemental fact of nature, as part and parcel of her. The fact that she never talked about this suggests that she accepted it, as the package of what she was. It was a form of innocence. It did not, as far as I can judge, ever make anyone unhappy except herself, because she became wounded, and hurt, by what she ultimately could not have.

Yet the tension it created was a part, albeit a subordinate part, of the exuberance that soothed, in the final instance, with its absolute assurance. Everyone has their dark side, their demons, their anxieties. Those who succeed, in whatever field, are not those who dominate, or subject others to their power, but those who *balance*. Peggy might have appeared in full command, but like a long jumper she was full of anxiety before she began the run and the leap. Rehearsals were often, and became increasingly so, lived through in a state of turmoil.

That an artist or an actor must not be anxious is, on the whole, a very narrow-minded view. Existing without anxiety is not only impossible for some who are called on to deliver their utmost skills in any field of creativity, but to be without anxiety is a completely false indication of greatness. Inevitably the more power a person possesses, the greater can be their anxiety so long as he or she are not in absolute accord with the power they possess.

Eternal youthfulness was the quality of the Beatrice Peggy played in the Stratford production of *Much Ado About Nothing* in 1950. Perhaps just having renewed her artistic vows by playing Juliet in the balcony scene with Paul Scofield in a programme devised for the

London Coliseum called *Merely Players*, she felt this exuberance as especially feminine, or even feminist, because her Beatrice was less of the grande dame, boyish, eccentric, essentially free in spirit. This was identified by some perceptive critics, notably Richard Findlater, as among the best Shakespeare productions they had ever seen. Certainly Gielgud thought Peggy's was the most original Beatrice of the trio he had played with, the other two being Diana Wynyard and Margaret Leighton.

Peggy, who was taking over Diana Wynyard's Beatrice of the 1949 season, immediately rejected Wynyard's grand dresses. While commenting that she had no great reputation as a comedian, Gielgud found her performance 'a revelation': 'an impish rather tactless girl with a touch of Beatrice Lillie.' It is important to register that young admirers, such as Peter Hall, who had already been fired by Peggy's 'English containment and decency contrasted with a wild passion', were now beginning to see in her possibilities for the advancement of their own future careers.

Next, at Stratford, she played a compassionate Cordelia, both understanding and rightly self-assertive, to Gielgud's Lear. Then she returned to London to the restored Old Vic, which had taken nearly ten years to be repaired after bomb damage in 1941, to play Viola in Hugh Hunt's production of *Twelfth Night*, in which exuberance triumphed over melancholy. Michel Saint-Denis stepped in next, in the power-riven politics of the Old Vic, to direct Peggy, after his usual, lengthy rehearsal period, in Sophocles's *Electra* in the spring of 1941.

For reasons which are perhaps not too difficult to detect, the production with Michel Saint-Denis this time did not work out. Something had been unresolved in Peggy's previous relationship with him, and Electra was a role that required a wholehearted commitment to passion in an atmosphere of security and trust. Saint-Denis represented on the one hand something which Peggy entirely respected and sought to implement, namely a permanent working theatre company with an accent on style. His influence on young actors and directors through the Old Vic Centre and School, which he had started in 1946 with George Devine and Glen Byam Shaw, had been growing and Peggy agreed entirely with his philosophy that 'There is only one theatre as there is only one world, but there is a continuity which slowly changes and develops from ancient to modern style.'

On the other hand Peggy, although over forty, was now a mother with young children and she could not allow herself to become emotionally involved with her directors as she had in the past. Vera Lindsay, former mistress of Saint-Denis, had a small part in *Electra*. Saint-Denis was now fifty-four, and had met Suria Magito whom he later married.

There were a lot of confused and muddled signals between the director and his leading actress. Robert Eddison, who played Orestes, found the rehearsals at times highly fraught, recalling that, in his great 'recognition' scene with Peggy, she would burst into tears so they had to abandon the rehearsal. When he asked Saint-Denis if it was his fault the director replied, 'No, no. Atavistic memories.' Saint-Denis, typically, left the answer both oracular and ambiguous, so no one was sure whether the atavism might have referred to his own former involvement with Peggy, or her subconscious baulking at Electra's feelings for Orestes.

Pauline Jameson, who understudied Peggy, found no such discord. Peggy, she said, sat in the stalls while Michel used to give her the 'most wonderful' notes. But Jameson, who sat next to them, often felt out of her depth. 'Everything was so deep. I loved him. There were a lot of people from his school, but they were afraid of him.'

'As we get older we settle into some kind of recognition of our own personality; I admired her for wanting to think in that way,' said the actor Clive Swift in a discussion about Peggy. She was, it would seem, very much at a period of change, of perhaps slowly but painfully finding herself during this production of *Electra*.

The reviews reflected this uncertainty. The most perceptive of these, written by A. V. Cookman in *The Times*, anticipated the later view of Priestley. 'Perforce a portrait in miniature,' Morgan called it. Peggy had 'neither the stature nor the vocal splendour Electra required if she is to thrill our nerves, shake our hearts, but her performance is never less than interesting.' This was echoed by *Queen*, with her 'anguish' and 'frenzied lamentations' exciting 'more pity than horror', which agreed in turn with the *Daily Mail* that the lank-haired, hollow-eyed, bare-footed Miss Ashcroft lacked elemental power. While declaring Peggy to be the greatest actress in the English-speaking world, the *Sunday Chronicle* refused to believe this was the real thing. It was a performance 'akin to that which Stanley Matthews might put up if displaced from the wing to right-half. It was of the same magnificent stuff as Freddie Brown's recent triumphs as an emergency opening bowler for England.'*

Electra failed to capture the public eye, and was not even a success at the box office. Perhaps the most significant point to be made about this play and Peggy's role in it was that greatness in an actress was not measured by ability to shine in the great, passionate dramatic roles. It was, in accordance with the general English view and expectation of women at the time, largely a refined quality, which Peggy so perfectly exemplified. She played her Shakespeare heroines, such as Viola, in a muted, teasing way. She had the passion inside, but kept it interior, still very much in the background. She was not only afraid to show the dark side of her soul in public, but also perhaps she was not prepared to confront and understand it herself.

Even in Michael Billington's engaging and wholly approving biography, vetted by Peggy herself, there is a sense that she was at this stage on a descent into the vale of tears, 'or dark slough of despond', which over the next years not only continued but deepened. She never again became involved with a director, and at the same time she turned more and more to the idea of a permanent company as the best means of fulfilling her ambitions. The critic T. C. Worsley had noted in Peggy's performance, 'even a hardness which we might not have thought her to possess', while Billington added that here was striking testimony that she was 'tapping hitherto unused strengths and, as her rehearsal tears indicate, drawing on some vein of private emotion'.

The Old Vic Centre subsequently collapsed, with Saint-Denis, Glen Byam Shaw and George Devine resigning as directors. Peggy was shocked. Again her ideal or hope of a permanent company and continuity of dedication was shattered; she wrote a very distraught letter to Rylands, voicing her disappointment at this disaster which would damage the reputation of the Old Vic. But this letter is not entirely lacking in self-centredness, which normally Peggy in her dedication avoided. As usual her feelings were expressed and executed in a modest, self-abnegating way.

Peggy knew instinctively that her talent, not of the most dramatic and spectacular order, would be best served by working in ensemble conditions, just as, for example, the talent of Gielgud, Richardson or

---

* Freddie Brown had taken five wickets for England in the final Test against Australia.

Olivier would not. The director, in ideal form, was the god, or at least mentor, she needed and looked up to. She was not *sui generis* the stuff of great stars. She would no longer become the starry-eyed, romantic lover of her director, looking up to him as the supplier of the father-love, by his impassioned care and advice, she had lost. She sought herself, now, to become the mother in a company which itself was, in a larger sense, a mothering, nurturing presence. Also, possibly, as she grew older, the Jewish element in her character became more important; after all 'if you have a Jewish mother then you are Jewish', said Clive Swift. Robert Morley also thought her gritty determination and strong ambition came from the fact that she was part-Jewish.

Curiously enough Electra, an emotionally challenging part, was followed by another role which demanded something approaching a complete emotional strip-tease. The part of Hester Collyer in Rattigan's *The Deep Blue Sea* was perhaps made possible for Peggy to play because Jeremy Hutchinson was by now a rising barrister, a junior in Chambers, but involved in some well-known cases. He was well able to provide a background security in which Peggy could do the parts she most wanted.

She hesitated over the Rattigan play. Although Binkie Beaumont did his best to persuade her, she feared – and it was always the same fear – that she would not be able to make the audience sympathize with Hester Collyer. Kenneth Tynan, then a rising critic, pointed out in his review when the play opened in March 1952 that its shape was 'roughly analogous' to that of *The Heiress*: 'Deserted by her man at the end of Act Two, she rejects love itself at the end of Act Three. But its mood is quite different: seedy, frayed and suburban, whole worlds away from the poetic haven which Miss Ashcroft is popularly supposed to inhabit.'

At any rate Peggy played against her desire for sympathy in the role. Frith Banbury, the director of the play, reckoned that she was now so totally in control of her own technique with body and voice, that both would do what her mind told them to. Was she happy doing so? It is hard to know from what she said about it subsequently. Banbury commented that she 'didn't want to undress spiritually in public', but she dismissed this as nonsense. In fact it was true.* She

---

* What she said to Banbury was, 'I feel as if I'm walking around naked in front of everybody.'

flinched from the idea of self-revelation in public. Hester was close to her character, a woman of impeccable middle-class bearing with a passionate sexual nature.

The Deep Blue Sea ran for nearly two years, but after six months Peggy, as usual, left the cast, while Celia Johnson and then Googie Withers took over her role. Tynan wrote that by not playing for sympathy – 'a simple device' – she 'overwhelmingly gained it'. But Tynan was not tuned to emotional depths, only superficial effects, and he often neglected the hidden weight (or sympathy) beneath the outward display of power. He called her a 'melted candle, burned down and beautiful'. As always Tynan metamorphosed her into part of his own mythology, while adding, perhaps, a new element to her armoury of well-acknowledged skills so he could harp on his own, lifelong preoccupation as a critic: 'Miss Ashcroft can convey a serious, *raisonné* interest in sex, an ability which alone would be enough to set her apart from her English contemporaries.' This last bit was nonsense, because Celia Johnson and Margaret Leighton, to name but two, both possessed the same ability. But Tynan was accurate at a deeper level: could Peggy unconsciously have a serious interest in sex which, for her, seemed by now to be close to an emotional dependency or a slight form of addiction?

Hester was an extremely difficult part, as Anthony Cookman perceived in his *Tatler* review, 'having to remain for the greater part of the evening on the verge of suicidal despair and quite unable to explain herself. She is infatuated; she is ashamed of the infatuation; and she hates herself. She is a sick woman rather than a heroine; yet the actress succeeds in communicating, not only a sense of genuine suffering, but a saving bravery of spirit which earns our sympathy.'

In presenting a woman who needed an ideal love which she could not have, was Peggy reflecting her own life, or was she returning to Juliet and Shakespeare's notion of the very nature of love itself, as passion, being impossible and mad? To her High Court judge of a husband she is a valued possession, capable of being summarized in Shakespeare's words, 'Th'idea of her life shall sweetly creep / Into his study of imagination.'

At this time Peggy was at last separating love, as a romantic, self-consuming passion – on whose dangerous seas she had always been prepared to risk herself – from the real thing. Hester seeks suicide because she cannot find the ideal love for which she searches: her lover, the RAF pilot, then test pilot, has burnt himself out emotionally, and alternates between the golf course and the bottle.

But again Peggy did not quite release her full emotional power.

Peggy had met Rattigan twenty years before when he played in the OUDS production of *Romeo and Juliet*. He had been a musician who appears with Paris to play the reluctant bride to church. 'Faith, we may put up our pipes and be gone.' Looking down on her drugged, seemingly dead body, Rattigan had noted disapproval, or so he thought, at his delivery. His play had supplied the centrepiece in Peggy's trio of love-plays at this juncture in her career. The third, perhaps inevitable play to which *The Heiress* and *The Deep Blue Sea* were leading, was *Romeo and Juliet*'s mature companion piece, *Antony and Cleopatra*.

PART TWO

EXPERIENCE
1953–1991

Western Man is drawn to what destroys the happiness
of the married couple, at least much as to
anything that ensures it.

Denis de Rougement

The best critics and the best artists are usually to
be found among those who have inherited a mixed
strain. In them opposing stresses coexist, grow to
maturity, and neutralize one another.

André Gide

ELEVEN

The Sacrament of Adultery

William Blake would have been disconcerted if, while he was re-reading the noble lines, 'Tiger, tiger, burning bright,' a real large live Bengal tiger had put his head in at the window of the cottage in Felpham, evidently with every intention of biting his head off.

G. K. Chesterton

What gave Peggy the required violence of passion to play Cleopatra which followed *The Merchant of Venice* 1953 season? According to David Lewin, in an interview Peggy gave to the *Daily Express*, she declared Cleopatra to be a vile woman: 'a wonderfully vile woman. But it was a chance to be completely and fully feminine! In my last three plays, I ended as a drunk in one, I was an unattractive spinster in the other, and in *The Deep Blue Sea* I just had to suffer every night, twice on matinee days. And don't you dare say I suffered exquisitely. I hated it.'

'A vile woman'? And yet the chance to be 'completely and fully feminine'? Michael Redgrave, aged forty-five, now in his prime, and having just played Lear and Shylock, was Antony: once a schoolmaster, his ruling on the nature of actors was written specifically with this production of Shakespeare's masterpiece on love in mind. 'No creative artist,' he wrote, 'is complete without a fatal flaw. In life, as in art, he is paradoxically only at full strength when his spirit grapples with this flaw. He may not be aware of it – indeed, he must not be too aware of it. But the battle has begun.'

For Peggy, indeed, the middle-aged battle for identity had already begun. Unconsciously, perhaps – she was now forty-seven years of age with Hutchinson still a relatively young man of thirty-nine – Peggy felt the differences between them growing stronger, although she still relied on the security provided by the success of Hutchinson in his profession. As the younger man perhaps he had once leaned on, or looked to Peggy to provide him with the security he needed – especially with his own difficult, confusing mother – to reach full emotional maturity. He had grown up a great deal and, witty and masterful as he was, he sought fresh fields to conquer. Also, he must have longed for someone to be on the spot to entertain, to take to the opera, to be compatible and sociable with the wives of other rising barristers. For Hutchinson, like his father, was ambitious and destined to reach the heights of his profession, and marriage to an actress as dedicated and as absent as Peggy was a lonely business.

The hectic days of commuting had not by any means arrived for performers. If you played in Stratford, you stayed in Stratford. Peggy lived an independent life. She had her own house. According to Lewin, she gaily paddled her own canoe from this house which was situated half an hour upstream from the theatre. In the Stratford Company were William Devlin and Tony Britton, handsome, manly actors who both at various times became her lovers, although her great and overriding feeling – and above all loyalty – to Jeremy and her family remained intact. But, protected by her privacy, she turned a blind eye – or so it seemed – to her own tendency to 'err' or wander sexually from the marriage, just as she had done earlier with Robeson, oblivious to the effect this might have had on others. Inevitably this must have been eating away at the security of the marriage, even though in her own mind it could not have been very important. Perhaps more significantly, it must have undermined her relationship with Eliza, for although she never failed to be a devoted mother, something of her double life must have been sensed by the child who grew very angry with her mother.

Yet, while being unfaithful, while being prestigiously married, secure in her home life, a loving mother, and playing this magnificent role, Peggy was perfectly – as we have described the dynamic tension of the actress – in balance. She chose to play Cleopatra as a 'wily Greek', with a pale skin and vivid red hair. 'I think that an Egyptian would be more sphinx-like and veiled than the woman Shakespeare drew.' This was not by any means the traditional, voluptuary approach, but the actress in love. What made the part so suitable for Peggy was the power of language which Shakespeare gave to Cleopatra. There was something especially Peggy-like about the serene, detached and opulent metaphors which rolled off Cleopatra's tongue and with which she portrayed her love and admiration for Antony, often in his absence. This again harked back to the ideal love, the exaggerated feeling and sense of loss felt by the child who has been deprived of her father. Pure romanticism was limitless aspiration, and this transformation of heavenly symbolism which Shakespeare, masterly in his depiction of supremely egotistic lovers, gave to Antony and Cleopatra, was especially suited to Peggy's ability to bring extreme, passionate feeling down to earth, even – as was often described of her – to miniaturize it. Cleopatra's seductiveness showed itself more in words and images than in her actions. So Peggy also went for the cunning, the wit, and the sadism in the part: 'tyrannical caprice and loose-mouthed lickerish dominion', one critic, fairly loose-mouthed himself, was to call it later.

Cleopatra is one of the characters of Shakespeare who takes on an independent life outside the play. One can, as with Falstaff, imagine her in other situations; above all, perhaps, in her slipperiness, her volatility. Peggy, with her director Glen Byam Shaw, went all out to attain that chameleon quality in Cleopatra, the scheming adventuress, the outright bitch and shrew, ringing the changes from the trivial and petty, to the spiteful, to the regal, to the overt sensualist. Yet at the core for Peggy was the romantic, adoring woman, which was what made the play so popular in that still-romantic age. Janet Suzman, who played the role nineteen years later, recalled a thirty-minute talk she had with Peggy about the line, or rather half-line, which Cleopatra uses to describe Antony: 'That head, my lord?'. While Janet Suzman interpreted the comment as judgmental and even cynical, Peggy could never be swayed from her loving viewpoint, determined that those four words should be played as the 'most complete expression of total adoration for Antony'.

Redgrave had suggested for the first entrance of himself with Cleopatra that both of them run on stage together. Again this is a rather romantic, almost hippy-like image. 'Cleopatra,' wrote Redgrave, 'has a sort of giant daisy-chain, a long rope of waterlilies and snares Antony with them on the line, "If it be love indeed, tell me how much".' The four weeks of rehearsal went by so rapidly that Peggy avoided her usual crisis over who she was, and who the role was. 'There wasn't time for fear.'

Unusually, Peggy departed from home for more than nine months as head of this *Antony and Cleopatra* company, which as well as playing at Stratford, toured The Hague, Amsterdam, Brussels and Paris. During this time Eliza and Nick were looked after by their stern but faithful nanny, Nan, while Peggy, with her great sense of fun,

115

would organize and participate in pursuits with her other theatrical family, the Stratford Company itself, which ultimately she would term affectionately 'the Co'. She led a cricket team of women against the men of 'the Co', captained by Harry Andrews who played Enobarbus: the men batted left-handed with the exception of Robert Shaw, who wanted to make no such concessionary gesture. She organized picnics, boating on the river, parties for the evenings. She adopted more and more the role of mother in a much closer and more practical way (and with much more immediate and appreciative support) than she could do with her own children. But then, the nine months over, she went back to real motherhood, and the role of the left-wing Hampstead barrister's wife.

Neither of the children will talk now of Peggy as a mother, or reveal how they inter-reacted. Eliza was almost thirteen, entering adolescence, a strong, temperamental personality whose love–hate feelings towards her mother frequently erupted in anger and criticism. Peggy reacted to these outbursts with silence, hurt feelings and deep guilt. As a close personal friend said later, 'Peggy was always desperate to help her children. But Eliza was a pretty tempestuous character, a very neurotic, difficult girl.' As usual Nan 'was the keeper of all the secrets'.

Peggy's next role was that of Hedda Gabler, a complex, insoluble character who is mercilessly observed by Ibsen in her self-destructive spiral. This was a part Peggy performed without self-consciousness and with complete ease, almost as a take-off, some noticed, of Helen Gardner, the well-known Oxford literary figure and critic. Indeed it was her academic contacts, such as Dadie Rylands, who set her up for this *tour-de-force* approach to a woman with a male super-ego.

Peggy approached the role entirely from the outside – as Olivier might have done had he been playing it. It therefore provided no conflict at all for her to play Hedda. Although the play was a tragedy, Peggy's performance had the mechanical efficiency of great comic playing. She did not need to interiorize the role at all: she 'became it' naturally as it unleashed, in complete security and confident self-assertion, one side of her being, the side which found its outlet in intellectualism, in Bloomsbury, and in fairly heartless sexual betrayal to which no deep feelings were attached. Naturally enough, Kenneth Tynan, who failed utterly to respond to the verse beauty and many-sidedness of her Cleopatra and who had upbraided her for her

Kensington vowels and being 'a nice intense woman', caught – possibly because he had a similar heartlessness himself – the essence of her playing of the role in a memorable phrase. The whole display Peggy gave, he wrote, 'is a monument to *nymphomanie de tête* which might be roughly translated as the nymphomania of Hedda'.

A nymphomaniac, if only of the head. This caused no problems at all for Peggy. 'Certainly,' she said, 'Hedda is one side a monster: one side she was a marvellous human being, but she was spoiled by circumstances – by the narrowness of society that didn't allow a girl of ambition to work her own way out. She was the victim of having a father complex. She was the victim of snobbery.' It was an intellectual exercise, just as her approach with George Devine (who played Tesman) – 'digging potatoes' to find out the depths of the role – did not in any way put her on ground where she felt insecure emotionally. What did Peggy find? That Hedda, as Michael Billington recorded, was a 'self-obsessed egoist, a snob; more her father's daughter than her husband's wife, frantically jealous and without the courage of her own inclinations'.

When this production was first tried out in Dublin it was greeted by gales of laughter from the audience, as the comic, external elements of the character-depiction in the play were so strongly heightened. When the play opened at the Lyric Hammersmith in September 1954, however, the balance between traditional gloom and humour had become just right: it was Max Beerbohm, having seen Eleonora Duse in the role in 1903, who perceived how much Hedda needed to be injected with some humour.

The balance, too, was just right in Peggy. Miraculously, and with that sense of mystery none can ultimately penetrate, she soared. The thinning dry hair of the intellectual woman had been her first external observation of the character, followed by her amused eyes as she delivered snubs, the play of her cruel mouth, the mechanical but barely controlled hysteria of her laughter: in sum, *nymphomanie de tête*. Alec Guinness, the most astute theatrical observer of other actors – as well as the most cunning self-concealer of all time – made no bones about what struck him. It was her callousness and her indifference, which made it seem so 'unlike Peg'. Visiting her backstage after the performance, he was amazed that it had taken so little out of her. When he pointed out to Peggy that it was unusual for her to be so 'up' at the end of a performance she answered, joyfully,

'Oh it's so wonderful. It's such a relief because there is absolutely nothing in Hedda at all, there is no feeling. She is a woman of no feelings, everything is calculated. It makes no demands on me at all ... I feel years younger doing it.'*

This was revealing talk from Peggy. She meant that Hedda made no demands on her because she didn't tap feelings within her which were difficult to play; feelings which caused conflict, or contradicted her own self-image. Hedda's feelings were still locked into her father, while Peggy, always the perfect lady, probably felt underneath and in the dark, other side of her personality, which she was ever too polite and generous to express, many of Hedda's feelings of hatred, especially self-hatred and boredom. Hedda gave her an opportunity for letting go all this dark side in the comfortable, secure, family atmosphere of a theatre company.

Indeed, the whole production could be pointed to as an object lesson in how playing certain roles can help an actor or actress to attain their full stature by supplying personae which both channel and develop the personality. An author's creations of character 'can teach you', Peggy once said, 'a great deal about psychology.' It possibly explains why very great actors and actresses can go on growing and growing into old age, not only as artists but as unique personalities. But for this chemistry to work they have to develop the skill of choosing the right roles. Just at this moment in her life, when clouds were beginning to form over her personal life, Hedda supplied a heaven-sent release.

As a token or symbol of the general widespread acclaim given to her performance Gielgud presented Peggy with the script annotated by Mrs Patrick Campbell when she played the role of Hedda. Awards now began to shower upon her: she had already been given the CBE in 1951; when the company took *Hedda Gabler* to Norway in 1956 she was awarded the King's Gold Medal by King Haakon. With her rare combination of 'emotional receptivity and intellectual capacity', she showed the Norwegian public how Hedda should be played. 'I felt the audience there loved Hedda,' she responded later. 'They don't condemn her as we condemn her.' The following year she was made DBE.

---

* At one point during the run she collapsed from food poisoning and had to take time off. She made the point that the family had no television. 'I have no time to watch: I don't think it's good for children. It is bad for their eyes.'

Was George Devine, who played Tesman, at this time a lover of Peggy? Undoubtedly he had been a great influence on her during the playing of *Hedda*, while at some time he was certainly her lover. At any rate, she was now in her George Devine period, which also engaged her left-wing sympathies.

We shall pass quickly over the next six months of Peggy's working life, when, in 1955, the Royal Shakespeare Company split into two companies. Laurence Olivier and Vivien Leigh led the 'A' team at Stratford, while Gielgud and Peggy took the other half on a tour of eleven European cities, six British provincial cities, a run in London at the Palace Theatre, and a final stint at Stratford just before Christmas.

There was nothing much new in this for Peggy: she repeated her Cordelia to Gielgud's Lear in a production by Devine much derided for its decors and costumes designed by Isamu Noguchi, the American-born Japanese artist. Noguchi, according to Peggy, got in the way of Devine's magnificent and unrhetorical production, illustrating the characters (Lear looked like a Gruyère cheese, Kent like a Michelin man) instead of freeing them of specific association.

Her second part was that of Beatrice in *Much Ado About Nothing*, which she had now played on and off with Gielgud for six years. It was on this tour, in Zürich, travelling on a boat, that she broke down sobbing, and poured out her heart to Gielgud about her love for one of the actors with whom she had had a relationship and who had now left the cast. His rejection of her had made her desperately unhappy.

The actor in question was Tony Britton, distinguished, handsome Shakespearian actor many years her junior. Their close attachment had lasted several years, having begun when she played Portia, he Bassanio, at Stratford in early 1953. Britton was 'frightfully British and charming ... an old-style British gentleman, an attractive, red-blooded man' whose involvement in Peggy's life, according to Peter Hall, caused 'raised eyebrows among the smart Tennent set'. What could she see in him, they asked.

Probably there was a great deal to see in him but Peggy always had to be in love. She needed it. Or at least in love with love. Like Juliet, her favourite role, love was the prime mover of her personality, her *raison d'être*. Like the great actor Frédéric le Maître in *Les Enfants du Paradis*, who falls in love with Garance, it seemed an article of faith that she was always romantically and painfully in love. She could well have declared, as le Maître advised actresses, 'What do you mean you don't know what to do? ... When I act, I am desperately in love, desperately, do you understand? ... But when the curtain falls, the audience goes away, and takes my love with it ... You see, I make the audience a present of my love. The audience is very happy, and so am I. And I become wise and free and calm and sensible again, like Baptiste!'

In Peggy's case it was much more discreet, careful, and restrained. The many-sidedness, the 'infinite variety', of her life was particularly apparent at this time: not only did she continue with the Apollo Society readings – a remarkable one of these had been a star feature of the Festival of Britain in 1951 when she had appeared with John Betjeman – but she took time off during the summer holidays to be with her children. Then, the moment she was created a Dame, the 'Red' Dame as she was dubbed by Binkie Beaumont, she left the hallowed world of Shakespeare to appear in Brecht at the Royal Court. As Hall said, 'She needed to lead a complicated life, and she needed to be on the brink and sometimes she toppled over – or damn nearly. It's a paradox because she was, or seemed, the very last word in all decent virtues, and yet she was frequently leading a double life.'

It was around this time that Peggy met and began a friendship with Hall in which they became each other's confidants and he a 'highly valued younger brother'.

She was even leading a third life at this time – as a figment of Rupert Hart-Davis's dream-life. In November 1957 he wrote to George Lyttelton, his own, slightly self-conscious confidant,* that he was married to Peggy when both of them were twenty-two, and that it was a 'sad failure'. They were much too young to know what they wanted, while actresses, he continued, should never marry, 'especially young ones'.

At that time he and Peggy lunched together once or twice a year in a Soho restaurant and had a 'lovely nostalgic–romantic talk of

---

* Could they have contemplated publication one day? Despite Hart-Davis's denials, the style often suggests that they did.

shared memories of long ago'. Hart-Davis had not thought of her for months when one night he dreamed they were lunching together as usual and she asked him, 'Do you think you could ever be in love with me again as you were when we were young?' To this he answered, 'The lightning never strikes twice in the same place, but the sun shines on for ever.'

This did not make Lyttelton curl with embarrassment, as it might well have done Peggy, to whom Hart-Davis wrote informing her of the dream. She, or so said Hart-Davis, was 'much pleased', although hardly could have reacted otherwise, and maintained the friendship. 'Entirely lovely,' rejoined Lyttelton.

But the reality of Peggy's third marriage was now becoming more and more painful. Indeed, she and Jeremy Hutchinson were spending far too much time apart. And the dream was to be finally shattered when she found out that Jeremy had fallen in love with another woman.

TWELVE

Bagpipes and Windbags

A man loveth more tenderly
The thing that he hath bought most dear.

Chaucer

This tangle of relationships might seem only too familiar and everyday to a person living in the 1990s, with its frantic mobility, its instant oblivion, and its fragmented, or indeed non-existent, sense of continuity. But in the mid-fifties it was unusual for a middle-aged woman and mother to be so socially eclectic and so widely dispersed in her contacts. Peggy would increasingly, now, as time went on, build up and maintain several networks of friends and admirers apart from her family, and to do this required immense energy and thoughtfulness which she seemed to find in abundance. Above all she commanded loyalty, and also received it in unbounded measure.

Brecht's little parable of *The Good Woman of Setzuan* is probably due for a long eclipse in the history of the theatre because it is essentially a work foisted on its public by a paternalist, Communist East Germany and a philosophy of propaganda which is well-nigh extinct. Indeed, it is to be wondered if many of Brecht's more didactic plays would ever have found audiences in England, had it not been for the exaggerated expenditure of East German state money on the Berliner Ensemble. This became the envy of many directors and actors in England at the time. Those especially with left-wing hopes and aspirations flocked to the Brechtian banner.

The Good Woman is a peculiarly antiseptic piece of moral propaganda, or at least investigation. Although its theatrical dynamics, its dialogue and its characterization are lively and engaging, it is hard to make sense of now, or to feel its impact. It seems to be little more than a naïve tale, in which both heroine and villain belong spiritually to the strip-cartoon order, with flimsy Chinese trappings purporting to have a 'moral'. But it does have one challenging role for an actress, that of Shen Te, 'the angel of the slums' who sells herself for a living and who transforms herself, every time the going gets particularly tough, into her ruthless cousin Shui Ta, who bales her out. Brecht makes much of the dual personality, especially in this play and in *Puntila*, but the episodic, alienating way the story unfolds hardly whips up great excitement although the text, especially that of the songs, is imbued with a wonderful lightness of heart which Peggy enjoyed.

She found it difficult to arrive at a 'proper style' in which to act *The Good Woman*.* Playing the 'cruel bestial male cousin' in a half-mask helped her. Her cocky unpleasantness worked well in this part of her role: the grinding nasal voice was quite effective too, but as for Shen Te, 'sexily though she blinks, all hints of whorish earthiness are expunged by those tell-tale, prim Kensingtonian vowels'. No prize for guessing who wrote this.

On 27 October 1956, during or just before the Hungarian Revolution – which demonstrated the inhumanity of the lie by which the Berliner Ensemble had created its reputation – Hart-Davis had been on his rounds of Peggy reminiscence, visiting Oxford with Comfort, his second wife, to see her in *The Good Woman*, telling Lyttelton it was here in 1929 that he and Peggy had plighted their troth. They had called round to see Peggy in her dressing-room after the play and Hart-Davis found the whole occasion 'disturbing'. Perhaps he sensed a deep unease in the private Peggy. In January 1957, only two months later, he had mysteriously reported 'finding' her at a party in Robert Lutyens's studio for the unveiling of a portrait of Hart-Davis's sister. Who else but he could have invited her? 'The news of Eden's resignation [over Suez] increased the jollity still further.'

Meanwhile her professional relationship with Peter Hall was deepening. Peggy Ashcroft had inspired in no mean way Hall's ambition to become a theatre director. After a distinguished performance in Enid Bagnold's *The Chalk Garden*† – a 'highly polished distorting glass' held up to life, directed by Gielgud at the Haymarket – she returned

---

* At the Royal Court at this time the director Tony Richardson remarked, 'We don't want any of that Saint-Denis rubbish in this theatre,' which provoked 'outrageous cries' from Peggy Ashcroft. William Gaskill: *A Sense of Direction*, p. 42.

† Edith Evans, who played Mrs St. Maugham, would have liked the Ashcroft role of Miss Madrigal, said Gielgud, and resented and criticized her. Rupert Hart-Davis found *The Chalk Garden* 'witty and wonderfully unstereotyped'.

to Stratford to play Rosalind in Glen Byam Shaw's production of *As You Like It*, a role she had last done in 1932. But Hall's *Cymbeline*, his first production at Stratford – which opened in July 1957 – was for both Peggy and the young director a stirring triumph, although it took him a week of rehearsals to move away from his rigid, pre-blocking of the actors' moves. Peggy herself put an end to this, saying, 'Pete, that move's wrong. I can't do it.'

Leslie Caron, the beautiful French-American dancer and film star, then married to Hall, watched the pair work together. She commented on Peggy's sense of fun, her wonderful passion, talent, and generosity, but added she was domineering. 'She loved having this handsome young man, learned and respectful. She was very fond of boys like Peter. But she was very finely strung, like a racehorse. You needed to take care of her if she was to come to the opening night in good shape.'

The production was condemned by Harold Hobson for its 'superficial extravagances and gaieties', but his reaction was the exception. The *Daily Mail* uncharitably pointed to Peggy's lack of youthfulness ('she gallantly essayed the frail delicacy of the young heroine. But too often she was more matronly than maidenly'). Most others praised her 'unfailing freshness', her sweetness, warmth and lightness of movement that 'many a young actress might envy'. Except for Kenneth Tynan, that is.

Tynan attacked Peggy, at this time, and also at others, because he needed in a performance either an intellectual lever, or a passionate dilettante appeal to the senses. The ordinary, strong appeal of soul left him cold. Radiance, light, unalloyed joy, these were not delights to the hedonistic spirit of Tynan. And when it came to the matter of a critic's actual vocabulary, Tynan also had to be different: 'pure-heartedness', 'grace', 'faith', 'goodness' – these, with the qualities they conveyed, headed the Tynan blacklist. But Peggy, as Imogen, radiated all of them.

Peggy's next play, *Shadow of Heroes* by Robert Ardrey, was also directed by Hall. A documentary drama about the events leading to the 1956 uprising in Hungary, the play had a cast of fifty, with the growing appeal of politically committed theatre. It ran only two weeks, supplying the needed adrenalin of failure to those who championed a theatre which was *engagé*. Naturally Tynan wrote an enthusiastic review, although commenting that 'West-End actors are seldom at their happiest when playing people to whom politics are a matter of life or death.' An anonymous review condemned Peggy's performance as Julia Rajk, wife of the Foreign Secretary whose liquidation had left her with a rankling hatred of the Kadar government, as 'inept,' especially in the speech before the Petöfi Club which was supposed to start the Revolution, by demanding posthumous justice for her husband. There wasn't in her soul, the review ran, 'the iron that must have existed in Julia Rajk's'.

The next four years saw Peggy established in, and repeating, two major roles, one by Ibsen and one by Shakespeare, both of which she played on stage and on television. Rebecca West in *Rosmersholm* and Margaret of Anjou in *The Wars of the Roses* are both dark parts which brought her career as a classical dramatic actress to a peak which she maintained effortlessly. But there was a price to pay, and she paid it in full.

Before she embarked on the first of these two parts, a new regime began at Stratford, of which she became an integral part. Peter Hall, both on the strength of his unusual and stimulating production of *Cymbeline*, and his enormous potential as a director, was offered the post of directing the Stratford Company. One of his first thoughts, in forming a company along the lines of the continental tradition established by Brecht and the Comédie Française, with perhaps a dash of Copeau and Saint-Denis, was to try to form a permanent core of actors under long-term contract. He tactfully and sensitively wooed Peggy to become the central star, the queen bee, Helen Weigel, or prime mover of his enterprise: flattered and yet modest, the very ordinary, down-to-earth and practical Peggy said yes.

Viewed from the outside, Hall would seem to suffer from an extremely engaging *égotisme à un*; he elaborates and self-dramatizes, as few theatrical directors can, or have been able, to do. It is to be doubted how deep his ambition to form an ensemble of long-term artists actually went, because he was by no means a Copeau dedicated to selfless, spiritual values, which Copeau saw as being tied up with the sacredness of drama, nor was he an individual, self-fuelling genius like Peter Brook whose dedication was to explore something in himself. He was at the same time something more, as well as something less. Hall has – and he is in many ways a representative of the ruling spirit of his age – always been a bit of this and a bit of that. He is the theatrical incarnation of Andrew Lloyd-Webber's music. Above all he is a superb entrepreneur, a man who can juggle, as his biographer Stephen Fay records, fifty-two different appointments in one day involving at least a score of projects, and manipulating hundreds of different people in numerous different locations in fulfilment of the-show-must-go-on principle. In short, he is maestro of the pleasure dome.

But there was also much more to Peter Hall than being the most enterprising and successful impresario of his day. He was and is a man of subtle intelligence, highly articulate and also extremely sensitive in a way that incorporated both the King's College, Cambridge, please-yourself tradition of aesthetic Bloomsbury (or modern Renaissance), a dominantly bisexual culture, with a modernist, Freudian bias – and its Downing College, Cambridge, antithesis of Dr F. R. Leavis. The latter championed high moral purpose, dedication to value and tradition, and puritan hard work. Above all, as a Cambridge scholarship boy with strong melancholic leanings and a nonconformist background, Hall fused those two apparently hostile philosophies.

It is not, therefore, hard to see that while he was ostensibly and outwardly devoted to so many values which earned him ill-odour and bad publicity, Peggy should become his ideal. Early on, as an adolescent, his imagination had been caught by her Duchess of Malfi: both were interested in European literature and, above all, in Russian and French theatre. With her pedigree and experience going right back to Stanislavsky, and her now secure reputation as the greatest Shakespearian actress of her day, she was a natural prize for someone such as Hall, out to catch the very best.

Hall assumed that Peggy, agreeing to lead his new Royal Shakespeare Company on a three-year contract, believed in the 'idea' he put forward. But was a woman such as Peggy ever so theoretical? The answer must be that it was Hall she believed in, instinctively sensing and grasping his potential. If, after her experience with directors from Gielgud, Devine, Komisarjevsky, Guthrie, Saint-Denis through to Frith Banbury and Glen Byam Shaw, she didn't understand them by now, then she would never understand directors. And she was at an age of discretion and perception when she could sift what was given to her, or told her, with more sensitivity and discrimination than before. When she no longer needed directors as men, to prove their mastery over her rather than hers over them, by taking them to bed, she could be objective in a way that was perhaps up to then unattainable for her. She had, possibly, discovered a love of greater value for her director, a chaste and mother love instead of a confusing, while at the same time comforting, carnal attachment.

Her closeness to, love for, and professional collaboration with, Peter Hall, and later with Trevor Nunn, were perhaps so important to her in the last thirty years of her life because in that most vulnerable period, especially at rehearsals, she needed to feel at ease and trusting, to show her naked self and to be nurtured into creativity, above all to be *understood* and encouraged to give of her best. As Hall said, the director holds the talent of the great actor or actress 'in the palm of his hand, like an egg'. The temptation, which must be resisted, is to squeeze.

Yet the next part she played for the Royal Shakespeare Company could have foundered disastrously: Katharina the Shrew in *The Taming of the Shrew* which opened in June 1960. Peggy was fifty-two. This was the first time she had acted Katharina. It is a young woman's part, surely, in which the basic tooth-and-claw of outraged woman-hood should be allowed to let rip, and where the irony, perhaps, was that Shakespeare himself had had, as his wife, the older termagant woman Anne Hathaway.

The Shrew was almost a disaster because Hall chose a *doppelgänger* self to direct it; a man fiercer, more academic, than himself, yet untried in practical theatre. This was John Barton, who had, while still Lay Dean at King's College when Hall was a young, upwardly-rising director, acted as his artistic confessor and directorial *alter ego*. Barton was a generous and brave choice, generous because Hall owed Barton a great deal, brave because Barton was most at ease mustering on stage numerous talented undergraduates, and instilling, sometimes in quite a draconian, schoolmasterly fashion, discipline among the male ranks which included Derek Jacobi, Ian McKellen and female ranks including the Drabble sisters who became distinguished novelists.* Before those young actors had fallen for the temptations of the 'Great Actor's Ego' few could resist Barton's authority, but now there were great dangers in such a choice. Barton had never directed the tough rank and file on the professional stage. And that

---

* Antonia (A. S. Byatt) and Margaret.

tough rank and file had a deep-rooted suspicion of the academic mind.

So the old cry went up which had been levelled at Coghill and Rylands during the *Midsummer Night's Dream, Duchess of Malfi* seasons: that academics did not understand actors. In fact Barton did understand actors (and actresses) extremely well. He just had an off-putting manner, and a strangely autocratic, highly eccentric nature. As the years passed and he weathered his first disappointments as a director, he came to be highly valued and much loved by actors who could see at heart that he was not a prima donna but a selfless, devoted man of the theatre. But in 1960, when asked by Hall to direct *The Taming of the Shrew*, he was an untried newcomer, finding it hard to kick the glittering yet sticky dust of King's College away from his heels.

Who should be cast as his antagonist, in this play, but the hell-raising Peter O'Toole, then twenty-six years old, almost half the age of his Kate? O'Toole was tipped as the rising Olivier of his generation, but he had adopted a style that set a new standard for the age to come: namely, that if you wanted to be noticed you had to be drunk, you had to outrage the public. Admittedly at that time it was still to some extent a decent, controlled outrage, unlike its logical and natural development in the 1990s. Indeed, it was the thin end of a wedge which has spread into all the arts. So we have O'Toole declaring, in his obligatory 'wild man' interview, 'Oh yes, I get drunk and disorderly and all that. But I don't think that there is any danger of me destroying myself. I like to make things hum. I like occasionally to shout at the sun and spit at the moon.' How romantic this is in comparison with the publicity excesses thirty years on.

The casting of O'Toole and Peggy was Hall's idea and at first Peggy demurred, insisting on auditioning late into the night, at a London theatre, where she and O'Toole played together – to gain the measure of their quarrel compatibility – the loving row of Cassius and Brutus in *Julius Caesar*. Peggy wanted to do this because she had played Cassius thirty-six years before at school with Diana Wynyard. She told both Barton and Hall, who was present, 'You and John come and be quite honest.' They convinced her she could do it: 'It was,' said Barton, 'the best quarrel scene I've ever seen.'

'I don't think she was ever secure as an actress,' remarked Barton later, adding that one bit of Peggy was very daring, the other cautious. 'For a famous actress she always had doubts.'

Hall's casting of Peggy as Kate was brave. Many people, not least the critics, must have been asking themselves how long she could last without exiling herself to the older roles (such as Paulina in *The Winter's Tale*, which in fact she did play in the autumn of 1961). Just as the daughter of the regiment used to be thought of as a daughter of the whole regiment, as 'ours', so Peggy had been long considered, perhaps not altogether consciously, as the nation's daughter. Was there – her private, much guarded personal life apart – anyone in her generation who had led more perfect a life, who was more exceptionally and happily gifted than Peggy? And more fêted as such? The answer was indisputably none.

Yet, it must follow as a matter of course from inevitable human weakness, therefore, that people should begin to ask, 'How long can she last?' Especially as she was still tempting providence by playing roles such as Kate. There is also the observation that to be fifty-two and playing a 'jeune première' in 1960 was much more extraordinary than it would be in 1990 when the artificial preservation of youthfulness had become one of the obsessions of the age.

Off-stage, according to Clive Swift, playing a small role in this production, Peggy had a definite crush on the commandingly youthful O'Toole: there was, he said, a 'tremendous frisson' when he came into the Green Room and she was there. Although she could be 'frightfully po-faced' if she didn't like someone, O'Toole's arrogance and such statements as 'Any actor who doesn't feel he is potentially a king should get off the stage and hide up a bamboo tree. No, it's success or failure as a person that's important,' did not detract from his appeal. Peggy's complete infatuation with O'Toole manifested itself in rushes of blood to the head, distracted glances and self-preoccupied musings. To Swift it seemed – and without her in any way making a pass or it in any way developing into an affair – that she fell in love with O'Toole.

It could be argued that as Kate she needed to do so, as the performance would otherwise have been null and void. O'Toole was at the time married to the beautifully cool and demure Sian Phillips, and they had a three-month-old girl.

Peggy enjoyed at best, then, a kind of giddiness, or self-intoxication in her admiring love for O'Toole, which refreshed her, and revived eternal youthfulness in her. A true rapport developed between this mother-and-son Kate and Petruchio. But while Peggy could understand Barton's analytical approach and academic manner, O'Toole and Patrick Wymark (Old Capulet) could not. Peggy told Hall, when the three of them went to see him and asked him to step in, that Barton was 'so obsessed by detail that they couldn't get hold of the play'. But Barton remained unaware of the effect he was having, claiming the rehearsals were fine. O'Toole in particular baulked at Barton's heavy and inexperienced handling of him. This now erupted in rows, one in particular in public at that well-known Stratford inn, the Dirty Duck. Towards the end of rehearsals Hall did make an appearance to smooth over the differences, purge Barton and finish the job himself. Barton consoled himself that O'Toole 'turned against everybody from time to time'. But it had been Peggy who said *The Shrew* would be a catastrophe if Barton was not replaced. In fact Barton clung to Stratford for years, using his erstwhile loyalty to Hall as his main prop. He did no production there for three years but taught verse-speaking and devised an anthology, *The Hollow Crown*. He held a curiously ambivalent position resulting ultimately in the greatest success of Hall's directorship, namely *The Wars of the Roses*.

The outcome of *The Shrew* was an unexpected and unqualified success. While Peggy was never an obvious choice for the part, wrote T. C. Worsley, 'a great actress can find some merit in almost any part ... [Ashcroft] finds enjoyment in this one. She enjoys every moment of her tantrums, of her humiliation, and of her surrender. And what she enjoys we inevitably enjoy, too.'

Worsley added in his review – and this became the general consensus – that Peggy and O'Toole were admirably matched, she with her perfection of assured technique, he with his fresh and swaggering talent. Yet it was a very traditional and complacent reading of the play, and one perhaps we should find reactionary today. As Eric Johns wrote in *The Stage*, this was a shrew who was better tamed than troubled; that one became too conscious of a refined gentlewoman who was trying to emulate a shrew; that Peggy never managed to find a withering tongue to lash out the lines; that she never blazed like a raging fire, but that once, however, she stooped to be conquered, her shrew tamed became deeply impressive. In her hands the play emerged as a plea for forbearance and dignity in suffering: one or other of the sexes had to be top dog.

Hobson, in his review, found it incredible that Peggy could actually increase her reputation in this strident role. This she did, he wrote, by a miracle, for there was 'a radiance hidden behind Katharina's sullenness, waiting to be released, and at the end Dame Peggy is a woman liberated, not a woman cowed'. Even Tynan was impressed by her 'sulky girl who has developed into a school bully and a family scold to spite her sister, Bianca'.

In fact she identified the nature of 'real laughter', a commodity which has almost disappeared from the theatre, for it does not stem from the cruelty of subjugation, all too prevalent, or a dirty-minded suggestiveness or vengeful aggression, but is a quality which comes from the heart. This is not a laughter which results from being stimulated, as many people might naturally imagine, although there was a great deal of that in Barton's production, but from being soothed.

The one dissident voice among the plaudit-mongers was that of Bernard Levin. He wrote that in this production Shakespeare was not only killed stone dead, but the earth shovelled over him and stamped down. Katharina hops on one foot, then on the other; Petruchio plays leap-frog; he enters playing the bagpipes; Biondello turns a somersault. And so on. Why don't the cast belabour each other with giant sausages, or empty buckets of whitewash over each other?

THIRTEEN

Counsel for the Defence

Just as the great doctors of the Church often began their careers – though with no loss to their essential goodness – by making acquaintance with the sins of their fellow men, and from the knowledge thus acquired, achieved their own personal sanctity, so does it often happen that great artists, even when their natures are essentially evil, may learn from their very vices to recognize the existence of a general moral law.

Marcel Proust

It was the last week of rehearsals for *The Cherry Orchard* in December 1961. Michel Saint-Denis was again directing Peggy, this time as Madame Ranevsky in a version of the play by John Gielgud. The Algerian designer, Farrah, who had worked with Saint-Denis at the Centre Dramatique de Strasbourg, had been given a contract by Hall to work with the Royal Shakespeare Theatre, as the Stratford Memorial Theatre had become. By means of this he could settle in England, and therefore avoid the harassment and threat which being an Algerian in France entailed in 1961, the worst year of the Algerian war. Farrah had connections with the National Liberation Movement, or FLN, through his family, and on one occasion on the way to England he was arrested at the Gare du Nord by the police and questioned violently for hours before being released.

Saint-Denis was very specific about what he wanted the characters to wear. He wanted Gaev (Gielgud) to be very faded, while having once been to the best tailor. When Farrah, a short stocky man with a round and smiling face – utterly, comically, incongruous on the English theatrical scene – went to Nathan's the costumier to fit Gielgud, he found him superbly accoutred in the most stylish clothes, and surrounded by an entourage. The 'little brother of Henry V', Farrah described him, 'grandfather of Shakespeare, travelling with an invisible Buckingham Palace. I couldn't place a button.'

Farrah went to discuss what to do with Saint-Denis. 'Look,' Saint-Denis told him, 'there is a big crisis in the whole generation of English actors! Burton has done a great Hamlet on Broadway. Anything that looks grand, or polished is out. Tell Gielgud his costume is too stagey.'

Farrah duly went back to Gielgud and tackled him in his halting English. Gielgud complied immediately – 'Yes, yes, of course, that wouldn't do' – with the shabby-faded look.

With Peggy, Farrah had even greater trouble. Ranevsky had to be, according to Saint-Denis, 'all emotion ... very fuckable'; Saint-Denis had been taken by Copeau to see Olga Knipper, Chekhov's wife, play the role. But Peggy was the antithesis of the fashion-conscious Gielgud: 'I don't think she realizes the way she looks', was Farrah's polite way of describing her dowdiness. She wanted to keep her own hair – it was 'short, dry, and she never went to the hairdresser. Her hairstyle "belonged to the *Banlieue*"'.

Farrah found a wig from the dresser which cost a fortune: it was, he said, 'of wonderfully attractive hair quality', and looked '*magnifique*' on Peggy. She had done one dress rehearsal with her own hair, but now the second was due. Farrah was lunching with Peter Hall when he was summoned to Peggy's dressing-room. There he found her crying and in a state of fury over the wig, which she wore. She was not only storming with anger, but weeping with anguish and complete desperation at the thought of going on stage in it: 'She looked beautiful. I wanted to make love to her,' Farrah observed. There was a technical rehearsal going on. Cyril (the wardrobe manager) was watching, 'following like a fox'. She saw Gielgud and was just about to let fly her passion when Gielgud forestalled her. 'You look magnificent,' he said, 'just the thing. Perfect.'

'People have got a blind spot,' concluded Farrah philosophically. During the rehearsal period he himself received some appalling news from home, namely that his brother had been shot dead by a French *para* somewhere in Algeria.

I should like to be able to report at this point in the story that Peggy, while drawing on the innermost qualities of her soul and feeling to deliver, as she did in these years, performances such as that of Madame Ranevsky, Paulina in *The Winter's Tale*, the Duchess of Malfi a second time – which became touchstones of restrained classic acting – led off-stage an uninterrupted and stable life as a mother and wife. Alas, it was not to be so. For by now her marriage to Jeremy

Hutchinson was becoming definitely unstuck, and this weakened her inner stability and put her through the most serious identity crisis of her life.

Peggy herself, at a level neither she nor probably her husband, with his Bloomsbury, liberal outlook, had taken seriously, had nevertheless hardly shown a pattern of wifely sexual fidelity. Hutchinson might have turned a blind eye, yet he must also have cared deeply. One may question again how deep the sexual involvement went, and indeed if Peggy was strongly interested in the sexual side at all. Laurence Olivier wrote that he disappointed Vivien Leigh sexually because 'all that' went into his acting; 'You can't be more than one kind of athlete at a time ... the acting of great parts most definitely was and always will be athletic, depending on inner if not on visible energy.' Olivier went on, 'One has often heard that the most magnificent specimens of boxers, wrestlers and champions in almost every branch of athletic sport prove to be disappointing upon the removal of the revered jockstrap.'* Noël Annan has already been quoted as saying, 'I always wondered about Peggy ... whether she was interested in sex. A purely subjective judgment.' And, further, of Leonard Woolf: 'No one has explored what Leonard did sexually. He wasn't able to go to bed with Virginia.' But Hutchinson himself was now in the process of becoming attracted to another woman.

In the 1950s Hutchinson had built a reputation as an effective advocate, often acting for the Crown. In 1953 he prosecuted Laslo Szilvassy for damaging Reg Butler's sculpture of 'The Unknown Political Prisoner' in the Tate: the accused called it a vulgar mockery of war. He was junior prosecuting counsel in the trial of Lord Montagu for homosexual offences, in 1953, but when, after the failure of the first case, a second was swiftly brought, he declined to take further part. Amusingly, he defended the Honourable John Fox-Strangways, an earl's son, against dangerous driving, asking his client, who was found not guilty, 'You didn't like having a superintendent, a posse of seven policemen, and three police cars outside your house when you

---

* Olivier admitted in his television interview with Melvyn Bragg in 1982 that he was subject to premature ejaculation.

had guests for a shooting party, just because you made a slight dent in a lorry?' 'No.'

In June 1961 Hutchinson was made a 'silk', or Queen's Counsel, and would seem, from now on, only to have defended cases. As junior counsel in the defence, for Penguin Books, at the Old Bailey trial for *Lady Chatterley's Lover* in 1960 – a trial which caught public attention at every level – Hutchinson had already made a name for himself. He had read to the court one passage describing sexual intercourse between Lady Chatterley and the gamekeeper, and was to be called by the press 'the man who succeeded in making the world safe for Lady Chatterley and her lover'. He was to champion one *cause célèbre* after another, especially in the fields of pornography, obscenity and treason. After the prosecution of *Lady Chatterley* was successfully quashed – one witness called by the defence was E. M. Forster, George Rylands's oldest friend, now living in King's College – Hutchinson defended the sex film *Language of Love* against an indecency charge, saying it had 'probably been enormously helpful to the $1\frac{1}{2}$ million people who had seen it'. He also defended John Cleland's *Fanny Hill*, the eighteenth-century novel of female erotic escape, producing as his chief witness Marghanita Laski who described it as 'very cheerful' and a 'gay little book'. When he asked her about the lesbian encounter early in the book, Laski replied, 'Fanny never returned to it and thought there was something wrong with the other woman for liking it.'

It is one of the paradoxes of the English legal system that to defend those accused who become more infamous as a result of their trials is both more profitable and more sanctifying than to act as the prosecutor who wins his case. Hutchinson soon became the legal champion of the left-wing Establishment. As such he escaped 'the stigma of siding with the Old Corruption'. Described by Noël Annan as 'the finest advocate in his time at the criminal bar', he 'refused to prosecute for the Crown'; when he took silk he 'continued to strike terror into the hearts of police officers in the witness box'. He attacked, in 1973, Sir Robert Marks, the Metropolitan Police Commissioner, over the questioning of suspects in police stations, and Marks's observations on shady lawyers. Ultimately he was made a judge, and elevated to the peerage during James Callaghan's Premiership as Lord Hutchinson of Lullington.

Hutchinson will also be remembered for defending George Blake, found guilty of spying for Russia in 1961, William Vassall, convicted for spying in 1962, and Dr Guiseppe Martelli, the Italian physicist of the Atomic Energy Authority, whom he succeeded, by 'humiliating' MI5, in clearing of spying for Russia in 1963: 'The jury took the curious view that to own spy equipment and be in contact with the KGB was insufficient evidence of spying.' The same year he defended Charles Wilson, the 'Great Train Robber', who later escaped from jail, and Christine Keeler, in the scandal which brought down the Macmillan government that year. He also defended Jeremy Thorpe at the Old Bailey in 1979, and Howard Marks, the Oxford graduate jailed for three years for smuggling cannabis, in 1982. Soon after defending Tom Keating, the artist accused of conspiracy and fraud relating to the sale of old masters in 1979, Hutchinson became chairman of the Tate Gallery Trustees.

Apart from these sensational trials, Hutchinson also defended less literary books, plays and films against which pornography charges were brought. He defended the film *Last Tango in Paris* in 1974 and, perhaps most spectacularly of all, the homosexual rape scene in Howard Brenton's *The Romans in Britain* in 1981–2, the outcome of which more or less put an end to any kind of censorship, even private, in the theatre.* When the private prosecution by Mrs Mary Whitehouse, self-appointed guardian of moral standards, was eventually brought to public trial at the Old Bailey, the Attorney-General withdrew the prosecution. Hutchinson led the team of lawyers defending the case, which was backed by the National Theatre budget of £72,000 and £20,000 of legal aid. He was reported to have said, on winning, 'You get your knickers in a twist if you launch private prosecutions.'† He clearly loved the limelight, possibly even more than his wife, although like her he was highly restrained and even self-effacing when he appeared in it. As the *News of the World* wrote, 'To be the husband of a famous woman and yet to be a distinguished figure in your own calling is given to few men.' This was during the Guiseppe Martelli trial. When, in 1969, Hutchinson defended *The

---

* The Lord Chamberlain's Office had been abolished in 1968.

† The triumph which greeted the quashing of Mrs Whitehouse's private suit was described in the *Daily Telegraph* as follows: 'Most repulsive is the exultant crowing of this gang ... [their] conceit and arrogance, their smug conviction that they are the arbiters not only of taste but of practically everything which goes on in our country has long been offensive' (19 March 1982).

Mouth and Oral Sex by Paul Ableman, a 'pot boiler written for an American publisher', Margaret Drabble was the star witness. 'Barristers are very close to show business; he certainly was,' commented Ableman. The publisher received legal aid, a fact which led the American author to remark, 'This is a wonderful country where pornographers get the best lawyers in the land.'

'A barrister is an old taxi plying for hire' is the motto of Rumpole, John Mortimer's fictional advocate, for the English system. This rests on the principle that a barrister takes on a client irrespective of, among other things, any belief or opinion he may have formed as to the 'character, reputation, cause, conduct, guilt or innocence of that person'. In America a different, more vocational approach is favoured.

Much criticism has been levelled at the English cab-rank rule, called by Hutchinson 'the very basis of advocacy in this country', from the complaint of Rumpole's wife that it is 'just a way of making money from the most terrible people', to the more desperate cry that no one could obtain a conviction in an obscenity case when the defence has the advantage of John Mortimer QC with his 'passionate devotion to the defence of the freedom of pornography'. Hutchinson himself has regretted that throughout his career at the Bar, 'I have met people from time to time who have addressed me on the basis, "I was very surprised to see you mixed up in a case like that". That is the attitude of so many laymen to the advocate.' Yet the observation that the best advocate wins has led many young barristers to be dubious about the ethics of their profession.

Rumpole claims that it is an advocate's 'sacred duty to take on anyone in trouble. However repellent I may happen to find them.' The defence against criticism of such a practice is that the adversarial system in the end is more fair than any other. 'The truth is more likely to be revealed, and error and bias avoided, if all the issues are rationally debated by the presentation of divergent points of view.' Judgments of right and wrong are to be made only *after* this process is completed. Hutchinson himself was proud that he had spent 'so many hours in defence of alleged child abusers, rapists, traitors and even terrorists ... To cross-examine children and unhappy women or even corrupt policemen ... is but painful work.'

Ableman was struck by Hutchinson's disarming manner in court during the trial of *The Mouth and Oral Sex* and described him as 'tall, like a maiden aunt, close to the lawyer of fiction or television, rhetorical, skilled in use of language, witty, of the rank of one written up by a writer ... his eye could flash fire if required'.

Thus Hutchinson throughout the 1960s, while always a pillar of respectability, asserted his liberal credentials. So did Margaret Drabble, who never, according to its author, disputed the fact that the book may have been rubbish and may well have felt uncomfortable when a newspaper asked, 'What's Margaret Drabble doing, defending crap?'

As usual in such cases the prosecution was rather inept, with the literary critic David Holbrook, the main witness for the prosecution, making much of the use of 'fuck' and 'cunt' in Ableman's book, while Drabble's defence swayed the jury and deeply impressed Hutchinson. He recalled the prosecuting counsel reading out a passage about oral sex, then asking, 'Miss Drabble, can you explain to me and the jury how we've got on without this for two thousand years?' There was a long pause. Drabble looked at her feet. 'I think Christianity had quite a lot to do with it.'

It didn't do Hutchinson any harm, remarked Ableman: 'It didn't do Drabble any harm. It did me a lot of harm.'

For some years, and in Peggy's repeated absences at Stratford and abroad on tour, Hutchinson had been seeing another woman with whom he had fallen in love. This was June Osborn, widow of Franz Osborn the concert pianist, a Jewish refugee from Nazi Germany who was many years older than her, and who had died in 1955. They had one son, Christopher.

Like Hutchinson, June Osborn had an upper-class background, which was more aristocratic than his. Her mother was Diana, Countess of Westmorland, widow of the late Earl of Westmorland; her step-brother inherited the title. June's sister was the first wife of Viscount Ward of Witley, a Tory Air Minister in Macmillan's government.

June was thirty-three years old when Osborn died. She was 'ravishingly beautiful' according to Julian Bream the guitarist, vivacious, devoted to good causes such as helping mentally handicapped children, and a 'great friend' of the Queen Mother. Her son Christopher attended Harrow. In sum, there could not have been a more enticing prize for the self-assured, quiet advocate who had grown out of his need for the security provided by Peggy's age and fame.

June Osborn lived in St John's Wood, not far from the Hutchinsons in Hampstead. A curious complication at the same time in the life of this ravishing widow was her friendship with Edward Heath, which became something like her public 'cover' while her love-affair with Jeremy continued. Indeed, some newspapers in 1962 and 1963 gossiped about her ten-year friendship with Heath to the extent of speculating whether she might marry the future Prime Minister. They shared a love of music, while June was quoted as calling him 'a wonderful politician, and would make a great leader'. They were 'near' one another on skiing trips in Switzerland. When she was asked whether she thought Mr Heath should get married she said, 'It is much harder at forty-five than at twenty-five. One sees so many failures these days, don't you think?' (She was forty-four, Heath forty-seven). How gentle were the tones of newspaper wooing gossip in those halcyon days. Even *The Times* had not yet abandoned anonymity (and with it undeniably a greater sense of objectivity) for its correspondents. June and Heath even went together, daringly enough, to the première of the film *The Yellow Rolls-Royce* at the Empire, Leicester Square, and afterwards to a reception at Claridge's. Heath commented, 'We are just very friendly. I don't think there's any more to say. She is also a good friend of Mr Anthony Asquith, who directed the film.' A wonderful Heathian remark this: 'I don't think there's any more to say.' Later it became almost John Major's motto.

June, in a frank newspaper interview in July 1965, kept up a more enthusiastic note. Believing, she said, that a man needs a woman's support, Heath 'has a woman behind him. I am right behind him, urging him on ... a most attractive and wonderful man. No woman in her heart could feel otherwise.'

No one suspected how deeply Hutchinson was involved with June until the divorce of Peggy became public at the end of 1965, and June was cited as committing adultery with Hutchinson. When Peggy found out about their affair, and no one can recall exactly when this was, her fury and hurt knew no bounds. It could not have helped her to know that June was six years younger than Jeremy, nor that the affair had been going on for five years or more. 'What really upset her,' said the guitarist Julian Bream, one of Peggy's closest friends of later years, 'was when she had found out another love-affair had been going on behind her back for many years. This shattered her feminine pride.'

Later on Peggy told Janet Suzman that the one great love of her life was Jeremy. When she learned of his affair with June she was very loath to leave, very reluctant to divorce him. The year before her discovery, she and Jeremy had been looking for a country house together in the village of Lullington, and settled on Deep Thatch. In December 1961, during the final week of rehearsals for *The Cherry Orchard*, she wrote to Leonard Woolf, whom she had recently befriended through Trekkie Parsons, an old love of his, and wife of Ian Parsons the publisher, that Jeremy had made an offer for the house and they were in suspense as to whether it would be accepted. She commiserated with Leonard on reading of the recent death of his sister-in-law, Vanessa Bell, saying that she had not seen her many times, and wishing that she could have known her better.

Later still, when Peggy was recording *The Rape of Lucrece* for George Rylands in Cambridge, she told Woolf that Hutchinson was at work on his next case, that of Vassall. This time, as Peggy pointed out to Woolf, he was not defending car frauds, While the new defendants – that's to say the Committee of 100, charged for their incursion into the RAF base at Weathersfield – had not yet decided whether they would appear.

But it was in an undated letter to Leonard Woolf, with a quite unmistakable change of handwriting, that Peggy reported that Hutchinson wanted to leave her and marry June. Not only did she write untidily with a thinner pen, but she crossed out Manor Lodge, her Frognal address, and substituted 'St Thomas's' – the nursing home to which she had retired when the full impact of the June–Hutchinson liaison, all her defeated hopes and her lost love, had sunk in, and she became ill with worry and despair. But it had not been a warm relationship, said Trekkie Parsons, 'Something had died out of it a good many years before.'

After telling Woolf emphatically that she did know how fond she was of him, but perhaps he didn't know how marvellous he had been for her as well as to her, Peggy went on to declare that she felt without direction or balance at that moment. Everything was, as Joxer said in O'Casey's *Juno and the Paycock* 'in a state of chassis'. She had no idea what she would do when she left the hospital, but it was reassuring to know that she could always visit Woolf at Monk's House.

Hutchinson, understandably, has always been reluctant to talk about the separation which caused Peggy such distress. Peggy herself dreaded the publicity. Nick was still at Bryanston where with Jocelyn Herbert's son, he directed plays. When eventually Peggy came out of hospital – and she was severely depressed, telling Woolf in another letter how in the routine of hospital life the days passed unnoticed and without character – she felt enormous reluctance, even fear, about accepting another stage part. She even felt like giving up the theatre. At the very peak of her fame and reputation this was the moment when she almost abandoned acting for good.

FOURTEEN

No Other Purgatory

Similarity is the mother of friendship.
Euripides

'I've never known Leonard admit he was ever wrong about anything
in his life,' V. S. Pritchett said of Leonard Woolf. Like Peggy he had
lost his father when he was young, in his case at eleven. In 1961,
the year of Vanessa Bell's death, he was eighty-one. He spoke very
slowly, very deliberately – 'he had to be sure that what he spoke was
true'. This may have brought back memories of his wife's death
twenty years earlier: with Virginia he began the Hogarth Press, which
was 'the child they never had'. Theirs was an exceedingly happy
marriage in spite of the continual threat of suicide and insanity; while
his antipathy to religion increased with the years, he became in time
more interested in his Jewishness. Above all, although older than
Peggy by twenty-seven years, there wasn't any sense of him being
old. He was infuriated by death: 'I would elect to live for ever if I
could.'

Peggy found Leonard, in her grief and sorrow over Jeremy, as Trekkie
Parsons recalls her saying, 'a refuge, a rock'. What made it better in
her eyes was that he was also a man chained to the rock. In her present
distress her attachment to him deepened quickly. 'You were honoured
if given a place in the family,' said Peggy who henceforth in her life felt
she could go and stay whenever she wanted to, not feeling a visitor but
just fitting in with Leonard's life. They would have a bread-and-cheese
lunch. Trekkie cooked the supper in the kitchen, or, if she had gone
home to Jugg's Corner near by, to entertain her husband Ian and his
friends – Leonard would do the cooking. 'Sometimes,' Peggy said, 'he
would let you cook it yourself' (she laughed at this thought). 'But it
had to be done as he wanted it.'

When Peggy had her 'sort of breakdown', Trekkie Parsons recalled,
Leonard became not so much a refuge to her as a counsellor. He had
known Jeremy as a little boy and was deeply pained at the separation.

Trekkie thought Leonard had 'really great wisdom; he had what is unusual – a first-rate brain and a first-rate heart'. All who knew him well benefited from these. To others, as could well be expected, Peggy shrugged off her breakdown, keeping the cause of it private. For example, to Dadie Rylands she wrote in October 1962 from St Thomas's that she had taken on too much: she was now 'out of the lists' and shortly hoped to return home in a better state.

Peggy began a very lonely life from the time she separated from Hutchinson. She was lonely but she was 'unique', said Trekkie. 'I always felt she was a very crystal person, and so funny. All three of us together, so funny.' Their company was always lively, as she said, 'very merry'. Peggy was concerned about her children, 'like the pelican which pecks its breasts and gives its blood to its young'.

But there was, said Trekkie, 'nothing soft about Peggy. She was tremendously sporting.'

Peggy remained spiritually and emotionally in the doldrums through-out most of 1962, slowly recovering from her breakdown but always fearful of returning to the stage. The shock of separation was both productive and destructive, for while it released new power and energy, both these were unfixed in their orientation.

Curiously enough, this inner crisis coincided in Peggy's case with the greatest international near-catastrophe the post-war period has known, that of the 1962 confrontation between President Kennedy and the Soviet leader Khrushchev over the installation of missiles with nuclear warheads in Cuba. To Peggy, a fervent anti-nuclear campaigner, this seemed the ultimate folly of a nation which possessed nuclear weapons – that it was now on the brink of total destruction. As she wrote at this time to Woolf, the news was really unmentionable and that one would be better off blind or deaf. The liberal, artistic community of Great Britain and the labour movement in general, were totally and zealously attached to unilateral pacifism.

The outer, public, gesture-making Peggy was calm, ever reasonable, solid. The inner Peggy, the private Peggy was turbulent, unhappy, angry. John Barton, out of favour at the Royal Shakespeare Company following *The Taming of the Shrew* but refusing to resign, had devised *The Hollow Crown*, in which she now appeared. This toured through-out Europe, and while in Paris she won the Théâtre des Nations award. But although this showed off the anthology-speaking Peggy to perfection, and reassured and re-rooted her in her beloved Shakespeare, it was by no means a demanding role, or a challenge with which to combat the disastrous turn her private life had taken.

This challenge finally came at the end of 1962, when Hall asked Peggy to play Margaret of Anjou in his ambitious scheme to stage the Shakespeare history cycle, beginning with the three parts of *Henry VI* condensed into two, and adding *Richard III* and the establishment of the Tudor dynasty to make a trilogy. This would give Margaret a character-span of some fifty years, from the twenty-five-year French ingénue to the raving old Queen of Richard Crookback's court. There was a driving, almost crude melodramatic thrust in the trilogy as adapted by Barton from Shakespeare with many interpolations of his own, even a Brechtian, comic-strip element which made the plays particularly apt for their time, that of the Cuban missile crisis, and the newly discovered Shakespeare-our-Contemporary angle of the Czech critic Jan Kott, which had influenced the previous season's resounding success of Brook's *King Lear* with Paul Scofield in the title role.

Yet what did this history cycle mean to the interior Peggy, upset and disastrously at sea due to her separation and impending divorce from Hutchinson? Primarily it meant a channel into which she could pour all her hatred, grief, and sorrow, all her sense of betrayal at the hands of a man, all her huge, reawoken sense of the loss of her father. For now she had lost that which had been most precious to her: the reincarnation of that father, the soothing, healing process of having her own dependable husband and flourishing family. Margaret of Anjou was a character who above all had enemies. 'Don't we all need an enemy?' she might well have asked herself at that hour.

Peggy saw Margaret first of all as what she called 'a tough cookie'. She was unfaithful, devious, a liar. But she found the daubing of the Duke of York's face with the blood of his son 'going pretty far'. She could not justify it, but 'understood' the 'ability of a woman who has the head of her lover, Suffolk, sent to her in a parcel to have a sense of violence, a grievance which explained many of her actions'.

When they rehearsed this scene, Peter Hall's revealing direction helped Peggy to understand that it was Margaret who was the weak one and 'York the power in that scene. He has the strength of

144

endurance and she does what she does out of hysteria, hatred and violence.'

The insights seemed to flow between Hall and Peggy at this time. Both of them were suffering the end of their marriages (Hall's to Leslie Caron); both found a release, a salvation, in their dedication to work. Peggy, with Margaret, the natural leader both of the trilogy and of the company at large, became a fervent supporter of Hall's idea of a permanent company. As Trevor Nunn said later, 'This is where her fervour was; it's that girlish, intoxicating fervour. She needed things to be very simple: "If we all pull together this can be best; sacrifice of individual to the whole"; simple banner things she believed in with gale-force ferocity.'

When she arrived in Stratford for the history cycle Peggy informed her friends that she was settled in her cottage at Hampton Lucy ('The Cottage'), and had just been along to her first rehearsal. She found it very strange after such a long time away, but very exciting. Then she had the feeling of doing a 'new play' by Shakespeare because, apart from it being so little known and less seen, 'ours', or so Trekkie recalls her saying, 'is very much a "version", three plays cut to two and manuscripts instead of printed texts'. It is fascinating that holding a typed script of Shakespeare became so remarkable for her. He had always been in book form.

Janet Suzman, who played Joan the Pucelle in the first play, remembered Peggy on the first day of rehearsal: 'I was short-sighted and I saw a young girl sitting on a skip – I remarked on the "very straight young back" '.

Peter Hall told them at the read-through, 'Please don't mumble.' He commented later on the result: 'Everyone mumbled except for Peggy.' Hall himself tried to restrain Peggy from acting flat out, which she always did at rehearsals. ('She didn't know how to rehearse; she acted full out; wore herself out.') They used to call her Dame Peggy, said Janet Suzman. 'Fuck Dame, stop calling me Dame' – out it came explosively as she shocked the company.

The rehearsals were a trying time. Disintegrated by marital problems, worried by money, daunted by the prospect of failure for his most ambitious project, Hall quickly collapsed with a near-complete nervous breakdown. He retired to his Stratford house, sat in a darkened room and built a battleship of matchsticks; he suffered periodic fits of weeping and strong feelings of suicide. A Harley Street psychiatrist suggested electric shock treatment. Hall was, he said himself, 'Like a child who doesn't want to take an exam because he fears he will fail.'

While he was away John Barton and the assistant, Frank Evans, kept rehearsals going. Peggy, with her experience of breakdown not long past, visited Hall and offered advice. Then, encouraged by Peter Brook, Hall decided to give the medicine of work a try. Advised to rest for three months, he came back after three weeks. Puffy-faced and grey, sitting slumped and physically debilitated in one armchair, he presided over the enterprise, while Paddy Donnell, the general manager, flustered and ever-attentive to his ailing chief, ministered support, a veritable Nightingale to the directorial genius.

Given this setback, what could have proved more heartening than the ultimate triumph of the productions themselves? It seemed as if Hall's collapse was a precondition of the creative excellence of the whole. Certainly the enterprise became in its essence very Shake-spearian, following the comic or tragic pattern of so many of his plays, namely decline, collapse and despair, then regeneration and renewal. Up to then Hall had been such an icon of buoyant, boyish energy that many came to look upon him with very different, and perhaps more admiring, eyes: first, that he could put his health and soul so continuously on the line; and second, that he was prepared to own up to his weakness and live out a nervous illness in public instead of withdrawing into the private shade of a nursing home. It taught Hall, as he said, that he didn't 'have to be happy or to feel well to do his best work'.

Peggy tapped into formidable hatred and barbarism to act Margaret, above all in her dealings with York, for she and Donald Sinden played at deadly enmity to one another on stage. Sinden firmly and amusingly pooh-poohed the notion of the almost obligatory love scene with leading man that had by now attached itself firmly to Peggy, the sense that, as another actor commented, in 'vivid plays' you're 'inevitably taken up with your opposite number'. 'My dear fellow,' he said, 'I'm sorry to disappoint you, but nothing so exciting.'

Sinden said Peggy had this marvellous Ellen Terry quality that he himself had observed when Terry appeared once as a washerwoman in Sardou's *Madame Sans Gêne*. 'She comes on stage telling the audience, "I'm Ellen Terry, but tonight I'm a washerwoman". The audience reacts, "Of course you are, you didn't have to tell us."'

Tell me who influences you and I'll tell you who you are: three snaps during the first world war – Peggy; Major William Worsley Ashcroft on leave with Peggy and brother Edward; her mother Violet, who died suddenly when Peggy was 19; and in later life literary Edward, who hero-worshipped De Gaulle; and Elsie Fogerty, the bass-baritone bachelor lady.

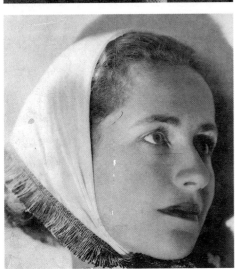

Marriage and adultery: Etonian Rupert
Hart-Davis (*top left*); 'Come-and-seduce-me'
Theodore Komisarjevsky (*top right*), who wore
his baldness like an expensive fur coat; Jeremy
Hutchinson (*lower right*), doyen of criminal
lawyers, who described Christine Keeler at her
trial as 'a central figure who has intrigued the
world in the last twelve months'. Peggy in
1938 as Lady Teazle in *The School for Scandal*.

The pursuers: Walter Sickert, R.A., who painted Peggy on a Venetian pedestal; 'Mr. Beastly' – J.B.Priestley (*lower left*) – who gave her a part in life she did not play, and wrote her a play in which she did not appear. Peggy in the late 1930s.

'She could be a friend of my mother's', said Elizabeth Jane Howard of Peggy, pictured here with Olivier in John Drinkwater's *Bird-in-Hand* at the Birmingham Repertory in 1927 – Peggy and Olivier only acted together again once; Peggy and Paul Robeson, as the 'lascivious Moor'.

The Queen in *Richard II* with Gielgud, after her return from New York in 1937.

The essential was to be a child of fourteen: as Juliet, with Marius Goring, 1933.

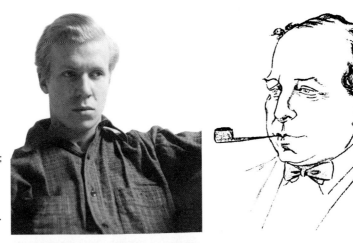

'Hanging and wiving goes by destiny': the 1937 suitors – (*right*) William Buchan, son of the writer John Buchan (later Lord Tweedsmuir); Michel Saint-Denis (*far right*); Burgess Meredith (*below*) with Peggy in Maxwell Anderson's *High Tor* in New York.

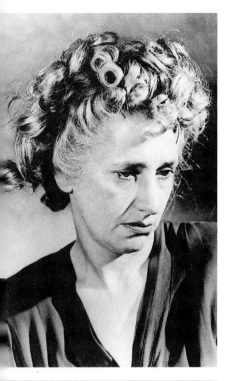

Stepping off the pedestal: (*left*) drunk and vulnerable as Evelyn Holt in Robert Morley and Noël Langley's *Edward My Son*; dressing-room téte-â-téte with daughter Eliza and the Morleys (Robert and elder son Sheridan) – is it the same woman?; collecting her Ellen Terry Award for this performance.

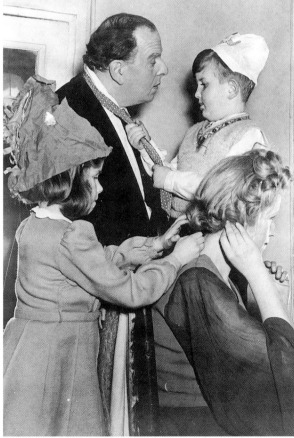

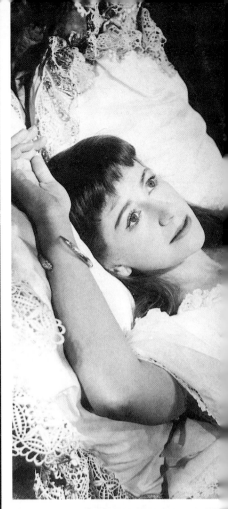

Plain, unloved, gawky –
but rich: as Catherine
Sloper (*top left*) in *The
Heiress* (1949); is she (*top
centre*) Cleopatra (in *Antony
and Cleopatra*, 1953), making hungry where most
she satisfies? or Imogen (in
Cymbeline, 1957) overflow-
ing with soul? – the faces
are almost the same; (*top
right*) as Shen Te (in *The
Good Woman of Setzuan*,
1956), 'Prostrate under the
weight of good intentions';
Tony Britton (*lower left*),
the ideal romantic Bassanio
to Peggy's Portia (1953);
Mark Dignam (*lower, second
left*), a partner in Ibsen's
Rosmersholm (1959);
Bloomsbury father figure
Leonard Woolf (*lower, third
left*): was Bloomsbury
ultimately a theatrical con-
cept?; Edward Heath (*lower
right*) one of Peggy's three
most hated Prime Mini-
sters, smiling with good
intentions.

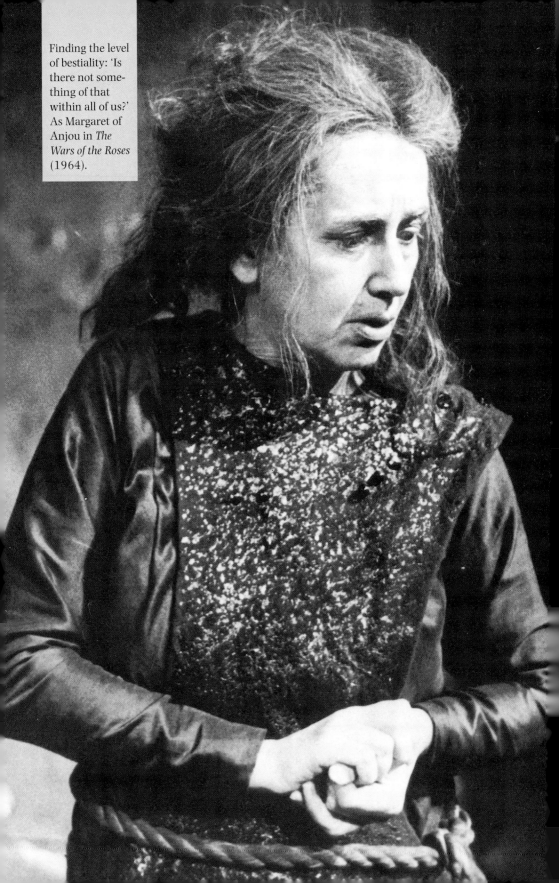

Finding the level of bestiality: 'Is there not something of that within all of us?' As Margaret of Anjou in *The Wars of the Roses* (1964).

Living in the shadow
of black feelings:
as Mrs Alving in
Rosmersholm; as
Hedda 'digging
potatoes' with
George Devine as
Tesman (1954).

Defending Katherine of Aragon in *Henry VIII* against Shakespeare (1969); and as Katharina, paired with Peter O'Toole in *The Taming of the Shrew* (1960): the 52-year-old Peggy with the 26-year-old hell-raiser.

George ('Dadie') Rylands (as Angelo in a Marlowe Society production of *Measure for Measure*, 1948): he taught Peggy to speak verse direct from the heart; William Douglas-Home (right), Ralph Richardson and Peggy together for Douglas-Home's *Lloyd George Knew My Father* (1972).

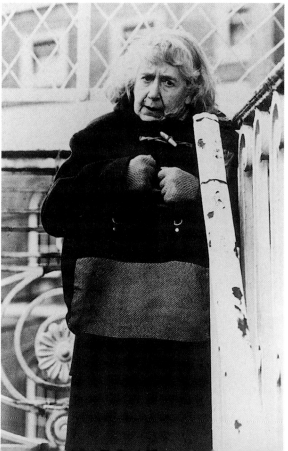

Not yet up to the neck in it:
as Winnie in Samuel Beckett's
Happy Days (1975); fully
submerged as Lillian in
She's Been Away by Stephen
Poliakoff – but with girlish
mischief.

As Mrs Moore in *A Passage to India* (1984): a cameraman
in an early film told her that if she had all her teeth out and
her nose straightened she could be a star.

Peggy the campaigner (Glenys Kinnock behind):
she felt you had to be political, but that actors
were used too much for causes.

Sinden offered caution on the degree to which great actresses were 'nice' people, or could be expected to be such, quoting Ernest Milton on Eleonora Duse, on the evidence of film easily the best of that older generation of great actresses. 'Duse,' said Milton, 'an *awful, terrible* woman.'

At first Peggy and Sinden found it difficult to get on. Sinden was about to surprise everyone with his handling of York, as at this time he was still considered very much a product of the Rank Charm School although he had had solid Shakespeare and Stratford experience; as York, he was to give a ferocious and then heart-breaking performance when Margaret turns on him. But not, apparently, before Hall had told him, 'You're doing it wonderfully, Donald, but now I want you to do it the hard way.'

Sinden said of the critical scenes he and Peggy rehearsed together, 'She made everyone around her better.' He constantly felt himself stretched by her presence and when they opened, would ask himself, 'Can I match her tonight?' But they were suspicious of each other right up until the first dress rehearsal. Here, in the long and emotionally exhausting scene when their hatred for each other first erupts, they gave the scene all they had. Both then left the stage entirely spent in feeling. They sank down side by side on a bench. Peggy gasped, 'You were best'; Sinden riposted, 'You were funniest.' This, said Sinden, made her laugh immoderately and from then on the ice was broken. It was a 'joyous moment'. They would 'openly chat, discuss, analyse . . . On such moments breakthroughs are made.'

Peggy continued for years after *The Wars of the Roses* to care about 'Don' as many of his friends call Sinden, although she was quite hard on him at times. They were also to appear together in Trevor Nunn's 1969 production of *Henry VIII* at Stratford and at the Aldwych Theatre. Sinden found her collection of acquaintances astonishing. For instance, she was mad about Danny Kaye and would talk about him enthusiastically, and when he came to London Kaye would take her out to dinner. As for her verse-speaking, Sinden, surprisingly, was not totally approving: she achieved, he said, 'enormous success with a falling inflection – there's many an actor sleeping on the embankment for lack of an upward inflection'. Barton had a similar view. 'I thought she could have been a bit more vulgar – not enough colour out of words and speech patterns.' While he found her acting 'very exciting and moving', he didn't find her handling of language 'that terrific'. It was the truth and humanity of the character that was important to her: 'I wanted her to go further.'

At the time of *Henry VIII*, Peggy as Katherine of Aragon, Sinden as the King, she was suffering severe pain from arthritis in her knee. In the great trial scene the script demands she kneel at the foot of the throne, but when they started rehearsing Peggy found she could not kneel. Nunn had the four bottom steps to the throne cut out and replaced with foam rubber. This made problems for Sinden who, when Henry came down from his throne, found himself hitting the bottom step and bouncing.

Sinden observed further that Peggy could not put her foot down easily and, in order to call attention to something, had to 'psych' herself up. For example, during rehearsals of one scene of the history cycle she was disturbed and on a collision course over something she disliked, working herself up to an explosion. Sinden made some facetious remark to her along the lines of 'Does it matter?' Whereat she turned on him, saying, 'Mind your own fucking business!' A day or so later she apologized profusely.

Unlike many actresses Sinden noted how she was torn between being a leading lady and a rank-and-file company member mixing ordinarily with the extras, queuing in the canteen for food. 'She hated it,' he said, since she was, in spite of the committed gestures of democratic behaviour, 'totally molly-coddled. She could be as sweet and lovely as she liked because she knew at the back of it everyone was looking after her.' There was no envy in what Sinden said and the statement contained a profound truth especially relevant to theatrical stars. It is never very difficult to be gracious, humble, and self-deprecating when the world accords you total adulation and material comfort. Why, then, are so many people surprised by this?

Hall rehearsed Peggy while propped up with cushions and wearing dark glasses. His collapses came and went but he kept going. Peggy, in spite of her own anxieties over her huge role, was extremely supportive, although she herself, as Hall said, was emotionally frail, even though confident. There were always 'lots of tears in the dressing-room'; lots of 'I can't go on'. She was as irrational as a sixteen- or seventeen-year-old. He saw this as part of her process, while she was in no way vindictive or incoherent: 'She always got out of it.'

This period was for Peggy a time of excruciating difficulty, but there *were* pleasures. As she wrote to Leonard Woolf, she loved where she was staying in Stratford, while the country was looking more beautiful than ever. The trees seemed to her greener than in the south, perhaps because there were more of them. She could walk straight into the meadows that went down to the river, while Charlecote Park was full of deer. Her best news was that Eliza, who had also been a real trial to her, had returned from Paris where she had gone to stay and seemed really herself again, brimful of spirit and zest.

Peggy was now a commanding and yet pervasively steadying 'presence' in the company. David Brierley, who succeeded Paddy Donnell as general manager of the company, commented how she was always 'complete', how she did not command 'any kind of curiosity'. She never offered herself as 'a tempting subject'. Her ability to connect with every generation was 'absolutely amazing'; while for cricket she had an 'unhibited passion which was totally engaging'.

Her interest in cricket must have gone back to her childhood and most probably to her father who, we imagine, shared both her enthusiasm and her desire to play the game. During rehearsals of *The Wars of the Roses* she had a radio transmitter in her bra since, according to John Barton, she was also listening to the Test Match in the middle of the performance battle scenes with the transmitter under Margaret of Anjou's battle helmet. The natural cricket parallel for *The Wars of the Roses* being a match between Lancashire and Yorkshire, Peggy fixed both teams to play at Stratford one Sunday for charity, herself opening the batting for Lancashire with Chris Washbrook. She was bowled out by Len Hutton for sixteen. 'Quite seriously,' she told John Barton, 'to be batting with Washbrook and to be bowled out by Hutton is the greatest moment of my life.'*

It is perhaps easy, with hindsight, to see how at this time and in later years much of her desire to be an integral part of a family, no less than its guiding motherly spirit, became transferred to the Royal Shakespeare Company with younger actresses such as Janet Suzman and Susan Engel as surrogate daughters, and Hall, later Trevor Nunn, as surrogate sons. Peggy had a powerful potential as a *mère de famille*, which was not fully realized by having only two children: perhaps, indeed, it was barely awoken. From listening to accounts of her

---

* 'The Dame,' commented Cliff, the Aldwych Theatre doorkeeper: 'cricket crazy'.

family life, one has the impression that she had more emotion, more love, more energy, for Eliza and Nick than she could properly find the means to express. 'Her attachment to family was always palpable,' said David Brierley, repeating the most-repeated fact about Peggy. She was a mother. There was even an article in the *Evening Standard* about how worried she became when Nick and Eliza were once stranded in Switzerland without any money, a story with decidedly Thatcherian overtones, for Margaret Thatcher was notably and very publicly anxious on occasion about her son Mark. But Tamsin Day-Lewis, daughter of Cecil Day-Lewis and Jill Balcon the actress, as a child remembers Peggy socially as never being very 'present'. Jeremy was the jolly, 'unscripted character. One noticed him being a character far more than her.' Tamsin recalls, as Eliza's friend, a disapproving heaviness towards her. She felt herself disliked by Peggy.

Ten years earlier she had conceded the role of Hester in *The Deep Blue Sea* to Celia Johnson, in order to spend time with her family during the summer holidays. Binkie Beaumont allowed this, so each of these very different actresses – Celia Johnson with her much greater film reputation than Peggy – gave the part her own imprint. Frith Banbury considered Peggy 'the more tragic ... Celia the more pathetic. Whereas Celia brought tears to the eyes more readily, Peggy hit you in the stomach. Peggy's technique was the more assured. [Celia] added a sense of utter desolation which tore at one's heart.'

'Hitting you in the stomach' described perfectly the impact that Peggy made as Margaret of Anjou, on both press and public. She was the only young Shakespeare heroine, as Peggy herself said (apart from Cressida, a part she never played, perhaps significantly), who was 'black'. (She forgot Lady Macbeth, who can be played young.) At the start of the play, Margaret of Anjou was not a sympathetic character, while by the end she becomes the embodiment of the curse which is one of its main themes. She goes, as Peggy said, 'about as far into madness and decay as any character ... the audience must see that she has lost by the end; as she, of course, loses the entire way through.'

'Will audiences stomach it?' one review ran as its headline. Winston Churchill had called the Wars of the Roses 'the most ferocious and implacable quarrel of which there is factual record'. It is perhaps significant that Barton's adaptation selected and emphasized the bitterness, the anger, above all else, at the expense of the essentially slower and more phlegmatic, more intuitive, more universal spirit that Shakespeare revealed in his own, more meandering and circumspect plays.

But the spirit of the times was very much behind the Theatre of Cruelty aspect of *The Wars of the Roses*. Like the treatment of the Stratford stage floor – expanded steel treated with acid and covered with tarnished copper – this was Shakespeare in contemporary context.* It *was* sensational, emotional, stripped of order and reason, although of course back-handedly asserting the values of such. In this production Peggy was 'bitter ... fanatic ...', playing 'white-hot' and 'spear-sharp', according to Bernard Levin. Perhaps the French accent, which Hall at first disliked – possibly it reminded him too much of Leslie Caron – but on which Peggy absolutely insisted, gave her the needed distance, the needed protection from herself, the necessary element of caricature which, for myself at least, remains as firmly implanted in the memory as Olivier's staccato delivery of 'Now is the winter of our discontent ...' The glottal rolling of her 'r's' died down a bit in the third play, yet they served as a framework for what the critic Philip Hope-Wallace called 'one of the most grandly "growing" performances I have seen ...' Above all, for Hope-Wallace, this was a termagant 'keeping herself alive, one felt, by the sheer passion of inner hate'.

One must not, of course, allow the idea of Peggy's great performance in *The Wars of the Roses* to overshadow the others. Her own modest spirit would deny any such emphasis. She confirmed the excellence of the acting which had emerged from a solidly based company used to ensemble work. Ian Holm, Brewster Mason, Donald Sinden, gave spectacular performances, while undoubtedly the greatest, the most compelling display of histrionic genius, came from David Warner as Henry.

Inner hate? David Lewin noted in one of the few personal interviews Peggy gave at the time, which appeared in the *Daily Mail* with the title 'You can't chase success', that Peggy not only had no airs of the star performer: she had the tranquillity which came, suspected Lewin, 'from an assured and satisfactory home life with her husband Jeremy

---

* John Bury, designer of the productions, when he appeared at rehearsals in a filthy boiler suit, was abused by a Stratford designer of the old school: 'Go home, you fucking cement mixer.'

Hutchinson the barrister and her two children, Eliza, 20, and Nicholas, who is 16'. Little did Lewin know what lay behind the façade.

She told Lewin how she had always been very lucky. She had never had to struggle. She worked quietly and effectively. 'Lucky' was a word Peggy repeated twice. She might have been like Julius Caesar who, as reported by Plutarch, told the sea captain, 'You are carrying Caesar and his luck' during a particularly dangerous sea voyage to Brindisium.

Yet she was drawing on something private, something very personal for this inner hate. As Janet Suzman expressed it tersely, 'We all bring our life's baggage on the stage.' At this point the baggage consisted of her fears about being able to perform again after her nervous breakdown. As Barton had noticed when she was easing herself back into performance with recitals of *The Hollow Crown*, she was nervous at that time about 'learning lots of stuff'. She did not want to move out of the recital mode, so she did not take off with the same panache. She wanted to remain in the world of recitals, not to 'move out of dinner jackets'.

Julian Bream remarked how doing recitals helped her back into the theatre. He was struck, when on tour with Peggy in the north of England, by the fact that they went together to stay with Rupert Hart-Davis. This was at Hart-Davis's home near Richmond in Yorkshire, described by Peggy as being at the bottom of a green bowl of steeply rising green fields, having an enchanting variety of trees around it, with a waterfall nearby tumbling down to a very deep and brown fast-moving stream.

Bream thought this was quite unusual on the part of both Hart-Davis and Peggy. Hart-Davis looked now, said Bream, 'like one's favourite brigadier'. It was, he commented, 'a most wonderful gesture on the part of both of them'. They got on wonderfully well: 'paradoxically intimate' they were, 'in a distant way'.

Bream described perfectly an aspect of Peggy's life which had grown very important to her. Friendship was really beginning to hold as much value for her as a marriage which, it now seemed, was impossible to save or recreate in another permanent form. It was tragic that life denied her what she most wanted, a stable marriage and a united home life.

The Wars of the Roses spanned the years 1962 to 1965. To celebrate the four-hundredth anniversary of Shakespeare's birth, in 1964, the

RSC added to it the rest of the English history plays, starting with *Richard II* and following this with the two parts of *Henry IV* and *Henry V*. At the end of 1963 *The Wars of the Roses* was recorded for television, with Peggy's performance emerging at a much quieter, more real and satisfactory lower key than her self-conscious acting performance in *The Nun's Story*, the only major film she made at this time, directed by Fred Zinnemann. But behind the triumph of this production the collapse of her marriage was all too evident.

Curiously enough Hutchinson and Peggy divorced when both were at the peak of their careers. As a newly appointed QC in 1961, his defence of George Blake having failed, Hutchinson was appointed Recorder of Bath in 1962. During 1963 he had gained the acquittal of Guiseppe Martelli. Reluctantly, now, in 1964, Peggy was suing him for divorce just as she was being named *Evening Standard* Actress of the Year. While waiting for the case to be heard, Hutchinson was briefed to defend Kempton Bunton, accused of stealing the Goya portrait of Wellington from the National Gallery. When the divorce case came up in court just after Peggy's fifty-eighth birthday, in December 1965, neither Hutchinson nor June Osborn denied the allegations of adultery and the judge said he found the allegations proven.* But Peggy also admitted adultery on her side, and the judge, exercising what is called 'discretion' over this admission, ordered Hutchinson to pay the costs.

Hutchinson and June Osborn were married in early May 1966. June told James Lees-Milne later, at a party given by Lennox Berkeley the composer, that she and Jeremy had recently dined at Chequers with Edward Heath, now Prime Minister, but in spite of that invitation she had been coldly treated by Heath since her marriage to Hutchinson. On the eve of her wedding she had sent him a message through a mutual friend explaining, presumably by way of extricating herself from any sense of attachment to Heath, that he had never so much as held her hand, far less breathed a word of love.

Yet the dinner took place. Hutchinson and June motored from London to Chequers for a 'small dinner party of musical friends exclusively'. Heath was by no means cosy but if he felt any sense of betrayal by June he would seem to have kept it to himself – betrayal perhaps not

---

* Peggy sued under her married name, Edith Margaret Emily Hutchinson. Her two previous marriages had been dissolved in 1922 and 1934.

so much by her behaviour as by his sense of being deceived over her adultery while he was publicly taking her out. It is in fact impossible to know how near June Osborn had been to becoming Mrs Heath. It could well be that this highly reticent man had been deeply fond of June, and had taken seriously the idea of marriage to her. As Lees-Milne commented on Heath's character: 'He shuns all conversation, all intimacy. He is terrified of talk which is not about national or international topics.' Who can ever know the truth? Heath showed June and Hutchinson the Nelson memorabilia and other relics of Chequers, and also his bedroom. June asked if this had always been the Prime Minister's bedroom. No, Heath replied, certainly not the last Prime Minister's bedroom. He would never have slept in Harold Wilson's bed: 'I wouldn't do a thing like that. I couldn't.'

June Hutchinson was lively on the subject of beds. She had a great friend, she told a confidante, who in her teens used to lie in the same bed with Prince Philip, a bolster between them. Destined for Princess Elizabeth, the Prince refused to transgress the bolster. When disbelieved June quoted Tennyson, saying only the young were capable of such restraint.

Peggy thought Heath an evil man. She also disliked Wilson – for being too right-wing, not radical enough. Later she was to hate Mrs Thatcher, although Ronald Millar the playwright and Mrs Thatcher's speechwriter, claimed they had a similar sexual fascination. 'She trails a coat,' Lees-Milne wrote of her; 'is fanatical in her political views, marches against the Industrial Relations Bill and any other assertion of national, traditional fitness. Tiresome these women are and impossible to have intellectual commerce with.'

The upshot of the divorce was that, by the end of 1965 Peggy was thoroughly depressed and furious. Unsure of the outcome, away from her home in Frognal much of the time, she had, as she told Trekkie Parsons, been living mostly out of suitcases, and 'feeling like a refugee'. She poured out a lot of her depression to her friends, especially Leonard Woolf, and Julian Bream, who had by now made available to her a small cottage next to his own house in Dorset. It was, she wrote to Woolf, no more possible to say thank you properly for the feeling of love and friendship that he gave her than to explain why she should feel so bad when she showed him she was depressed. 'Unlike' Dr Johnson, when she tried to be philosophical 'uncheerfulness' would keep breaking in.

All pain, she concluded, was resolved in the end and if she learned not to feel possessive she would never feel dispossessed. She could not quite 'rise above it' with true Bloomsbury Valour, but she would carry on trying. Her next letter to Leonard ended with the words: 'love from one of your catastrophes'. The truth was that, in spite of her recent DBE and having a theatre in Croydon, her birthplace, named after her, the secret Peggy, the one she assiduously hid and kept from the world, was deeply unhappy. To herself she was a catastrophe.

FIFTEEN

Chance or Providence?

All time is the right time for saying what is just.

Sophocles

And what of the roles Peggy never played in her life? Chief among these was that of wife, the hardest perhaps to identify, and certainly the role most despised or ignored in today's value-systems. Perhaps there would always be an inequality between the life of a great theatrical actress and that of an ordinary married woman, and while Peggy despised the word 'star' and hankered after the mundane, her gift – no fault of hers – would always make it impossible for her to succeed in the latter role.

It would be rash to speculate on the whys and wherefores of marriage dissolution. At some time in the 1960s the whole set of ground rules for married life would seem to have changed, and those who had been unhappily or even happily married, or who had accepted the yoke of marriage, no longer felt disposed to abide by the traditional set of rules. It did not happen overnight. But the tide was turning on every strand. In Hutchinson's case the break was clear-cut. He had met another woman, fallen in love, and wanted to marry her. Whatever his motives, his secrecy, his hidden adultery upset Peggy deeply. But was hers more condonable? It certainly could not have been so secret. The years of Peggy's attachment to him, at first intense in romantic feeling, were set suddenly at naught. Aged fifty-eight she was on her own.

In the settlement she and Jeremy made, which friends had the impression gave Peggy little or no alimony, she kept the house in Hampstead. So she notes to Leonard Woolf in early 1966, when she did one of her characteristic switches from Shakespeare to the avant-garde, rather like the Brechtian characters from *The Good Woman of Setzuan* or *Puntila*. This time it was a play by Marguerite Duras, formidable intellect of the French theatre and screenwriter of *Hiroshima Mon Amour*, a film which has had a worldwide influence. From now on until she gave up acting in the theatre in 1982, at the age of seventy-five, she played almost twenty major stage roles, ending appropriately with the Countess of Rossillion, the greatest and most mature woman character created by Shakespeare, and perhaps significantly as far as Peggy was involved, a mother and a moralist rather than a wife, for the Count of Rossillion is not still alive.

Indeed, it is perhaps easier to characterize Peggy in these last years as a widow than as a divorcee. This is the part she played sometimes merrily and with a lecherous twinkle in her eyes, always with gaiety. She certainly seemed, with her huge crisis over, to adapt to or accept the change of life her new status entailed. But then of course, in spite of all the declaimers and elaborate gestures of modesty, she was Dame Peggy still; she kept her beloved Manor Lodge, with its large, quiet and secluded garden close to the heart of Hampstead. She had her 'Nan', guardian of the family secrets. In 1966 above all she had her children, Nick, who was twenty and Eliza, twenty-four. Nick had shown little propensity or desire to study but had a bold, strong personality, anarchic, left-wing principles and a talent for directing. His mother encouraged all three and Peter Hall took him on as an assistant director at Stratford.

Trevor Nunn himself, only a few years older but by now a seasoned hand from the many productions he had done at Cambridge, again under the watchful eyes of John Barton and George Rylands, and then subsequently in repertory theatre at the Belgrade Theatre, Coventry, was assigned Nick as his assistant on his production of *The Revenger's Tragedy*. 'He was very bright,' said Nunn, 'very receptive and quite gaunt, thin-faced.' Nunn observed that Nick was capable of looking either austere or aesthetic. Nunn found him highly talented and stimulating, except that he had a great anti-Establishment animus, expressed in finding targets for his scathing wit among older players, directors, members of the management. He would send up people mercilessly, said Nunn. He was 'capable of getting me into a schoolboy state of laughing at anything and everything from the day he found me able to laugh at him'.

It is not really surprising, with a background of English society at its most élite and snobbish, that Nick should react so strongly and dislike the theatre so much in England, and indeed be angry at society in general. Perhaps there were deeper reasons, too, connected with his mother's fame and his parents' divorce, which made him want to leave the country. He did so a few years later, moving to Vancouver,

Canada, and forming a Mobile Caravan Company which took theatre to the Rockies. But before he left he spent much time at his Hampstead base with his mother. During her sixtieth year, for instance, she wrote excitedly that she had been to see Aristophanes's *Frogs* with Nick. They both found it very moving, and she picked out as breathtaking the moment when the chorus took off their masks and made their plea for Athens.

If Nick, always the apple of his mother's eye, was about to spread wings and settle in Canada, Eliza, with whom Peggy had a stormy relationship, had already flown, although only as far as Paris, a much nearer haven, where she was studying art. Peggy herself took every opportunity to travel and just the opening she wanted came along to provide relief. She was invited to Israel to give a poetry recital with Rylands. She was staying with Hart-Davis in Richmond when she elaborated her plans. She and Dadie were to stop at Athens on the way there; she wanted Dadie to do 'his unforgettable lecture' on Shakespeare's classical education. She was doing her own programme, 'some words on women and some women's words', but she also wanted to do a programme together with Dadie, possibly Shakespeare's sonnets.

In Athens they would stay with Barbara, her ex-sister-in-law, now living with the Greek painter Nicholas Ghika whom she married after running away from the poet Rex Warner. It'll be fun, Peggy told Dadie, or rather 'WE will make it fun'. They would bathe in a warm sea, and would probably have to fight off what both of them loathed: a certain amount of over-hospitality. 'Corragio darling friend', she exhorts Rylands, adding, 'No, I don't want to be LEFT ALONE!'

In the event it *was* fun: they had a natural compatibility as travelling companions, and while the days of Rylands's stormy and romantic love-affairs were over – he was now sixty-three, while his attachment to Arthur Marshall, his life-long friend, had lessened – Dadie's sharp conversational wit and gift for friendship were just what Peggy needed. Indeed she often invited him – and would in future years – to stay at the Bream cottage in Dorset. Even when they were apart, she would keep an eye on Dadie: she had, as Bream remarked, an 'instinct for keeping an eye on people'. She and Dadie would arrive at the cottage on Friday night. Saturday would go well, but by Sunday with two such strong individuals together there would be evident strain between them. 'They'd had enough of each other,' observed Bream.

Rylands at this time was extremely angry with Laurence Olivier about a programme he had 'concocted' of Shakespeare's sonnets for television. Rylands intended having Ian Holm as the male reader, Peggy as the woman. The BBC accepted the script, but Olivier heard about it and rang up Rylands, saying to him, 'I must be in on this. Come up to London and have lunch with me.' As Holm had not yet been engaged Rylands agreed to lunch with Olivier, who was wildly enthusiastic about the programme, but then his agent demanded such a huge fee that the BBC said they could not afford it. The idea fell through completely.

Hutchinson and June had lost little time in marrying. Small consolation to Peggy's hurt pride was that now, and until she retired from the stage in 1981, she reigned absolutely supreme on the English stage. Harold Hobson had written of her during the run of *The Wars of the Roses* that hers was a continuous summer of achievement which had begun with her appearance in *Jew Süss*. He recalled not the archiepiscopal cadences of Matheson Lang, he said, but the slim young Ashcroft in a high tower reading the Old Testament. About her, he wrote, there was 'a quality of tranquillity ... an immovable, sad peace which immediately concentrated any attention'.

Preserving, as he resoundingly praised her for doing, the great values of any part she played, he said that for anyone to have 'a career without setbacks' was itself a paradox. While being the only actress 'to rival Garrick and Wyndham and have a London theatre (admittedly at Croydon) named after her, she was unrivalled in so far as her career had not declined at all, as with most great actresses'. Hobson attributed this to Peggy's extraordinary power of communication, citing as an example her response as Catherine Sloper in *The Heiress* when charged with cruelty: 'I have been taught by masters.' 'No nuances, no subtleties, no dim suggestions here: only an elementary unqualified answer, but launched with such a grieved recoil from affection that it was unforgettable.'

Peggy had a similar moment in *The Deep Blue Sea* when she told how she had fallen in love at the local golf club. 'From that moment

I knew I had no chance, no chance at all' – 'the very ecstasy of desolation', Hobson called it, 'the exalting path of her sorrow'.

This path of sorrow, which I have attempted to identify as unnamed grief over the early loss of her father, gave Peggy the confidence to explore the darker side of herself in the new drama of the absurd which had caught the imagination of intellectuals seeking something novel in the theatre, and possibly above all in pursuit of something teasing which, denied a creative gift themselves, they could use and ride upon to gain some recognition for their own powers of comment and analysis. The age of the enigmatic text and the middlemen who grew rich on interpretations had been born.

Beckett was the master, Pinter his chief English derivative and acolyte. Peggy with her great gift of communication, her flair for discovering genuine talent, and continuing ambition which she knew how to conceal with immaculate self-disclaiming, now put herself firmly into the world of verbal dislocation and non-communication summed up by the term 'Theatre of the Absurd'; although Albert Camus, the first proponent of the philosophical idea of the Absurd, had meant something entirely different by it than the practical, theoretical uses to which it was put by Ionesco, in his plays *La Leçon* and *Les Chaises* – something more optimistic than the negative attitudes that the actual words of many of the absurdist theatre texts convey.

Equally the involvement of great actors (and specifically actresses) in the exploration of spiritual deprivation and despair gave, almost of itself, the life-assertive quality to the texts which commanded attention. Actors are, have to be, by their very nature life-assertive because the first thing people go to see in a theatre, and pay money to see, is energy. This is why actors and actresses so often make poor husbands, inadequate lovers, ineffective fathers and mothers, and even less reliable politicians, moral theorists, or philosophers. They have to save all their energy for their performances, and the energy demanded of them is devouring and all-consuming. As role models and exemplars, in all but the quality of their art, they should be studiously ignored. This is why Peggy, in her wisdom, wanted her energy sources preserved from the prurient eye of the public. She suspected the audiences, and especially anything done for 'effect'. For example, much later she exploded at Helen Mirren for talking to the *Guardian* about sex and revealing the intimacies of her love-life. 'Why was she doing it?' she asked. 'She's a wonderful actress, she doesn't need to talk about it.' She genuinely thought such revelations trivialized the perception of actresses, and also trivialized the actresses themselves.

When Peggy performed in Marguerite Duras's *Days in the Trees*, which opened in June 1966, something inside her revolted at the nihilism in the play. But she squashed it down. She needed to do it. Her old desire to reconcile herself to the character she was playing, to justify her, was paramount during the rehearsals; she worried away at how to play this rich old lady trembling on the edges of senility who comes to visit her son, the only one of her children for whom she has any affection, who has become in middle age a compulsive gambler. As someone complained, not yet attuned to the new moral–relativist spirit, 'In plays like these almost anything can be said and then contradicted, and later perhaps even be restated, and the justification offered for such bewildering and obscure behaviour would be that life is absurd, people are absurd, so why look for the everyday disciplines of reason?'

But Peggy had already proved her range and flexibility with Margaret of Anjou. She had passed in the course of a single day from light-footed, ginger, sub-deb sub-bitch to bedraggled crone with glittering eye, rambling and cussing with undiminished fury – through maniac monster of rage and cruelty. To play a querulous old mother who chewed her lips and muttered bitterness at an uncaring world was child's play after this.

But she could not succeed without making it difficult for herself, which perhaps is the greatest tribute that could be paid to her greatness as an actress. John Schlesinger, the distinguished film director, was her mentor on this occasion. He had, the previous year, made his debut as a stage director with a play by John Whiting at the Aldwych, in an experimental evening called *Expeditions One*. All through rehearsal Schlesinger had been supplying notes which Peggy found hard to absorb because they went against the grain in terms of the sympathy she wanted to create, and herself feel, for the character. She couldn't abandon this need for what might be seen as some kind of moral approval for the part she was playing. But, in the final reckoning, the only morality she could recognize and observe was one of art. She had no religious feeling at all: art was her religion. When it came to it, and perhaps in some curious way this was related to her off-stage practice in sex, there was only one thing to be done. She had to go out there and do it in front of an audience.

Schlesinger related how, just before the curtain rose on the first night, Peggy was sitting on a bench in a state of clenched rage, and how she erupted with anger when Schlesinger tried to cheer her up with a good-natured expletive. 'Fuck! Fuck! Fuck!' she shouted back, giving a 'V' sign to the audience. So there we have it. A new 'gloves-off' period had been born. She gave, of course, a well-nigh perfect performance.

But as an unpleasant, 'indulgent' performance, it was not the one which the Duras play called for. And Peggy was competing at the highest level. Madeleine Renaud had played the part in Paris and made it her triumph. Would Peggy be able to equal it with that mysterious power I have already tried to define more than once? 'She plucks at her shapeless black dress,' wrote Tynan, 'fusses with unpinned white hair, gustily crams herself with mouthfuls of food and drink through which she lets straggle plummily her familiar vocal mannerisms ... Having spoiled her son, the old woman now spoils herself: eating hugely, carelessly offering charm and peevishly cutting it short. "What am I but her indulgence?" cries the son ... the mother's real emotion towards her son is horrified pride. She has raised a metaphysical monster.' It is not recorded whether playing the part brought Peggy any great pleasure, or if it was not all pain. But at least Leonard Woolf enjoyed and liked it, or so she registered to him in her next 'thank-you' for having stayed at Monk's Cottage: 'it was lovely to be with you after so long'. She remarked, or so Trekkie recalled, that she was always leaving her cheque book behind.

Fortunately she did not have to be in *Days in the Trees* every night of the week; as a box-office draw only for the initiated, it took its place quite rarely in the RSC repertory. At the end of June she went on holiday to Norway, able to absorb her suffering and restore her soul in the beauty of the landscape. Here she stayed with friends identified as Rosmer and his wife, 'her grandchild, a small black Aberdeen and four 2 month old puppies'. Her daily life was an idyll. Rather mundane, as she describes it, like a holiday brochure, catching fish, eating natural healthy foods, the scenery of endless rocks with gulls perched on them – and she concludes that it was like a scene from an Ibsen play. Clearly it struck a chord yet one wonders what the super-intellectual Woolf made of her simple, fresh, almost naïve enjoyment. No intellectual complication, yet with an unspoken sense of loneliness.

She almost succumbed to the problem she had with *Days in the Trees* in the other dark Duras play she performed some years later, in 1971, at the Royal Court. In this, *The Lovers of Viorne*, she was without the steadying hand of Schlesinger to reassure her that she needed no explanation as to why Claire Launes, the character she played, murdered her husband. Everything is dead about the murderess, her emotions, her desires, her intellect. The play is a complete exploration of this woman's remote and lonely life, slowed down not only by time, but by the interrogator, a sensible and humane seeker after truth. The investing of the facts of crime with Duras's strangely unreal and fascinating question-and-answer technique makes one ask whether she chose the right story for her talents. Peggy insisted on a searching after fact and reason: what Duras only wanted to show was a scanning of the picture bit by bit.

This was very much in accordance with the new philosophy which Duras and other absurdities propounded, with Jacques Monod the French philosopher as the then current figurehead of scepticism: that all forms of life were the product of pure chance – through unpredictable mutation – and, of necessity, Darwinian selection. These discoveries, wrote Monod in his *Chance and Necessity*, made it impossible to accept any system, religious or materialist, that assumed a master plan of creation.

You cannot derive any sort of 'ought' from the 'is', wrote Monod, who, like others were to do in the 1990s, sought to deny man any position in the centre of the universe or any objective moral values. Man is only a product, wrote Monod, of the evolution of the universe. Monod, who was once a Marxist, now predicted that 'the risk of the race committing suicide is very great. In my opinion the future of mankind is going to be decided within the next two generations.'

Well, if a generation is ten years, Monod was wrong. If a generation is twenty years, does anyone see the future of mankind being decided by the year 2011? Of course not. The curious fact about such beliefs, which Peggy shared theoretically (including her much-publicized views on euthanasia), was that when she had to play a character incorporating such an outlook, she could not go the whole way. In fact, vestigial religious feeling claimed the reason why she ultimately failed at playing Claire as intended by Duras (and why the play itself sank undistinguished and unrevived into the future). Only plays which incorporate some idea of an underlying design in creation seem to survive. Hobson expressed this with the profound insight to which he could often rise: 'There is a wonderful moment when Dame Peggy talks of her lost lover. Her face brims with tears that never fall. But she makes Claire mad. Her mouth works, her fingers endlessly twitch. Her way of life is of utter desolation and it is not surprising that she ended it by murder. In other words, Dame Peggy offers an explanation where it is essential that there should be no explanation. It is very fine but it is not Mme Duras's play.'

Of course, having descended into the dark areas she then needed her resurrection, her revival of faith, and it is uncanny how, after each descent into the particular cultural hell which the affluent society has devised to castigate itself, in order then to return to its pursuit of wealth, she would invariably revive her faith with upbeat, optimistic 'normal' plays and, on two memorable occasions in these last years, with Shakespeare. As Peter Hall said, she now took 'extraordinary care' about her workload, while she always thought he was mad, doing three times what he should have done. From this point she paced herself, turning down much work including Volumnia in *Coriolanus* which Hall wanted her to do, a play commissioned for her especially by Ronald Duncan, and numerous other projects. 'I always thought she rather underworked,' said Hall.

Henry VIII, in which she played Katherine of Aragon, was her first production with Trevor Nunn. Here she brought to fruition a friendship which had begun when Nunn had employed Nick as his assistant at Stratford. As a result Nunn had often met Peggy at her house where gatherings would frequently be a mixture of 'family fun and RSC insights'. On one occasion, Nunn recalled, she took them to eat in a Pekinese restaurant which was a rare, unexpected place in north London in those days and she had discovered was run by a Chinese cook who had defected from the Embassy. One evening the subject of Komisarjevsky had come up. She mentioned a couple of productions she had done with Komis: 'worked with him – married him', she said briskly. 'It felt like the most horrific gaffe,' said Nunn.

At this time Nunn was going out with Janet Suzman who had played Joan the Pucelle in *The Wars of the Roses*. 'Because of Peggy I had this fantasy notion to live in Hampstead to be close by.' He bought a house not far away from Peggy, on the edge of Hampstead

Heath in an area known as the Vale of Heath. Most of Janet Suzman's relatives were left behind in South Africa: she moved in with Nunn. 'That's where I saw Peggy an uncountable number of times for breakfast, lunch, dinner.' Trevor's link with Nick was terribly important to her, and he admired the way Peggy was determined to be part of what Nick was doing. He was always some sort of conduit for her feelings about him: 'She knew I rated him highly'. She would, when Nick had left for Canada, always show Nunn photographs of him, and later of his children: 'My link with Nick as much as any other factor was the thing that bonded me with her'.

When they first rehearsed *Henry VIII* Nunn found that Peggy had organized some extra lines for Katherine of Aragon's defence, which she claimed as being part and parcel of how the play worked. Nunn found her backstage reading a biography of Katherine: she was in tears at the injustice of her divorce and, worst of all, that Shakespeare toed the party line by excluding crucial things which Katherine said in her defence at trial. Through her tears Peggy said, 'It makes me so angry.' She thought that what Shakespeare and his probable co-author John Fletcher was presenting to the Court of James I was a slander on Katherine. She could not tolerate the idea that she was represented as being in the wrong. 'I have to be heard – because I'm Katherine of Aragon; her case is my case.'

Nunn's production turned out to be just what Peggy needed: earthy, almost gauche, with much tomfoolery and plenty of processions.

Donald Sinden, while haranguing the court on the first night, felt his beard becoming detached from his chin: holding the side of his face like a man with raging toothache he extricated himself commendably from this tangle, puffing out the thin pastry of his part with a dry and eccentric bluffness which Peggy adored. She endowed each moment of humble and downtrodden Queen Katherine's progress to a dignified end 'with an emotional truth which is the crown of great technical achievement: there is, in each line, a lifetime's work'.

She did two plays by Edward Albee at this time, again, rivalling or at least paralleling her French peer Madeleine Renaud. The first was *A Delicate Balance*,* directed by Peter Hall, which opened at the Aldwych Theatre in January 1969; the second, *All Over*, also directed by Hall, at the Aldwych in 1972. The author appeared at rehearsals:

---

* Vivien Leigh was originally to have appeared in this, but she died in 1967.

'such a pussy cat – absolutely delights in wrong-footing you,' said Hall. Peggy, who was magnificent in both plays, was a bit suspicious of Albee at first. He was, she commented, 'very likeable, charming, shy – (and I should think could be very unpleasant!!)' Initially she baulked at playing Agnes in *A Delicate Balance*, an 'elegantly tooled woman of steel' whom she thought of as something of a monster. To find the right 'New England sound' was absolutely critical, said Hall. 'These tonal qualities are as important to her as what she is wearing.' It was, she told Woolf, helpful having Albee with them: 'he has given us a far clearer idea of his intention in the play and I think we are getting it into perspective and I have ceased to regard myself [Agnes] as a monster!!'

The natural identification of herself (so natural by now that she ceased to 'regard myself') with the character she was playing by no means meant that Peggy ceased to be herself while playing it, but rather the reverse. She could extend herself with confidence and utter assurance into the role. The confrontation between her own authority, and the endlessly shifting sands of Albee's feelings, was even more evident in *All Over*, in which a great man's family faces his impending death. *All Over* circles endlessly with much of the self-involvement and self-pity of *Who's Afraid of Virginia Woolf?* but in a much more muted way. The feelings occasioned by death are little to do with the objective fact.

Peggy played the wife sitting out the dying moments. The character she played was not named, nor is the cause of her husband's demise. The family think mostly about themselves, as Peggy as the wife bitterly observed twice, the first time carving it with a grand and poignant caesura. None of their thoughts extend much beyond the subjective mood to which Albee almost entirely committed himself. Great chunks of the play seemed little more than a rambling literary symposium. By the end the great man had slipped away with, as Sir Thomas Browne wrote of a friend, 'not so much as an Expiration or Sigh'.

Hall treated the whole elegant mismash of feeling as if it were a masterpiece, exquisitely marshalling and composing the pauses. White-haired, plainly attired, with a single row of pearls, Peggy again brought her authority to bear on this central role, 'giving us solid and weighty stepping stones amid the endless rush of pain'.

SIXTEEN

Biographers Be Warned

Apes are apes, though clothed in Scarlet.
Ben Jonson

Like Albee, and indeed like Pinter, Samuel Beckett was a playwright of mood and depression. Indeed, avant-garde theatre at this time seemed overwhelmingly preoccupied with visceral change, for in the absence of any belief in free choice or of self-determination, man (and woman) had turned within. But unlike many of his contemporaries, Beckett was expressing a serious and original vision of life, a vision developed out of the raw material of the artist's life and himself, a raw, literal metaphor, born of many years of failure, loneliness and depression. Peter Brook claimed that Beckett did not say 'no' to the values of life with any satisfaction; he forges his merciless 'no' out of a longing for 'yes' and thus 'the despair is the negative from which the contours of the opposite can be drawn'. So, did this assessment of Brook's mean that the famous line from *Waiting for Godot*, 'God, the bastard, he doesn't exist', could be taken to assert Beckett's belief in God, or a wish he did exist?

Equally, Peggy's belief in God seemed to operate in a negative way. Did she, as in the *Godot* line, draw continually on belief while denying it? It was very much a phenomenon of the epoch, confusing and muddling to young people who idolized their actors and writers. Having the cake and eating it was all right while there was a big cake to divide, but what of the future? Even Pinter's plays drew, in their cynicism and amorality, on the presence, somewhere, of the stern Old Testament Jehovah.

It was perhaps just and inevitable, therefore, that Peggy should end up performing Winnie in Beckett's *Happy Days*. This was another Madeleine Renaud part. Peggy went frequently to Paris, visiting her daughter and seeing all of Renaud's great performances, not least her Winnie at the Théâtre de l'Odéon. Brenda Bruce had also performed Winnie in George Devine's production at the Royal Court.

In *End Game*, Beckett's second and last, almost full-length play, there is at least expectation: in *Happy Days* there is little more than memory. Even the language is reminiscent – of Beckett's own early work. Instead of 'The sun shone, having no alternative', from the novel *Murphy*, we have the 'The sun was not well-up'. Theatrically the action, or lack of it, remained as mockingly tedious as ever, with Winnie immured in her ever-encroaching mound – and Willie making one sortie from his underground tomb in a valiant yet futile attempt at contact.

This production of Beckett's *Happy Days* was accorded a singular and extraordinary honour. After leaving the RSC, to Peggy's annoyance, Hall was now the first director to run the National Theatre since Olivier had stepped down. But for the first four years of his tenure, which began in April 1972, the South Bank theatres had not opened. The first performance ever given in the National Theatre, at the Lyttelton, eventually took place on 16 March 1976. This, a matinee, was of *Happy Days*.

'I write down every single second,' Beckett told Hall, who had invited him to come over from Paris and show Peggy what it was about. Beckett's meticulousness nearly drove Peggy mad, especially the two weeks they spent perfecting Winnie's withdrawal of her mirror from her handbag. For Hall, it illustrated the 'impossibility of Sam being able to notice a whole aspect of his theatre – the humour of it'.

Both were wisely on their guard with Sam and the diseased sensibility which he exercised at one remove, so to speak, paranoid attention to detail, an obsession with getting each detail exactly as he saw it in the perfect performance in his own mind. When Billie Whitelaw played Winnie four years later at the Royal Court, with Beckett himself directing, Whitelaw became so desperate she phoned Peggy. 'I'm going mad,' Whitelaw told her. 'I don't know what to do.'

'You've got to ask him to leave, dear,' Peggy replied. 'He's impossible. Throw him out.'

'I said: "I can't do that."'

'She said simply: "Well, you'll have to." '

Beckett, whose lilting Irish accent became Peggy's own in this performance, wouldn't even go to the opening. He refused to see plays with audiences: 'He was too frightened,' said Hall, 'he didn't like to see the great beast unleashed on his play.' By the time of the opening, which was at the Old Vic on 13 March, prior to its transfer to the South Bank, Peggy had been 'quite ratty' at the physical perfection insisted on by Beckett, who regretted there was no known notation for recording the technical aspects of acting. The reviews were by no means wholly approving. *The Times* noted how Hall's production stretched Winnie's pain and cheeriness and her involvement with the trivia of her life so as to make it go as great a distance as possible. Her delivery, said Irving Wardle, was full of the Ashcroft music: 'floating sentences off into the air with a soaring lift at the end, and making emotive words glow like stones in a fire'. But John Barber, in the *Daily Telegraph*, felt Peggy missed the indelible Irish lilt of 'No pain, great thing that, nothing like it', as well as the 'casual briskness of the woman's equally indelible faith in God, the holy depths of her stoicism'. Robert Cushman in the *Observer* called her voice, 'Fortnum-and-Mason, gently overlaid with Irish'.

In April 1969 Peggy wrote from Dorset, where she often stayed with Stanley and Pamela Robinson, in one of her numerous bolt-holes, that she wasn't feeling too well. She had suffered a recurrent and 'particularly virulent bug' during the last performances of *A Delicate Balance* at the Aldwych which had blocked her head. She missed two performances because of ear trouble, but went back for the last three performances, then relapsed again.

This she related to Dadie Rylands from Iwerne Stapleton. The doctor had ordered ten days' convalescence, and while she was 'lapped in luxury' and it looked so exquisite, the winds were 'cruel' so she could not get out for a walk.

This gloomy news preceded (and may have had something to do with) her great announcement, the news that Eliza was to have a child and that she was therefore shortly to be a grandmother. After Peggy's difficulties with her prodigal daughter, Eliza had returned from Paris to tell her all – 'avec l'homme'.

This was a great deal for her to digest. She had heard of Pierre Loizeau, Eliza's boyfriend: journalist, poet – and, as she added approvingly, he was needless to say revolutionary, with anti-racism his chief passion.

Peggy found, on Pierre's trip to London with Eliza to meet her, that he was enormously interested in everything he saw. This being his first visit to England, she was glad to observe that he found everything exciting. He was thirty-six years old. Clearly he charmed

Peggy, who responded to his talkative French spirit. But he spoke almost no English. Like Julian (Bream) he had a built-in resistance to the idea of legal marriage, although, as she noted, it was perhaps more ideological than Julian's.

Peggy voiced the hope that he would change his mind and said she would never be surprised if they did eventually 'dwindle into' matrimony. (In fact they did, and so remain.)

She was longing to see 'le petit oiseau', as she punned, and was sure the baby would be born in London, but in the event her eldest grandchild, named Cordelia Manon, was born in Paris.

'Joyful' Peggy called the news, but the prolonged convalescence from her flu, the edgy, excited way she writes, suggests that she had mixed feelings and may have experienced some conflict over her own feelings towards her daughter, probably of guilt about her failed marriage to Hutchinson, anger too, perhaps, at the circumstances. At the same time she was prepared completely to suppress her more uncharitable responses and proclaim her happiness. She took to Cordelia Manon at once and by the time Eliza's next child was on the way, she had wholly embraced the role of grandmother, and as she joked 'half-French' grandmother. Indeed when Emilie Rafâel was born, at 7.45 a.m. on 10 February 1975, she had to put her 'skates on' and go to Paris at once to see the child. Manon, she remarked at once, was taking it all very stoically and, for reasons now strikingly odd – 'hygiene' – she was not allowed to see her sister. But she would, she added, be able to see her mother tomorrow. Peggy herself was put, on her visit to Paris, to sleep in Eliza and Pierre's bed: 'very sweet of them', while she was, she tells Dadie, very relieved that the birth went well, making reference to a newly-born as 'a fragile bark' that somehow always manages to survive the tempest.

On the other hand, Peggy told Dadie, in Vancouver, where Nick was not working, there seemed to be a split between him and his girlfriend. She had not heard from him for a long time, and had only discovered it by telephoning and not finding him in. This sent her to a high level of anxiety. Like most mothers, she imagined the worst because she did not know what exactly there was either to hope or dread to hear.

Three months later the devoted grandmother returned again to Seine Port where she found the little Emilie now a delightful and lively 'person' – who beamed and laughed when she was not asleep or eating. She had a remarkably expressive way of talking to herself on waking which made everyone laugh. She noted that while Eliza was very well, parenthood was taking its toll on Pierre who was smoking too much and had an incessant cough.

She herself was also not feeling well after her trip to Paris on this occasion, for again she had succumbed to a nasty throat infection which stopped her going to stay with the Parsons at Jugg's Corner in Sussex. She inveighed against the Almighty. 'God seems to have got it in for me at the moment,' she told Trekkie, who wondered at her atheistic referral to God. She was performing Winnie at this time. 'I'm told no talking! Poor Winnie!!'

Her letters to Dadie are dotted with occasional references to the Deity, and, as she grows older, with more and more résumés on the state of her health. Her letters to Leonard Woolf also listed much of what she enjoyed reading, clearly under Woolf's influence. She returned to Virginia Woolf's *To the Lighthouse*; she enjoyed very much 'The Song of Solomon' in the Old Testament, commenting to Woolf, 'I wonder how the Pope interprets that!'

She shared Leonard's intense dislike of Michael Holroyd's life of Woolf's close friend, Lytton Strachey. 'Really it is a bad book,' Woolf had commented, in which Holroyd failed completely to understand his subject, having been 'taken in by Strachey's epistolatory self-dramatisations!'

Biographers should beware of the families of their subjects, or, as in this case, their surrogate families – Bloomsbury friends. Noël Annan concurred, praising Leonard's condemnatory review but later claiming that Woolf was really more upset than anything by the revelations about Strachey's homosexual affairs. 'It's puzzling, isn't it, what happens when all the letters and juvenilia are laid out on the table? It seems to impede, rather than aid, understanding.'

Annan continued with a passage which seems especially relevant to Peggy the actress: 'I think perhaps biographers should be warned that letters, & even diaries, do not necessarily reflect the inner man; that there is no single inner man, but lots of characters often in conflict with each other presenting different faces to different people.' Annan further praised Woolf for puncturing a lot of biographers' shibboleths, such as the notion especially dear to them, that 'if only you dig deep enough you will always find a man of profound depth of emotion'. Peggy was more direct in her response. The "consolations" (of Boethius?) was her bedside book, she told Leonard just after her sixtieth birthday, and they consoled her for the boredom of Holroyd. She did not know if she would ever reach the end.

If Peggy had, like Strachey, no great depth of emotion in herself, she had all the rich and varied emotions that her great 'performer' friends such as Julian Bream and George Rylands could also project in reading or in playing. What she could be especially was a medium for great and deep emotions, without necessarily feeling them herself. What she did feel, and one gains this overwhelmingly from her letters, were very earthy, sensible, ordinary emotions about life, her family, her marriage, caring for her friends, especially in their infirmities. She cared unusually for other people.

Leonard Woolf died in 1969, soon after the birth of Peggy's first grandchild and the appearance of Leonard's final 'child', as Peggy jokingly referred to *Growing*, the last of his autobiographical books. Peggy enjoyed it enormously, she told him just before he died, as she had always enjoyed shutting her eyes, sniffing the jasmine, and imagining she was at Monk's Cottage again.

Her sexual side remained private, although perhaps it might ultimately be explained as a quite understandable desire for love and affection which could be achieved by no other means than by giving herself sexually. Just after the birth of her first grandchild, in May 1969, she began rehearsals again with Peter Hall, this time of her first Harold Pinter play, *Landscape*. She was to perform in two more plays by Pinter, the double bill of *Landscape* and *A Slight Ache* in 1973, and *Family Voices* in 1981.

Pinter was twenty-three years her junior; they shared, frivolously, one great enthusiasm, cricket, which Pinter considered God's greatest invention. Cricket had given Peggy some of her most memorable experiences: writing, for example, to Leonard Woolf a year before he died, from Barbados where she was on holiday, she says that the Sobers' innings was 'unforgettable', and that she was hoping to see Cowdrey, Graveney and Parks.

Pinter's writing had just that ferocity and ease which she admired. Pinter, in fact, recorded his view about her performance in *Wars of the Roses* to Michael Billington: Peggy's 'ferocity and tenderness' were what made her so singular, he said. Ferocity, Pinter went on, 'seems quite an accurate word: it hadn't occurred to me till I said it. But it's to do with an absolute focus and concentration and a kind of immediate insistence on excavation of the moment: a refusal to let it out of her grasp.'

But also he delighted in Peggy's vulnerability on stage, for, he said, allied to the ferocity there was a kind of panic that the image would elude her, that it needed 'a further grasp to sustain the moment'. At the same time he applauded her technical perfection. He said to me that she found it hard to satisfy herself. 'She would worry and worry about a thing, sharpening and simplifying it with great precision and determination. She did chip away at her acting.'

Pinter was uneasily married to Vivien Merchant, his first wife, and had recently ended a long, extra-marital relationship with the television presenter Joan Bakewell. Peggy herself was three years divorced. Clearly there was something very special in Peggy for Pinter and, reading between the lines of his observations, one can sense that extra fascination she held for him which was to lead into something near if not actually realized as a love-affair. 'We went around a lot together,' said Pinter. They attended plays, visited Glyndebourne and drove in the Sussex countryside: 'she would navigate'. He would lunch at her house, loving the gentleness and sense of history he found there. She had 'such a wonderful library of 20s and 30s poetry'. Pinter's early work had been criticized, as had the work of Osborne and other new-wave playwrights of the 1960s, for being unable to present or see women as people; in particular, Pinter had been singled out for criticism for portraying women only as 'mothers or whores'. It may be that this friendship with Peggy, coming at a critical time in both their lives, helped to illuminate and deepen insight into women.

Guarded and private like Peggy, like her Pinter also had, as Tim Pigott-Smith expressed it, a sense of fantastic loyalty to 'those he lets through the net'. If he liked someone he stuck by them through thick and thin. In fact, but for the difference in age, there was a great closeness in outlook between them. Both were much affected by the overthrow, in Chile, of President Allende's democratically elected government in 1973: 'We spent a great deal of time talking about its meaning.' Her need to believe in a cause was overpowering – and infectious. A cause for Peggy wasn't a great abstraction, said Pinter, but a 'concrete state of affairs'. She felt 'the issues, the humiliations suffered as a palpable fact'.

How can one describe their chaste love-affair? As a form of

sublimated consolation? For Peggy – and the feeling was stronger on her side than on his – it must have been autumnal, even though for Peter Hall the sexuality or sexiness that Peggy could communicate on stage was not 'something you can exaggerate, or put on, or fake: audiences were never in doubt'. Off-stage, still, as Hall had said, 'she needed to be in love'. The experience of being in love was crucial to her acting and 'she always was in love, romantically and painfully ... In her sixties she was so like a girl of fifteen.' And, moreover, the connection between this vulnerability and her work was critical to her: making her own talent work as a form of therapy. As Pinter had said, she was 'like quicksilver and her moods were also quicksilver: she could be very happy one moment and very sad the next'. Moreover, she 'lived on quite a high wire ... she wasn't placid by any means. She didn't divulge nor did she engage in dissertations on her past.'

While the background of Pinter's characters was indefinite, their fate indeterminate, their utterances often ambiguous, even obscure, the scripts were technically very sophisticated, carefully balanced, with their pauses and silences as exactly indicated as musical scores. Again the complexity showed in that the man, the playwright, was unlike the scripts: it was true he could be quite intimidating but he was warm, incredibly joky, and good fun.

But Pinter was 'knotted up' with complexes. As a much older woman, Peggy may have helped him solve some of these, for it was in her giving nature that she should pass on what she herself had been given by others. But both of them were against any revelation of what had attracted each to the other, or what made them tick as artists. It is ridiculous, as Tim Pigott-Smith pointed out, to give away 'the secret of what makes you work: you give up the most essential, if not the greatest residue, of your power'.

Peter Hall commented, 'The Pinter passion didn't come to an end until the seventies and the time of going off with Antonia.' Some of their friends were sure the relationship was far from platonic. Pinter insists that it was never consummated: 'If you're asking if we had an affair the answer is no.' But it was 'close and warm and very dear ... that very rare thing, a close friendship'. Pinter then saw less of Peggy as he became involved with Antonia Fraser, whom he married in 1980, and, as he said, 'naturally my life changed'.

Pinter's *Landscape* had been a radio play originally, about a couple, a chauffeur and housekeeper, speaking in parallel monologues, with a permanent 'rift' of non-communication between them which was signified by a cleft running through the set. The wife, Beth, dreams of a lover long past, whom she made love to on a beach, whom she had asked for a baby. The man, onomatopoeically harsh in language, talks of earthy matters like beer and his dogs. Peggy was sure that the gentle recall she had, was of him: in separate worlds now, she is recalling the tragedy of their estrangement. Pinter said of her performance: 'Frozen, forever in memories of lost or imagined love. She sat in the willed prison of her kitchen chair, at one and the same time grief-stricken and radiant. A miraculous synthesis.'

Landscape joined *A Slight Ache* in a double bill at the Aldwych in May 1973. In *A Slight Ache*, again written for radio some ten years earlier, Peggy played Flora, a housewife who prefers an itinerant match-seller to her middle-class husband. The play traces the usurp-ation by the 'shadow', a dirty old tramp-like figure, of the respectable well-heeled snob: this is primarily sexual and Peggy, now sixty-seven, displayed a surprising eroticism in the role, giving to lines such as 'when I was a Justice of the Peace, I had him on the front bench', an overtly sexual thrust. She caught, said Pinter, 'precisely the balance between the housewife and the erotic woman underneath'.

Peggy was devastated, Pinter upset, when in early 1979 she had to withdraw from playing in Simon Gray's *Close of Play*, which Pinter was directing. The part, that of a woman who never stopped talking, was described by Pinter as 'one of the best of Simon's creations'. She rehearsed for a week with severe cartilage pain in her left knee. She was, said Pinter, 'more and more in tears simply out of pain'; even so she could have been 'one of the funniest things anyone had ever seen'. The will didn't give in, but she 'finally just couldn't walk'.

On 12 October 1980 they played a 'Landscape Special', as Peggy called it, at the Aldwych Theatre for Pinter's fiftieth birthday. 'It went well and we had a packed house.' She was now approaching her own seventy-third birthday.

SEVENTEEN

A Friend in Norway

It is dangerous to associate with ghosts.

Goethe

One of the plays in which Peggy performed out of a sense of cause was *The Plebeians Rehearse the Uprising* by Günter Grass, which opened in June 1970. Again this was a left-wing play, but with a difference, because the target was Brecht himself, whom Grass attacked through the character called the Boss, accused of attending to his production of *Coriolanus* while Soviet tanks were called in by the authorities to crush a genuine workers' uprising.

The Plebeians was muddled propaganda, both for the workers and against Brecht's hardline communist principles. The intention behind it was perhaps good, but it was not a good play. Farrah, the Algerian designer, described Peggy's involvement as 'very idealistic. But this was not a good enough reason. It was very much a propaganda play, full of weaknesses.' Again taking the part played by Helen Weigel, Peggy had a problem with her hair, which Farrah called 'Lady Croydon suburban'. Farrah insisted on her wearing a scarf as the Boss's wife: 'even Weigel had a headscarf. I told her take this neutral, navy blue scarf.'

Peggy rebelled and sent for Farrah: once she had set her mind on something she would not change it, Farrah recalled, and they had a terrible drama: 'I wished,' said Farrah, 'I would never have to work with this lady again as a designer.' But Peggy kept the scarf, singled out by several critics as a distinctive feature of her playing of the role.

During the run Peggy called in Farrah one night because she had an Algerian man she wanted him to meet. Apparently a Rothschild girl had eloped with a young Algerian, who himself had fled from the police and followed her to England. She said the Rothschilds hated the idea of their daughter marrying an Algerian and Peggy wanted Farrah to give his assessment of the man: but she was, he noted, clever enough 'not to say come and give me your verdict'. In the event the two married and had a daughter. They lived abroad and later the man had an accident and drowned.

1973 saw the death of Hugh 'Binkie' Beaumont, the Welsh-born impresario who had dominated the West End theatre for almost forty years, and who, towards the end of his life, had been on the governing board both of the Royal Shakespeare Company and the National Theatre. It was he who had faithfully steered Peggy to stardom as Gielgud's leading lady, perhaps with more than an element of truth in the observation that his theatre (and Gielgud's) was so dominated by homosexuals that they liked actresses who were not sexy. Peggy reacted to Binkie's death with shock. She found it 'incredible', she said to Rylands. She could not think of him not being there. She went to his London home to see the two 'sweet' Italian servants he had, and the empty house finally convinced her. One had, she consoled herself, to be thankful that he went without pain or even without any warning. But he left such a blank behind. It made her think of Joyce Grenfell more than anyone else for Grenfell was the great revue artist Binkie had presented again and again.

By now Peggy was far from her 1930s West End origins, but her oft-repeated objection to returning to the past was overruled by a chance to act with Ralph Richardson, with whom she had not trod the boards since the triumph both of them had shared in *The Heiress* in 1949. Previously, in 1926, she had taken over the role of Margaret in *Dear Brutus* at the Birmingham Repertory Theatre, from Richardson's first wife Muriel, and then, four years later, had watched Richardson as Roderigo in van Volkenburg's production of *Othello* flashing the torch concealed up his sleeve to find his way over the darkened set.

Richardson, with characteristic astuteness, noticed there was 'something underneath the surface' in William Douglas-Home's apparently superficial West End play, *Lloyd George Knew My Father*. 'Don't ask me what it is,' said Richardson to Home, 'because I don't know. Nor will I ask you, because you won't know either.' With Robin Midgley directing, the impresario Ray Cooney asked Richardson whom he would like as leading lady.

'Edith couldn't do it now,' Richardson told him in a restaurant where they lunched. 'Old Edith couldn't do it, could she? I should doubt it, poor old Edith!' He stared into the middle distance, summoning replacements for 'poor old Edith' out of the four corners of the restaurant. 'Peggy,' he then said suddenly. 'I might give Peggy a ring.'

Peggy responded at once. 'O Rare Ralph Richardson', was how she thought of him – 'our greatest Theatre Magician'.

Again, and in spite of its obvious dimensions as a West End vehicle, so that one noted, reviewing the play, laughter automatically greeted the lines 'as if they had been spoken by members of the royal family or prime ministers at a party conference', Peggy and Richardson unearthed that 'something underneath' that Richardson had detected, in this case, the depth of resentment which the Richardson character still felt for his wife's unfaithfulness in the past.

During rehearsals Richardson and Peggy felt strong qualms about the opening of the play in Oxford and its pre-London tour. Richardson wanted to quit because he thought it just wasn't any good. Peggy was terrified of the first night in Oxford, fearing it was going to overwhelm her and make it impossible for her to put pen to paper in any sane way. She appealed to Dadie for support. How much she valued his friendship, she told him, which from Israel onwards had manifested itself in so many ways.

She now very much wished she had Dadie's hand to hold in what awaited her at Oxford. She feared for that dear fellow Ralph – 'as I also fear from him!! Well – it's only a play! & a very small one at that. But it curiously doesn't lessen the agonies!' She added that the smoke of battle may take some time to clear.

Although she did not know it at the time, this proved to be Peggy's last production in the West End. She could have run almost indefinitely in it but left after six months at the end of 1972, to be replaced by Celia Johnson who in due time also left, leading Richardson to comment, 'I've had two leading ladies shot from under me and I can't take any more.' So he went off, aged seventy-one, to tour Australia with the same play and Mu, his wife, in the leading role.

A little later he wrote to Douglas-Home about a play they proposed to write together in jocular mood called 'The Blood-Stained Mouse': 'There is not YET in my life at the moment no PRESENT – am working for a rival author of yours – comes even NORTH of you – had a beard – name of IBSEN. Awful fellow.'

Peggy was to join Richardson again in 1975 playing the 'awful fellow' at the Old Vic in *John Gabriel Borkman*; she took the part of Ella Rentheim, twin sister of Mrs Borkman who fights over possession of Erhart Borkman's heart and soul. Ella had long ago lost Borkman himself and she was not ravenous for his son's affection.

This was Peggy's fourth major Ibsen role, and it was to be her last, with the exception of the Ratwife in *Little Eyolf*, on BBC Television in 1982. According to Michael Meyer, she played this part like the 'lady of the manor: she couldn't act working class'. Prior to *The Wars of the Roses*, and since, on television, she had played Rebecca West in *Rosmersholm*, a production which had begun at the Royal Court in 1959 and transferred to the Comedy Theatre. This had been a typical Peggy triumph but not at all on the scale of *Hedda Gabler* twenty years earlier, architected, she herself claimed modestly, by Leonard Woolf who had given her a copy of 'Character Types', Freud's essay about *Rosmersholm* which emphasized Rebecca's incest guilt.

Devine read the essay to the whole company, while Peggy made it the centre of her interpretation. As explained by Peggy herself, 'Rebecca has loved Rosmer as a free woman. Then she discovers that Dr West, with whom she had an affair, was her father. She can't reconcile her ideas about freedom and her love of Rosmer with what she has done in the past. I think it's guilt that leads her and Rosmer to the mill-race. They are expiating their sins.' She found her own performance 'exhausting ... Ibsen seems to demand everything'. Her old difficulties with her ankle were playing her up again. She hated performing Rebecca in the television production, telling Woolf and Trekkie that she was glad they hadn't seen it – 'it was desperately disappointing'. She exploded: 'How I hate Television!'

On the whole the critics found her exactly right as Rebecca. Irving Wardle in *The Times* wrote: 'Rebecca amidst her ordinary domestic preoccupations is plainly obsessed with the bewildering consequences of having found it possible to love with utter selflessness ... it is Dame Peggy Ashcroft's triumph to make us believe completely in the courage and the honesty which make the sacrifice possible.' T. C. Worsley in the *Financial Times* found her as near perfection as an actress was likely to get. But Michael Meyer, Ibsen's biographer and translator, although not of the text in this production, thought her much too tame and naturalistic. A 'terrible' Rebecca, he said, 'much over-rated'. Alan Pryce-Jones in the *Observer* agreed with him: 'too discreetly naturalistic,' while at the very end 'there is a disordered poetry which eludes her'. Was she an actress who, as Meyer said, 'could do no wrong in the eyes of the critics'?

Rosmersholm was televised in 1965 in Michal Meyer's translation. *Ghosts*, the RSC production at the Aldwych in 1967, was Peggy's next Ibsen, in which she played Mrs Alving. She felt under-directed, it was very exciting, she wrote Woolf in May 1967, and 'I STILL have the last act to learn.' Rehearsals were difficult on account of a 'very inexperienced Oswald [John Castle] and this curiously uncommunicative director [Alan Bridges]. It is sad – for the play could be such a voyage of discovery.' After it had opened and Bridges had left the country temporarily to work abroad, Peter Hall called on Trevor Nunn to rework the production with extra rehearsals. Nunn, still in his mid-twenties, felt daunted but agreed to give it some directorial overview and try to untangle the difficulties. 'She was wonderfully generous and able to feed off anything I had to offer. She decided to take care of me.'

Reactions to Peggy's Mrs Alving were mixed. After severely criticizing the casting of Chloë Ashcroft, her niece, in the role of Regina, B. A. Young in the *Financial Times* reported that he could not take his eyes off Peggy in the scene when Engstrand tells the circumstances of their marriage to Manders: 'With hardly a word to speak, [she] told us of a whole lifetime of shame and suffering and patience.' W. A. Darlington in the *Daily Telegraph* noted that something in Ibsen's make-up had a special appeal to 'depths in Peggy Ashcroft's nature, or she would not be able to play his less appealing women so uncommonly well'.

On the other hand, Alan Brien in the *Sunday Telegraph* wrote that her technique was now so perfect, so transparent, as to be invisible, while her reaction to the news of her son's syphilis was 'as if she were George Eliot with a headache'. The *Liverpool Post* said she was 'stern, nervy, deadpan'. 'She could not act motherhood', according to Meyer: 'there was no warmth in her performance.' There would seem to be something incomplete about Peggy's mastery of Ibsen, as if her miniaturizing process, so long before described by Priestley, did not quite work, as if she was trying, continually, to extend herself, to extend her mastery over herself.

Yet when it came to the 1975 *John Gabriel Borkman* it appeared as if being unhappily in love suited Peggy perfectly and she could project into Ella Rentheim that whole lifelong power which came from her frustrated love for her father and which had never been satisfactorily transferred to, and earthed – or satisfied – in another. As Richardson said of the 'awful fellow' Ibsen, 'There was a continual struggle in Ibsen's life of conscience, of falling in love with strange little girls.' Could the same be said of Peggy's repeated falling in love with men? 'The continual question addressed to God would be: "Am I good enough?" The irony is that God's reply is: "Pack it up, old man". That's the eternal humour and what gives Ibsen his philosophic greatness.'

The rehearsals were fairly bumpy. Alan Webb fell ill; Wendy Hiller (Mrs Borkman) missed several rehearsals and lost her voice. Richardson, now in the most creative period of his long working life, was to prove himself the country's most complex and complete actor in this role. But for much of the rehearsal period he experimented endlessly, while his grasp of the text came and went eccentrically. Peggy found this very taxing, as she explained to Dadie: after *Borkman* opened, 'I shall be more than a bit fatigued owing to Ralph's verbal insecurity.' As Richardson himself quipped at one point, 'I've got the John, I've got the Borkman, I'm still looking for the Gabriel.'

They had a problem over the sofa on which Peggy and Richardson had to sit side by side. Richardson, who was tall, found it just right; for Peggy it was too high. Hall recalls: 'She asked me if she was being difficult and I told her she was. She said she was fussed and tired.'

But Ralph loved playing again with Peggy: he celebrated memories of her first performances with him in Barrie's – 'Christ what was it called? ... She'd been whipped out of drama school where she was a gold medallist and rushed to Birmingham.'*

'She is a marvellous craftswoman ... She does a lot of poetry reading, you know. I can't stand that. I neither like to give poetry readings nor listen.

'Her control is extraordinary. The bowing is so skilful.

'We have a very good cast and good sets. It might not come off. We could fall off the horse. A dangerous animal, the theatrical horse.' In the event it did come off. Peggy appeared just as Ibsen described

---

* She had played Margaret in J. M. Barrie's *Dear Brutus*.

181

Ella: 'more suffering than hardness in her face. There are traces of great beauty combined with a strong character.' She and Borkman became, as B. A. Young wrote, 'larger than life characters that are first and foremost characters in a drama'. After giving this grand histrionic display both she and Richardson, who end up on the mountain-top, slide down the sloping set on their bottoms to take the curtain call. Meyer was at last satisfied with a performance by Peggy in Ibsen.

For how long did – or could – Peggy go on creating the dramas of love on which she drew for energy? It seems she may have stopped with Pinter. But who knows, or could say? When asked how strongly the theme of guilt and retribution figures in *John Gabriel Borkman*, Richardson answered, smiling, 'Well ... there is the essential God and the essential Devil. However deep you scratch, people still have to love. That's the chemical ingredient of our life. Sin comes into the play, yes, and right or wrong.'

But sin had never come into Peggy's life. Like many successful artists* and creators of the age, she kept sin at arm's length by identifying causes she could champion or targets she could hate. In the place of the creator she put the artist and therefore, deep down and ultimately, in spite of her modesty, herself. In these last years of her life, although still, as she had been as a young student at the Central, 'clear-headed, down-to-earth, tough and sure of herself', she perhaps more and more came to accord with Ralph Richardson's pronouncement about people: 'We don't know exactly who we are, do we? We hardly know anyone else, really completely. We none of us know when we're going to die ... We're a mystery to ourselves and to other people.'

He was certainly a mystery to her. 'I couldn't do eight performances like Ralph Richardson, before he died,' she said of his last performance in *Inner Voices* in 1983. 'It's nothing,' he told her, 'just like doing press-ups every day.'

---

* Harold Pinter defined soul, when he talked of Peggy, as 'susceptible to any or many kinds of permutation and manifestations'.

EIGHTEEN

Perfection Walks Slowly

He is twice a conquerer who conquers himself in the moment of victory.

Publilius Syrius

Peggy continually missed, in the last two decades of her life, the presence of Nick and Eliza. But she had a double feast in store in 1977 when John Neville, director of the Citadel Theatre in Edmonton, asked her to play in *Happy Days* there, while Nick proposed taking her to tour the Rockies in his Mobile Caravan Company. 'Old men should be explorers,' wrote T. S. Eliot, unaware that only a generation or so on from writing that line women had, for better or worse, dismantled a traditional boundary so the line could equally be applied to them. Peggy, aged seventy, became an explorer in that great nineteenth-century tradition of eccentric women. She would now travel, she would take risks, she would explore the limits of human communication and live in the plays of Pinter and Beckett. She was now an arch high-priestess of art.

Indeed it was fascinating to see how her spirit, strong and unquenchable, devoured and absorbed into itself Beckett's manic-depressive pessimism. Unlike Shakespeare, who always gives something back to actors, Beckett's work – even *Waiting for Godot* – tends to infect its executants and bring them down. The list of suicides and breakdowns consequent to appearing in Beckett is lengthy and legendary: some, such as Peter Bull, who played Pozzo in *Waiting for Godot* in the first London production, could turn the depressing experience to hilarity, as when he wrote about it in his autobiography.

But for the most part even Beckett worshippers such as Billie Whitelaw, fascinated by the man, could only justify the plays on the basis of how they told their own life-stories.

But outward travel and physical adventure first. Peggy loved the British Columbia tour with Nick, his new girlfriend Patty and his children from various partners, telling Dadie she had a good idea of all the complications and problems of their lives. But she was encouraged by his positive response and future plans. It sounded as if, in his own individual way, he was marrying Bloomsbury to a new frontier style of theatrical endeavour. Peggy donned dungarees and lumberjack shirt and appeared in a play about a Canadian train robber (not defended by Hutchinson QC!) and said just one line.

After a few days of this – experienced therefore as a tourist – Nick took her for a three-day holiday to Vancouver Island where she relaxed by the Pacific rollers on the totally empty sands.

After all this flying about and visiting she arrived in Edmonton where she stayed on the seventeenth floor of the 'block' (the hotel) with John Neville's theatre just over the road. She found Neville delightful, 'very bright and has done his homework'. She came back to herself, she told Dadie, and apart from work she could take it very quietly there. She liked Edmonton, calling it 'impressive and rather beautiful in its modern way – & the bare rolling prairies all around are rather refreshing after the forests of B.C.'.

Happy Days bemused the Edmontonians, especially the 'brass-arsed' first-nighters. But Peggy, while not imposing her own life-story on Winnie, somehow lifted Beckett up to her fundamental optimism and sense of fun: it was as if she devoured Beckett's darkness and turned it to light in the affirmation of her perfect 'bowing'. It was, as Neville said, like 'listening to opera'.

Distant son and grandchildren, and, although nearer, daughter and granddaughters, were not quite enough for Peggy who, now increasingly lonely without a husband, turned to friends in the theatre as a surrogate family. Perhaps it was a measure of her continuing deep involvement to the end, her mission, so to speak, that she needed helpers and supporters, while she allowed herself to become a semi-institutionalized figure by signing letters among the usual circuit of do-gooders who liked to attach their names to causes in an often self-serving and suspect way. But in her case she was totally sincere.

Jeremy Hutchinson, now Lord Hutchinson of Lullington, may well have questioned the value of such gestures. At a lunch party in 1991 his wife June asked the assembled company including her mother, Lady Westmorland, her husband and James Lees-Milne, 'Have we done the slightest, tiniest bit of good minding so desperately about the worsening of the world physically, morally and all? Has our minding contributed one-tenth to lessening this appalling declension?' Lees-Milne answered, 'No. It has merely made us miserable.' The rest – 'all but Jeremy' – thought it had done some good to care about the state of the world.

This was Jane Austen's view of causes. It is by no means everyone's. It had not always been Peggy's. She had never read a newspaper when young: 'I remember someone talking about the Slump. "What's the Slump?" I asked. I hate politics. There's something odd about people who contemplate being a politician. What a life.' But Peggy had become a dedicated campaigner, as witnessed by Michael Foot, whom she much admired and who was a devoted Hampstead neighbour. She was, Foot said, a supporter of CND from its inception, and when her ideological passions were stirred, 'she would give unstintingly of her time and influence'. She wasn't, Foot noted wrily, 'a great supporter of John Osborne, and she was very critical of Ken Tynan'. She and the Foots would lunch together sometimes in her beautiful, magical garden. But apart from her public causes she would also support local appeals, donating generously (and anonymously) to the Keats House Appeal launched by the *Hampstead and Highgate Express* and raising money for the local history museum at Burgh House. She deplored the 'infinite unhappiness' in children: it must be pretty grim 'to be young now, without the possibility of a job'.

Tim Pigott-Smith recalled reading with Peggy in the Star Chamber, Westminster, poems of political content in aid of Charter 88: 'You get this call,' he said. 'You never felt in awe of her or of the event. There was an absolute assumption that you are equals and she had absolute trust in you.'

One night she asked Pigott-Smith to accompany her to the annual charity entertainment of the Gallery First-Nighters. Peter Hall, Harry Andrews and Rachel Kempson were also there. But after the first course of the dinner Jack Rosenberg, the president, had a heart attack. It was most bizarre. He was still alive but only just, lying, feet sticking out from under the table, shielded from public view by these famous actors. Peggy turned to Pigott-Smith, saying, 'I wonder how the mighty reaper will come.'

When the ambulance arrived they formed a line as Rosenberg was wheeled out. 'The show must go on,' he said, then died. But opinion was divided as to whether the comedy and cabaret show should go on. Peggy put her foot down and said, 'No.' Peter Hall announced the death of the president to the gathering. 'They were all very shaken and went back to Peg's for a stiff drink.'

'If I had to find one word to describe her it would be that she was so earthy,' Pigott-Smith commented, 'in the sense that she was rooted. It came, I suppose, from her political beliefs.' Comparing Peggy with Celia Johnson, Anthony Quayle, who worked with both actresses, made a similar comment. Celia was a comedian, while behind those great round eyes was hidden 'a devastatingly amusing mind'. But Peggy took life much more seriously. 'She's a crusader, she's *Pilgrim's Progress* to the end.'

She much deplored the spread of unlimited information. 'I can't pretend that I think the world is a better place. I know we can think of all sorts of evils in the past, but it now seems to me so nasty. One must never lose all faith because it's not all nasty, but we know too much about what's going on. We're told *everything* instantly and that affects us.'

She registered great unease when Essie Robeson's remarks about Paul and herself were published in 1989, placing herself beyond reach for comment; but she quite shocked two colleagues who visited her in Hampstead by saying, 'Let me tell you that whatever they say about negroes being more well-endowed than white men, it's definitely not true!' She must have both wanted to surprise with her Wife-of-Bath frankness, at the same time answer to herself in some redressing sense of justice over the past.

Sometimes she must have felt strongly that she had given her heart too freely and hurt herself too much. For it was she who went on and carried in herself the pain of loving.

Old age was lonely and disorientating for Peggy. In early 1991 James Roose-Evans, founder of the Hampstead Theatre, was lunching with a friend in a Haverstock Hill restaurant when Peggy came up and asked if she could join them, 'feeling rather solitary at the news of the Gulf War'. Roose-Evans subsequently bumped into her in the street. She was walking with a stick having hurt her knee. 'Old age is a bugger!' she complained, banging her stick on the ground.

On another occasion she grumbled about her knee trouble, which went back to the V-2 explosion in 1945: 'I have a slightly gammy knee, which is a big disability because you never know if you're going to keep your balance ... I don't like getting old. Everything about it is horrible. You don't get wiser well, perhaps a little. You get slightly deaf, go a bit lame and don't see as well as you could.' Her tranquillity, she said, was a myth. 'I'm a worrier. I worry about everything and anything.'

Harriet Walter first met Peggy when she was seventy-four, appearing in *All's Well That Ends Well*, directed by Trevor Nunn at Stratford and at the Barbican. It was fitting that her last Shakespearian role should be the Countess of Rossillion, Shakespeare's most warm and rounded portrait of a mother. The male protagonists, Bertram, the King of France, even Parolles, are sick either mentally or physically, but the women, Helena and the Countess in particular, shine out as exemplars.

Naturally, for this was her role in the play, Peggy became something of a mother-figure to Harriet Walter who played Helena. When Harriet first met her she was extremely conscious of Peggy's royalty stature, and as such she was 'more intimidating than the real royals'. Harriet said she felt quite ageist when she had lunch with her: 'I was so angry that I was reserved; she didn't detect I was nervous – bored, lonely, wanting to spend time with her; I should have been less reverential.'

Yet she soon found Peggy wanted to be an equal: 'she wasn't an actual mother who was a surrogate', and she had 'the perceptiveness of older women about what younger women were going through'. She knew how to refresh her creativity. And like any actor who has got to that age and still commands attention, her 'whole life was there in her face'.

Like everyone with low self-esteem, said Harriet of her character Helena, she wondered if Peggy, for all her sense of royalty and command, didn't have the opposite within her, an isolated and lonely side. She had, possibly, a 'hidden promise and availability', a sensuality which conveyed itself 'veiled in the face, expressing a great need or desire for male attention'.

Trevor Nunn, directing Peggy in *All's Well*, had his own troubles at this time; after fourteen years of marriage to Janet Suzman they were nearing break-up. Nunn tried to explain what was going wrong. Peggy, who was confidante to both of them, was dreadfully upset.

Eventually she said, 'I love Janet; if you are that unhappy, and it is that unhappy, you can't spend the rest of your life resisting it.'

But *All's Well* was a completely golden time for Nunn: 'It was only to be expected that when she came to live in Stratford for *All's Well* she would live in my house': she was 'there as friend and mothering me too; we spent countless evenings together.'

Peggy's performance as the Countess was exquisite: 'You simply lose yourself in the largeness of her spirit,' said Nunn. Harriet Walter commented, 'She existed effortlessly – everything fitted like a glove; the establishment of resources, regality, warmth, humour; fierceness; being in touch with her young self; in touch with being in love.' She sobbed real tears when she thought of Bertram being away from home – thinking perhaps of Nick in Canada.

They were aware at the last night in Stratford that this was Peggy's final stage performance: Harriet recalled going out to the car park afterwards to find her car, seeing Peggy, also alone, climbing into her car, a Honda, and recognizing something poignant and historic about this moment. 'One is grateful to the royalty,' Harriet said of her, 'one hates hierarchy, but it is useful to have it.' Peggy at this time met Mrs Thatcher: the two women, apparently so opposite to one another, chatted away with great animation. Was it just a public show, or was there recognition, perhaps unconscious in both of them, of some deeper affinity?

Dadie Rylands was five years older than Peggy: still extraordinarily vital, he was to remain so well into his nineties. He would scurry along like a crab, possessor of some extraordinary spirit, undaunted by the steep staircases of King's. Into lifts he refused to be drawn, remarking to me when I visited him, 'I don't go in lifts: they find you a week later!' Independent, fierce sometimes, quick in repartee, he would keep on at Peggy to give Apollo Society recitals very nearly to the end.

He kept her on her toes, for when, on one occasion, he had sent her a furious letter about some forthcoming engagement, she replied – this was at the time she recorded *Family Voices* for the BBC – explaining the hectic life she was still leading. She addressed him as 'Dear Crosspatch' and pointed out how much he was on the warpath but that even so she would reply gently. After quoting the Bible – 'a soft answer turneth away wrath' – she went on to explain her silence in a warm, undercutting way, listing her myriad activities, which included a little matter of making a film, reading a dozen or so plays, the whole of Easter-time passed belowground in Broadcasting House doing Pinter. Oh yes, and she had nine days, too, of her son at home.

Dadie had told her she could 'take your time making up your mind about the poems' he had sent her: she quoted this back at him, and to his queries as to where they would stay she replied they were booked in with Leonard and Trekkie, Julian Bream and their Dorset friends, the Robinsons. They had to remember one great drawback, namely performing in a church, as they had been asked to do. She was horror-struck at the idea, fearing it might prove 'acoustically ghastly'.

After this came numerous technical suggestions. This letter conveys the essence of Peggy's daily life, yet, as with all her correspondence, gives nothing away. One seeks in vain for her voice. Perhaps it is a mistake to look for anything original in her letters. As Donald Sinden has said, 'As long as I'm working it keeps me happy': this applied equally to Peggy all through the 1980s, her last decade. She remained to the end a solid trooper, while her range of acquaintance was, as Sinden also said, 'absolutely astonishing'. He contrasted her to Edith Evans, with whom she was often compared. Nobody knew Edith, she was 'nobody's friend'. But Peggy could be as sweet and lovely as she liked 'because she knew at the back of it that everyone was looking after her'.

Yet Peggy very much echoed Edith Evans in her attitude to money. Quoted in *Ned's Girl* by Bryan Forbes, Edith had said, 'How terribly wrong this money-first attitude is. Money, yes, in its place, but the good work first and then the money. The money-first system drains a country or a profession to the dregs and never really gives anything back. I *know* that it is the root of all evil. Not money, but money first.'

Her last radio play for the BBC was Tom Stoppard's *In the Native State*, the precursor of his stage play *Indian Ink*. She had played Lady Macbeth on radio in 1966 to Paul Scofield's Macbeth, but according to the director she and Paul 'didn't feel married'. Moreover, Lady Macbeth was not a role she enjoyed playing. This was true, also, of the wife in Strindberg's *The Father*, which she broadcast in 1971, again with John Tydeman as director, who said, 'She didn't get on with really evil people – she did want to be loved, although she eventually played it right.' Queen Margaret had 'a rightness, a political rectitude with which she would have agreed'.

Stoppard wrote with Peggy and Felicity Kendal in mind but Mrs Swan, the character played by Peggy, appears as a young girl in the last scene. Tydeman cast another girl in the role but Peggy, who was upset she was not playing it, told Tydeman, 'That's why I accepted the part.' She wanted the youthful side to offset Mrs Swan's pugnacious crudity, as when she defends her sister's sexual forthrightness: 'She used men like batteries. When things went flat, she'd put in a new one.' She pleaded with Tydeman, 'I mean it's radio,' who told her to try the part.

They rehearsed. Tydeman thought she could get down to thirty-five, but in no way down to twenty, and he told Stoppard, 'It's just not right – how are we going to tell her?' Stoppard said he would take care of it: 'Tom was wonderful and gentle, and told her he actually thought of the twenty-year-old as being another character and wanted someone else to do it. "What you are at twenty is not what you are at eighty," Stoppard told her. Peggy cried and implored them to let her do it, but finally gave way, accepting, in a truly Chekhovian moment, that she was no longer young.

She had, judged Tydeman, a 'very quick mind' but she was not an intellectual at all. 'She'd like to have been thought of as an intellectual and liked to become it.' But really she was closer to Gielgud whose attitude, on the whole, was, 'I don't really understand it. I just do it.' Gielgud was 'somehow a conduit'. He had an immense feel for it – 'instinct and impulse'.

'I think she missed Frognal very much; she missed her garden; she was working on plays and films; she looked in your face and smiled and was enchantingly pretty again,' said a Hampstead ex-neighbour who remained a friend. Why did she sell Manor Lodge after forty years and move to a top-floor flat in Belsize Park? Probably, as she was not someone to manoeuvre in the capitalist system to pass on a house before she died, because she wished to realize a lump sum and secure her children's future. The sum was £1,100,000, the purchaser the publisher Tom Maschler. Subsequently it changed hands several times and fell into neglect and planning permission limbo. 'The house has been allowed to stand there,' complained Jeremy Hutchinson in 1991. 'My former wife loved the garden and the house. She would have been horrified by what's happening to it. We bought it together in 1947.'

She still felt very orientated towards Hampstead: 'Oh let's go up the hill to Hampstead to a pub,' she would say to a friend. 'The one in Flask Walk where Kingsley Amis always goes.' Sometimes she would go to the heights of Hampstead on her own, and sit by Whitestone Pond. Margaret Drabble noticed her there one day. 'The last time I saw her was very eerie: she didn't recognize me at all. She was sitting at one of the lower ponds on the Heath, gazing ahead. A little child was straying near her. "Come here, little girl," she said, "what are you doing, little girl?" She was wandering a bit, looking distrait. The child looked at her as if she was speaking from another world.'

There was a lift up to her top-floor flat. You came up to her landing and there was a very difficult key. In order to get her grand piano into the flat she had to have an inch taken off the ceiling. A feature of the main sitting-room was that when you went in you looked straight across to a little roof garden with a white trellis: jasmine, honeysuckle, basil, begonias, geraniums, grew there; a kitchen led off the main room. It was a very modest apartment although it had the luxury of an electric escalator running down to her bedroom below. Visitors were struck by the austerity with which she lived and the few clothes she had; someone asked her what she was going to wear for a TV award ceremony in the mid-eighties and she replied, 'My old kaftan' – an old cotton kaftan which she had dyed. Her honours and awards were all piled away in a cupboard: mostly masks – she didn't know what to do with them, she said.

One day Catherine Lambert, widow of J. W. Lambert the theatre critic and a neighbour whom Peggy befriended in these last years, was rung up by the housekeeper to say Peggy had had a fall and been taken to the casualty department of the Royal Free Hospital. Catherine Lambert went along to the hospital but they had not heard of her. She walked around and then heard Peggy's voice: she was lying unattended on a trolley in a draughty corridor, face purple, lip bleeding. No one knew who she was.

Catherine Lambert insisted to a young doctor that she be treated properly, and he sewed up her bottom lip – teeth had come through it – and her head. She wanted to leave at once. Having got her back by taxi to Belsize Park, Mrs Lambert helped her to bed.

'What struck me was the poverty of her bedroom; the little cotton counterpane on her bed – all very shabby. I helped her on with a nightdress. "Don't stay with me," she said.'

Peggy had a number of minor complaints at this time: frozen shoulder; always the bad knee. For quite a while she had a New Zealand physiotherapist called Joanne who visited her. Many, now, were her 'surrogate' daughters, as people invariably called them, although this often seemed no more than fancy talk for young friends. Susan Engel said the same of herself and her husband Sylvester: 'surrogate children', because it was natural that with her children away she should adopt others of the same age.

She had plenty of helpers, 'doers, shifters, shakers', Janet Suzman surmised. She only felt 'really comfortable with men ... but she was on the telephone to me or others all the time. You'd get these calls: "Darling, what about ...?" We used to go out and have fish and chips. Young people liked to be with her. We all enjoyed being with her.'

Janet Suzman had the sneaking suspicion, which I share, that while Peggy had a great sense of fun she did not have much of a sense of humour as such. She went once with Janet to a matinee performance of *The Dybbuk* at the Aldwych. When they arrived the house was full and members of the audience were all shouting to each other, greeting each other and making such a hubbub that they couldn't take the curtain up.

'Oh my God,' said Janet, 'all these Jews!'

Peggy pulled herself up and her eyes flashed: 'I'm a quarter Jewish, you know.'

'Don't worry, Peggy. I'm the whole hog,' replied Janet, admiring her 'wonderful defensiveness'.

NINETEEN

Glory in Copper Pieces

Ship me somewheres east of Suez, where the best is like the worst.

Kipling

Peggy was never much of a film actress, in her own estimation, at least. Sadly she clung to the common cliché that film was not an actor's medium. She could not visualize in advance those original performances that she was able to offer so directly to the public toward the end of her life springing both straight from her own imagination and who she was. They were to happen almost in spite of herself.

Her cameo role in *The Thirty-Nine Steps*, which came very much out of Hitchcock's admiration for her as a stage actress – he attended all her major stage performances and admired her boundlessly – led to several insignificant roles during the 1940s. She wasn't at all the actress of suggestible looks, in contrast, for example, to Celia Johnson. Even at drama school, as Angela Fox had said of Peggy, she had been 'clear-headed, down-to-earth, tough and sure of herself', while Celia suggested the eternally feminine, and as a result had a much greater film career than Peggy: 'so pretty, vulnerable, almost ethereal; the tilt of her head, the touching, apprehensive eyes made the fat girl Angela Worthington wish she could do something for her'.

Peggy often told the tale of the cameraman who suggested to her that she could be a great star if she had her nose adjusted or shortened with surgery. She also needed, they said, her teeth fixed. Perhaps she was destined only to play earthy, direct characters on screen because, in more ways than one, she was not prepared to compromise, even to the slight degree of having a quite obtrusive mole removed from just beside her nose. Her next film of any note after *The Thirty-Nine Steps* was *The Nun's Story*, twenty-three years later, set in the Belgian Congo, in which she played the Mother Superior of a Catholic order.

Fred Zinnemann, the director, charmed her into the adoption of religious principles with which she never felt really happy. Zinnemann wanted the three women principals in the film, Peggy Ashcroft, Edith Evans and Audrey Hepburn, to spend several days in a convent to watch and, wherever possible, join in the observances. In Paris the nuns when approached with this end in view were liberal, intelligent, relaxed; in Belgium they viewed the whole thing with hostility, while the Vatican orders were as 'concrete' in opposition 'as a stone wall'.

In early January 1958, Zinnemann succeeded in 'stashing away' Peggy, Edith and Audrey in three different convents in Paris. Zinnemann would make a daily tour at 10 a.m. 'to see how they were doing. I'd arrive in the warmth of a taxi ... The winter was immensely cold and the convents were hardly heated ... All of them would come out of the cloisters absolutely purple with cold but fascinated by what they were involved in and very excited by the way they were getting prepared for their characters.' In April they filmed for two weeks in a leper colony in the Belgian Congo, where Peggy 'helped with the nursing'.

But Peggy was in no way attracted by the observances, although this was the year in which Alec Guinness, her old friend, played the Cardinal in *The Prisoner* and himself became a Catholic convert. She gives a crisp, authoritative performance in the film, as if holding the character of Mother Mathilde slightly apart and at one remove from her. In spite of Peggy's protestations and arguments the Audrey Hepburn character, Sister Luke, rebels against the Order and opts for the secular life. The film became the biggest money-maker of its year, although it had been feared that it showed too much documentary detail about the life of a nun.

Peggy was always reluctant to discuss her religious beliefs, although she was not a believer. After she had managed to overcome her deep and instinctive aversion to the cinema, during the television version of *The Wars of the Roses*, she did in fact gain greater popularity than one had ever supposed she could by playing three elderly women on film, all – to show the typecasting that old age brings with it – Englishwomen either visiting India or in exile there.

The first character was by way of being a prelude to the other pair, Barbie in *The Jewel in the Crown* and Mrs Moore in *A Passage to India*. This was in a television film called *Hullabaloo Over George and Bonnie's Pictures*, made for Melvyn Bragg's South Bank Show by James Ivory and Ismail Merchant. The script was written by Ruth Prawer

Jhabvala, the novelist. Peggy played an eccentric old Anglo-Indian lady who tries to obtain from India a set of rare miniatures in a Maharaja's collection. It was in the clash-of-two-cultures genre with which Peggy easily identified herself. Filmed in Jodhpur, Rajasthan, in early 1978, *Hullabaloo* was supposed to take a month, she wrote to Trekkie, Dadie, and Trekkie's husband, Ian Parsons, on 12 February from the Armaid Bhawan Palace where some of the film was shot, and where she was staying. She was being worked hard, although a 'fantastic' party had been thrown for them the previous evening in the 'vulgar' palace (sandstone outside, marble and art noveau-cum-Maples furnishing inside). They were staying with an eccentric Maharaja who lived in his penthouse, while his 'minions' ran the rest of the palace as a tourist hotel.

She must have been, in this early 'late' film – so to speak – collecting bits and pieces to hoard them away, for India was to become her film canvas. Her letters back home are full of positive observations, although still very much in her official, 'head-girl' style. The shooting of this film was a bit all over the place: 'improvisationable' was her word for it, although not to be found in any dictionary. She found it all to her liking, although, with a slight look down her nose, lacking in professionalism.

The days were very hot, but the nights were freezing, while the marble halls where they both filmed and lived were not heated. She grew tired of endless curries, but in contrast to the many visitors who went down with upset stomachs and were ill-at-ease in primitive surroundings, she delighted in the confused jumble of picturesque poverty she found in the streets of Jodhpur. The teeming variety of animal and dilapidated mechanical transport of the town – whose name in place of riding breeches joined the English language – caught her imagination: tikka-gharies, four-wheeled horse-drawn carriages; two-wheeled tongas, sometimes pulled by motor-bikes, and bicycles galore.

But the filming took much longer than a month: she kept a very brief diary containing fairly ordinary observations: the Maharaja and his dancing girls; sport – for 'sport was the great thing in old India', a credo that to indulge in endless physical exercise was the way to survive, that 'a jolly good sweat was tremendously good for you'. Then she spent twenty-four hours on the train to Bombay. After the filming was over she gave herself a luxurious seaside holiday in Goa.

She turned down the offer of a woman companion, and one senses that she felt better on her own.

In 1979 Stephen Poliakoff cast Peggy in his television play *Caught on a Train*: his first choice for the Viennese lady from Messner was Lotte Lenya, but her doctor said, 'No way can she cross the Atlantic.' Then he turned to Peggy, whom Poliakoff expected to be like a Queen Mary figure, for she had recently played her on television in the drama series *Edward and Mrs Simpson*. On visiting Peggy in Hampstead he was surprised by her informality, her directness, and her 'sensuality'. Peter Gill, the director, had told Poliakoff she was 'one of the sexiest actresses in England', and Poliakoff remarked on her very 'un-English' quality – 'when you met her more like a French actress'.

Poliakoff knew about Peggy's love-affairs: 'She had a lot of love affairs with a lot of famous people', including Sickert, whose portrait of her was hung prominently in Manor Lodge.* 'She liked writers and creators, people who created from nothing; very instructive, all that generation. They liked to get on with it.' She told him she had met A. E. Housman, and 'what a bitter man he was'.

She inveighed, at their first meeting, against James Agate as if he had written his bad reviews of her only yesterday: 'Oh, he hated me,' she said. She was also very worried she would have to take off her clothes on the train.

Later, after the success of *Caught on a Train* and her 'very flinty' performance, Poliakoff, who liked her 'ruthless clarity' and the fact that she didn't 'milk the part for sympathy', wanted to write something for Peggy to play in the theatre, possibly a work for the Cottesloe, the National Theatre's small house. She told him, 'I can't play a main part. I'm too old; I mustn't talk too much; I mustn't move too.' It was a very difficult brief for Poliakoff, and while the stage play came to nothing, Poliakoff later wrote another television film script for her, *She's Been Away*, in which she played an old character who returns home from many years spent in a mental institution. This was based on the recent disclosure that two nieces of the Queen Mother whom she believed to be dead, had in fact been alive and in a mental home. During the filming of this, Peggy took up and led the cause of saving the site of the Rose Theatre in Southwark from speculators. 'We stood together on the barricades,'

---

* It is now in the Tate Gallery.

said James Fox who also appeared in the Poliakoff film. Peggy told Fox, 'I shall be there at five a.m., and lie down in front of the sand lorries.' And so she did.

The Jewel in the Crown, based on Paul Scott's 'Raj Quartet', was a favourite with Peggy and, unusually for her, she thrust herself forward for the role of Barbie when she heard that Christopher Morahan was to direct for Granada. Barbie was an 'extraordinary living character', whose eccentricity greatly appealed to her. Morahan, as a former pupil of Saint-Denis at the Old Vic School, was working at the National Theatre at the time, where Peggy was playing Fanny Farelli in Lillian Hellman's *Watch on the Rhine*, a truculent Yankee lady in a run-of-the-mill political drama which added little either to her reputation or to Hellman's. She found it difficult to catch the Hellman rhythm and she could not stand the director, Mike Ockrent.

The Jewel in the Crown took her off to India for a further five months in 1982, just after she had finished her final stage appearance in *All's Well That Ends Well*. She liked India immensely. She stayed most of this time in the Simla hills where she shared a cottage – and sometimes, when it was very cold, the same bed-covers – with Rachel Kempson. The simple up-country bungalow with its primitive bathroom, whitewashed walls and muslin cloth ceiling was unattractive. The furniture was just cushions and bamboo chairs and tables, their feet standing in saucers of water to prevent the ants climbing up.

Out one afternoon on a boat on Lake Nogin she and Rachel Kempson were pestered by itinerant sellers. A boat full of furs pulled up alongside them. 'All right,' she chose a hat, 'I'll try that hat in mink,' she said to the pedlar. She put it on, preened herself and asked, 'What fur is this?' 'Cat', said the dealer. She threw it from her head with disgust.

Tim Pigott-Smith recalls how much the learning of the text bothered her. Her insecurity impressed him, and how she was open to all possibility. 'She asked us for accents (for Barbie) and Christopher directed her to Croydon and she was very rooted.' Morahan also made use of her lame knee, which had recently been operated on, for the stiff, wide-legged walk.

Fabia Drake, who claimed, as many did, Peggy as a close and dear friend, played Mabel Layton in *The Jewel in the Crown*. But Peggy had always found her insupportable: 'Please don't put me in the same hotel as Fabia,' she asked Christopher Morahan. During the filming her old rival Celia Johnson, who was due to appear with Ralph Richardson in Angela Huth's *The Understanding* in May 1982 at the Strand Theatre, died just before the first night. When told of this, Peggy commented sharply, 'She deserved it!'

Barbie, in the course of *The Jewel in the Crown*, loses her faith. An outsider in India, just not quite the pukka memsahib, she becomes, in what she most values, namely, her Christianity, an outsider to her deepest self. It is, as most of Peggy's later roles showed, a bleak development which again she somewhat relished. Here, perhaps, is further identification with the alienation from faith that being 'modern' entailed: a nostalgia, to which Beckett gave his authority, over the world having become an old place in which religious belief no longer counted. Singing snatches of hymns, Barbie tells the Indian boy Ashoch that she is a servant of the Lord Jesus. Reviving the south London tones of her early life, Peggy caught the flat vowels of disillusionment perfectly. And sexual disgust, as when Barbie lights upon the casual ugliness of Mildred and Kevin Coley copulating and is filled with horror at the 'mechanical pumping' and emotional 'inertia'.

The general reaction was that Peggy had dug deep into her own feelings of solitude and isolation to play Barbie so perfectly. If despair is not just as catching as anger and sexual licence, she managed not to catch it herself. But drama is out to exploit every state of mind and feeling, and Peggy did not moralize: she did, while remaining detached, create an extraordinary compassion, especially in the scene when she tells the boy Ashoch, 'My heart hardly beats at all, it's very tired and old and far from home.'

When David Lean approached Peggy to appear as Mrs Moore in *A Passage to India* the part had already been turned down by Katharine Hepburn. He would have had Hepburn play Mrs Moore as a New Englander, an indicator from the word go as to how far Lean respected E. M. Forster, his original source. Years before, with Rylands, Peggy had seen a stage adaptation of the novel by Santha Rama Rao at the Cambridge Arts Theatre, which had transferred to the London Comedy

Theatre.* She had also met Forster who told her, 'I hope one day you'll play Mrs Moore.' Her unspoken response: 'What me, play an old girl like that?'

Apparently Lean, when he decided to approach Ashcroft, was already as sure as can be 'that Peggy as Mrs M. would be on the list of Academy nominations'. He invited her to lunch at the Berkeley Hotel. Peggy told him she was now seventy-five and was 'beyond doing another work in India', but Lean riposted that he too was seventy-five. Peggy told Rylands that Lean won her over straight-away, and with the intimacy she could only use with Dadie, 'He's a knock-out, isn't he?' They spent lunch discussing Croydon, where both of them were born, to Peggy a source of amazement. Peggy owned up to not really 'seeing' Mrs Moore in Lean's script, and while she acknowledged his affection for the character he had no grasp, she felt, for the change she undergoes in the caves, which Lean's script left out.

Peggy asked Dadie to explain various chapters to her. She was reading the book for the *third* time – she underlined third – and finding it more and more ambivalent. She found Lean ambivalent, too. James Fox, who played Fielding, describes how Peggy asked for a read-through of the script and Lean agreed. But they found, when they came to this, that the script contained so many of Lean's meticulous camera directives, of which he was extremely proud, that they gained little from it. Lean kept stopping the read-through and telling the cast, 'I think what they'll do here is ...' He could only see the film in terms of where the camera was pointing. He cast his actors because he thought they *were* the characters.

This attitude soon irritated Peggy – she admired Lean's per-fectionism, but when he tried to explain his vision of the characters to her, she found it was very different from her own. She was concerned to remain close to Forster but Lean saw Mrs Moore as having a touch of the ghost about her and he commented that Peggy had no poetry in her – not a widely held view at all. At another time he voiced criticism that Mrs Moore was more sensitive, more intuitive, than Peggy was making her. When Lean asked her to look at scenes through the viewfinder, she didn't respond with any excitement or

---

* Mrs Moore had subsequently been played, in the BBC television adaptation, by Sybil Thorndike.

sense of challenge, but thought this just another example of Lean's passion for having 'everything set in concrete'.

Alec Guinness, ultimately considered a piece of gross miscasting as Professor Godbole by Lean himself, cheered up Peggy when he arrived. She wrote to Rylands that his presence was enormously comforting. Guinness at once fell in love with India, and went sight-seeing in Delhi. He and Peggy spent a lot of time together, and although Lean felt Godbole was a sort of spiritual first cousin to Mrs Moore, also with a touch of the ghost – 'two ghosts understand one another' – he was suspicious that Guinness, who hadn't really wanted to be in the film, was passing on to her his negative 'vibes' about Lean.

Both had a great affection for him, but Peggy remained critical. When he asked her, towards the end of the filming, to look at Aziz and blush like a girl she was stunned. If the suggestion had come sooner she would have had a great deal of difficulty in playing Mrs Moore. When she told him she couldn't possibly do it like that he said, 'Oh well, if you can't, you can't'.

Her unhappiness was also due to Lean's lack of sensitivity where the young actors – Aziz (Victor Banerjee) and Adela (Judy Davis) – were concerned. There was, she felt, a deep lack of respect for *their* attitudes to the part. Lean was not only an anti-analysis man, but also an 'aristocrat'. 'I heard him say he cast his play [sic] with people he knows are absolutely right for the part. It isn't a case of being absolutely right, is it? It's how to play it. And then you've got to allow that they have their attitude to the part.'

During one scene, filmed in the mosque, Peggy fell and twisted her ankle. A member of the production team related how Lean looked upon this almost as a plot against him which stopped him from forging ahead: 'He hated suffering and couldn't go near it. He recoiled from cripples in India ... I can't remember him ever consoling anyone personally.' Guinness also found it strange that even though he was staying in the same hotel as Peggy, Lean did not go and see her.

Another time, filming in the temple, when Peggy was at a loss and asked, 'David, what do you want me to do. What am I thinking?' Lean answered, 'Just act.'

They filmed in Ooty – a ten-hour drive from Bangalore and situated at 7000 feet. From there they moved for a spell in Coonoor, 1000 feet below. Here they stayed in Hampton Manor, or 'Fawlty Towers', as the cast renamed it, and Peggy felt the need to explain to Dadie that this was a television programme. According to her the hotel was run by a depraved nobleman, and was of such discomfort that she wondered at its five star grading. There was no silence in the Indian nights, cicadas and bullfrogs were active, even jackals could sometimes be heard. The last sound of all would be the *chowkidar*, 'moving around at night, clearing his throat and spitting'.

In this relic of the Raj she explored Mrs Moore's loss of religious faith with James Fox, who, as she well knew, during ten years of passing through a dark spell of drug addiction and withdrawal from his acting career, had embraced Christianity as an evangelical convert. Although this was some time ago she eagerly questioned Fox about his faith. 'She knew where I was coming from, and asked me questions about how I believe, what I believe.'

Fox knew of Peggy's atheism, but found she respected his faith without engaging in 'jolly put-downs'. A particularly jealous sister of an evangelical mission tried, however, to collar Peggy and engage her purposefully, but Peggy would have none of that. She had 'extremely wise and loving values', said Fox; she had discarded Christianity but not its core values or the person of Christ.

Peggy remained friends with Fox and his family to the end of her life, although knowing 'jolly well that I was a believer', said Fox. It was while making the film that she told him how the Church had refused, at the time of her betrothal to Komisarjevsky, to sanctify their marriage and that this had turned her against it. She was, Fox thought, a 'very contemporary person', enjoying the benefits of freedom, even licence, while maintaining an attachment to the underlying virtues of Christianity.

One day they spent wholly on a train, shunting backwards and forwards over a series of horrendous viaducts – with views and waterfalls of 'an absolutely (for me) unparalleled beauty'. Aziz performed his running-board acrobatics over terrifying abysses – the day was both wonderful and at the same time she was extremely thankful when it had come to an end.

In its outcome *A Passage to India* was a success both financially and, among certain sectors, critically. But, its visual splendours and some of its performances apart, it was not a coherent or sensitive film although it conveyed, to a great and singular degree, Lean's mesmeric power. And in the end Lean was right about Peggy's Oscar. It was true that, as handled by Lean, the camera 'loves intelligence.

It loves to detect what's going on behind the face.' She was awarded her Oscar as Best Supporting Actress. As Peggy had flu badly she failed to turn up for the awards ceremony, and there was a mix-up which resulted in Angela Lansbury collecting it for her. Her old friend Michael Redgrave died the following day.

TWENTY

The Earth

My brain I'll prove the female to my soul.
Shakespeare, Richard II, V.v.6

'She is always April or May,' said Anthony Quayle, 'never October or November.' Peggy smiled briefly. 'It is not accurate,' she replied. 'Now I am December.' 'Never was there a December more like June.'

Julian Bream confirms a general impression that Peggy was depressed towards the end of her life. But, he said, she never talked about her family. It would seem Eliza wore her down two years before she died: mother and daughter had never really got on, and this depressed Peggy. But she kept it all to herself. And we have not heard her daughter's side of the story, which may be very different.

In October 1990 Antonia Fraser gave a party for Harold Pinter's sixtieth birthday to which sixty of his friends and those he had worked with were invited, among them Peggy. They took over a neighbourhood restaurant, an oddly shaped room with pillars and distant corners, tables tucked away. Amid the clatter and chatter, Pinter recalled that this 'very small, quite elderly lady' stood up and made a short speech. The room grew rapt and silent and the still 'extraordinary, commanding voice' penetrated to every corner. The only moment that for Pinter equalled this was when Laurence Olivier, on the top floor of his Brighton home, picked up the telephone to answer it and shouted down for 'Joan' to take the call.

In April 1991 Peggy spent a joyful three weeks in Canada with Nick. She loved the set-up there: a theatre company combined with a farm. 'No more plays,' she said, beaming, 'no more films, no more television, that's it, all done!' Some said that the visit was inadvisable and it only brought on her final illness: yet maybe she would not have been so determined to go if she had not had some presentiment of the end. None denied it made her very happy to see Nick for the last time.

Her last holiday before that had been in Norway: in fact, when she writes to George Rylands from Norway one can understand that her idea of heaven was on this earth and no other. She was a thoroughly down-to-earth hedonistic atheist, with no belief in an afterlife. She describes Trome in Norway as her idea of paradise: she had always longed, she said, to take Dadie there to share in the simplicity *and* the luxury, the unostentatious spaciousness where the whole place is dominated by the sea and the rocks. In a way, strangely, it is as if she sees herself as a small figure in a large landscape or setting, just as, all those years before, Sickert had painted her on stage. We have, she tells Dadie, swum every morning under the blue sky with the wind blowing pretty hard. She had a vigorous pagan idea which she maintained to the very last. It was consistent, one of a piece, allied with her integrity, and it connected with a poem she wrote when she was seventeen, then allying herself to the earth. This had given her a body which raged with unfulfilled longings.

The curious fact of Peggy was that while she was atheistic she remained to the end a passionate devotee of Shakespeare. One may truly say she worshipped him, while paradoxically his spirit, although disguised in his writing, was profoundly Christian. In conversation with me in 1989 she even criticized Peter Brook's landmark production of *King Lear* in 1961 for omitting the remorse of the men who put out Gloucester's eyes, 'Where Shakespeare has that scene where they repent, and Peter cut out so that I think he deprived Shakespeare of some of his redemption'. But there were two ways of looking at *Lear*, she added: that it is 'redemption and that it is devastatingly defeatist'.

A prison, soon to be outworn, she calls her body in that earlier poem, but paradoxically, too, she was very fully in the nature of a Shakespearian woman. For Shakespeare, woman's nature was absolute, like the earth, like an element in nature itself. Revealed or hidden, forward or retiring, her disposition might be good or evil, but still was absolute.

There had perhaps always been a deeply buried death wish in Peggy which remained intact to the end. Did it not echo Juliet's 'if love be blind,/It best agrees with night'? Soon she would be gone –

Only a sound and scent of you, Earth.

For Shakespeare, it was the men who changed. And the best men were, as in *Measure for Measure*, moulded out of faults. The regret in

Peggy's life was, perhaps, that she did not find a man as broad, as universal, as able to embrace many-sidedness as herself. Yet still what had influenced Peggy most in her life was male intelligence and the creative spirit as possessed by those men with whom she became involved. For other skills she may have drawn on actresses such as Edith Evans and Sybil Thorndike, but they were parallel talents, not first and foremost influences. Jean-Louis Barrault observed that one finds in an influence something already contained in oneself, in embryonic form, and that 'to submit to an influence is to discover oneself more quickly'. Discovering herself Peggy had become the supreme English actress of the flesh and the spirit.

Peggy's greatest achievement was to become sensitive to the world and nature, and express this sensitivity through her highly sophisticated and carefully developed techniques as an actress. She must have been deeply and unusually cared for by her own mother for her to be able to create the extraordinarily rich and attractive view of the feminine personality that she did in her roles. She responded to Shakespeare and embodied his ideal of womanhood. Shakespeare never sought to humiliate woman, nor did he make her disconnected in speech, feeble and frail, as Dickens so often did with his female creations. Likewise Shakespeare never sought, through his invention, revenge on the female sex as a whole. He never created maternal figures as imaginative compensation for any lack of proper mothering himself. As Peggy said of him, 'I think Shakespeare must have loved women very much ... he felt that even when women were capable of acts of cruelty or violence, there was a compulsion of emotion or frustration which forced them on.' For all her much-vaunted socialism and egalitarianism this is not only a very traditional view of women, it is also profoundly unexpected. She did not approve of what G. K. Chesterton called the 'plodding, elaborate, elephantine imitation' of men by women. Yet she would have been furious to believe she shared any opinion with Chesterton.

> Come night ... come, thou day in night,
> For thou wilt lie upon the wings of night
> Whiter than new snow on a raven's back.

On 23 May, soon after her return from Canada, Peggy had a severe stroke and was taken for a second time to the Royal Free Hospital in Hampstead. 'The last time I saw Peggy she was in a deep coma after a sudden stroke,' said Molly Keane. 'She looked even more beautiful and peaceful than I have ever seen her in life.' She never regained consciousness for the remaining three weeks of her life. For Harold Pinter, her death was shocking. It came right out of the blue. Pinter saw her twice in her coma. 'She was like this': he held up a closed fist. 'Not dead, not asleep; alive as a tight fist. Still a will there, a furious will, not wanting to give up.' She died on 24 June 1991. Her funeral was secretive, like her life.

'Are you going to the funeral?' someone asked Donald Sinden.

'I'm hoping to, when I can find out where it is.'

Most of her remaining relatives are cagey, uncommunicative, and a little unsure about whether it was their secrecy or her own they wanted to preserve. As far as we can ascertain, no one asked Peggy what her beliefs about her own privacy after her death might have been. We shall never know. I suspect she would not have minded much one way or the other, although she may have confessed, as Lytton Strachey did to Mary Hutchinson, 'I am afraid my biography will present a slightly shocking spectacle.'

Peggy adamantly refused to write about herself, and always put pen to paper with great difficulty; when Fabia Drake wrote her autobiography, *Blind Fortune*, in 1978, Peggy was encouraged to try but refused. Later, when one editor, an old friend, exhorted her to come up with something interesting for a book about her, saying 'Imagine you're talking to the public over your tea-table,' she retorted *avec froideur*, 'I wouldn't have the public to tea!'

Geoffrey Hill, the poet, once wrote of Charles Péguy, whom he translated, that the French dramatist was attractive because of 'a moral imperative ... certain people do seem ... to bear about them some secret of life and experience that one would like to know more about.' With her memorial service at Westminster Abbey in November 1991 Peggy surrendered at last 'to what she avoided in life,' wrote Nicholas de Jongh in the *Evening Standard*, and became 'a truly public person'.

One mystery at her life's end remains outstanding: her will. Somerset House is quite unable to trace it. While various newspapers reported in April and June 1992 that she had left to the Tate Gallery the portrait of herself in Venice painted by Walter Sickert in 1934–5 (as far as we know, she never went to Venice with Sickert), the fact of her will's publication remains unverified. She left £900,000, but to whom and in what proportions, we cannot say except that there was a large outstanding tax problem and that her nephews, nieces and cousins received £500 each.

Peggy Ashcroft was the supreme English-speaking actress of her time. Her great performances had burned themselves into the memory of all who had seen them. But they were ephemeral, as all great performances on stage are, and they leave nothing behind. Her films, television and sound recordings give an idea of the enormous diversity and depth of her career but do not reveal the heart and universality of her power. A riot of convictions and emotions beneath her serenity, she often expressed not so much the part she was playing but something within herself. No head waiters ever recognized her. She was wary of analysis, and loath to question why. She believed in getting up and doing it.

Plays

d. = director.   Theatres are in London's West End except where otherwise stated.

1926
22 MAY Margaret in *Dear Brutus* by J. M. Barrie (d. W. G. Fay), Birmingham Repertory Theatre

1927
MAY Bessie Carvel in *One Day More*, adapted from Joseph Conrad (d. Ralph Neale), Playroom Six

Mary Dunn in *The Return* by Charles Bennett (d. Alexander Field), Everyman Theatre, Hampstead

JULY Eve in *When Adam Delved* by George Paston (d. Nigel Playfair), Q Theatre, Kew

SEPTEMBER Joan Greenleaf in *Bird in Hand* by John Drinkwater (d. John Drinkwater), Birmingham Repertory Theatre

NOVEMBER Betty in *The Way of the World* by William Congreve (d. Nigel Playfair), Wyndham's Theatre

1928
JANUARY Anastasia in *The Fascinating Foundling* by Bernard Shaw (d. Henry Oscar), Mary Bruin in *The Land of Heart's Desire* by W. B. Yeats (d. Henry Oscar), double bill, Arts Theatre

Hester in *The Silver Cord* by Sidney Howard (d. Henry Oscar), on tour

SEPTEMBER Edith Strange in *Earthbound* by Leslie Goddard and Cecily Weir (d. Henry Oscar), Q Theatre, Kew

OCTOBER Kristina in *Easter* by August Strindberg, trans. E. & W. Oland (d. Allan Wade), Arts Theatre

NOVEMBER Eulalia in *A Hundred Years Old* by Serafin and Joaquin Quintero, trans. Helen and Harley Granville-Barker

(d. A. E. Filmer), Lyric Theatre, Hammersmith

1929

APRIL Lucy Deren in *Requital* by Molly Kerr (d. Molly Kerr), Everyman Theatre, Hampstead

MAY Sally Humphries in *Bees and Honey* by H. F. Maltby (d. H. F. Maltby), Sunday night production, Strand Theatre

JUNE Constance Neville in *She Stoops to Conquer* by Oliver Goldsmith (d. Nigel Playfair) on tour

SEPTEMBER Naemi in *Jew Süss* by Ashley Dukes (d. Matheson Lang and Reginald Denham), Duke of York's Theatre

1930

MAY Desdemona in *Othello* by William Shakespeare (d. Ellen van Volkenburg), Savoy Theatre

SEPTEMBER Judy Battle in *The Breadwinner* by Somerset Maugham (d. Athole Stewart), Vaudeville Theatre

1931

APRIL Pervaneh in *Hassan* by James Elroy Flecker (d. Gibson Cowan), OUDS, New Theatre, Oxford

Angela in *Charles the Third* adapted by Edgar Wallace from Curt Goetz (d. Mrs Edgar Wallace), Wyndham's Theatre

JUNE Anne in *A Knight Passed By* by Jan Fabricius, adapted by W. A. Darlington (d. Jan Fabricius), Ambassadors Theatre

Fanny in *Sea Fever* by Marcel Pagnol, adapted by Auriol Lee and John Van Druten (d. Auriol Lee), New Theatre

SEPTEMBER Marcela in *Take Two From One* by Georgio and Maria Martinez Sierra, adapted by Helen and Harley Granville Barker (d. Theodore Komisarjevsky), Haymarket Theatre

1932

FEBRUARY Juliet in *Romeo and Juliet* by William Shakespeare (d. John Gielgud), OUDS, New Theatre, Oxford

MAY Stella in *Le Coçu Magnifique* by Fernand Crommelynck, trans. Ivor Montagu (d. Theodore Komisarjevsky), Stage Society, Globe Theatre

JUNE Salome Westaway in *The Secret Woman* by Eden Phillpotts (d. Nancy Price), Duchess Theatre

Season with the Old Vic Company at the Old Vic Theatre, September 1932–May 1933:

SEPTEMBER Cleopatra in *Caesar and Cleopatra* by Bernard Shaw (d. Harcourt Williams)

OCTOBER Imogen in *Cymbeline* by William Shakespeare (d. Harcourt Williams)

NOVEMBER Rosalind in *As You Like It* by William Shakespeare (d. Harcourt Williams)

[NOVEMBER Fräulein Elsa in *Fräulein Elsa* by Arthur Schnitzler adapted by Theodore Komisarjevsky (d. Theodore Komisarjevsky), Independent Theatre Club, Kingsway Theatre]

DECEMBER Portia in *The Merchant of Venice* by William Shakespeare (d. John Gielgud)

1933

JANUARY Perdita in *The Winter's Tale* by William Shakespeare (d. Harcourt Williams)

Kate Hardcastle in *She Stoops to Conquer* by Oliver Goldsmith (d. Harcourt Williams)

FEBRUARY Mary Stuart in *Mary Stuart* by John Drinkwater (d. Harcourt Williams)

MARCH Juliet in *Romeo and Juliet* by William Shakespeare (d. Harcourt Williams)

Lady Teazle in *The School for Scandal* by Richard Brinsley Sheridan (d. Harcourt Williams)

SEPTEMBER Inken Peters in *Before Sunset* by Gerard Hauptmann, adapted by Miles Malleson (d. Miles Malleson), Shaftesbury Theatre

1934

FEBRUARY Vasantesena in *The Golden Toy* by Carl Zuckmayer, book and lyrics Dion Titheradge (d. Ludwig Berger), Coliseum Theatre

OCTOBER Lucia Maubel in *The Life That I Gave Him* by Luigi Pirandello, adapted by Clifford Bax (d. Frank Birch), Little Theatre

1935

SPRING Thérèse Paradis in *Mesmer* by Beverly Nichols (d. Theodore Komisarjevsky), on tour

OCTOBER Juliet in *Romeo and Juliet* by William Shakespeare, (d. John Gielgud), New Theatre

1936

MAY Nina in *The Seagull* by Anton Chekhov, trans. Theodore Komisarjevsky (d. Theodore Komisarjevsky), New Theatre

1937

JANUARY Lise in *High Tor* by Maxwell Anderson (d. Guthrie McClintic), Martin Beck Theater, New York
John Gielgud Season at the Queen's Theatre, September 1937–June 1938:
SEPTEMBER The Queen in *Richard II* by William Shakespeare (d. John Gielgud)
NOVEMBER Lady Teazle in *The School for Scandal* by Richard Brinsley Sheridan (d. Tyrone Guthrie)

1938

JANUARY Irina in *Three Sisters* by Anton Chekhov, trans. Constance Garnett (d. Michel Saint-Denis)
APRIL Portia in *The Merchant of Venice* by William Shakespeare (d. John Gielgud and Glen Byam Shaw)
OCTOBER Yeliena in *The White Guard* by Mikhail Bulgakov, adapted by Rodney Ackland (d. Michel Saint-Denis), Phoenix Theatre
DECEMBER Viola in *Twelfth Night* by William Shakespeare (d. Michel Saint-Denis), Phoenix Theatre

1939

MAY Isolde in *Weep For The Spring* by Stephen Haggard (d. Michel Saint-Denis), on tour
AUGUST Cecily Cardew in *The Importance of Being Earnest* by Oscar Wilde (d. John Gielgud), Globe Theatre

1940

MARCH Dinah Sylvester in *Cousin Muriel* by Clemence Dane (d. Norman Marshall), Globe Theatre
JUNE Miranda (from Jessica Tandy) in *The Tempest* by William Shakespeare (d. George Devine and Marius Goring), Old Vic Theatre

1941

JANUARY Mrs de Winter in *Rebecca* by Daphne du Maurier (d. George Devine), on tour

1942

OCTOBER Cecily Cardew in *The Importance of Being Earnest* by Oscar Wilde (d. John Gielgud), Phoenix Theatre

1943

OCTOBER Catherine Lisle in *The Dark River* by Rodney Ackland (d. Rodney Ackland), Whitehall Theatre

1944

AUGUST Ophelia in *Hamlet* by William Shakespeare (d. George Rylands), on tour
John Gielgud Season at the Haymarket Theatre, October 1944–June 1945:

OCTOBER Ophelia in *Hamlet* by William Shakespeare (d. George Rylands)

1945

JANUARY Titania in *A Midsummer Night's Dream* by William Shakespeare (d. Nevill Coghill)

APRIL The Duchess in *The Duchess of Malfi* by John Webster (d. George Rylands)

1947

MAY Evelyn Holt in *Edward, My Son* by Robert Morley and Noël Langley (d. Peter Ashmore), His Majesty's Theatre

1948

SEPTEMBER Evelyn Holt in *Edward, My Son* by Robert Morley and Noël Langley (d. Peter Ashmore), Martin Beck Theater, New York

1949

FEBRUARY Catherine Sloper in *The Heiress* by Ruth and Augustus Goetz (d. John Gielgud), Haymarket Theatre

NOVEMBER Juliet in the Balcony Scene (with Paul Scofield) from *Romeo*

and Juliet by William Shakespeare, *Merely Players*, Coliseum
Theatre

1950

JUNE Beatrice in *Much Ado About Nothing* by William Shakespeare
(d. John Gielgud), Memorial Theatre, Stratford-upon-Avon

JULY Cordelia in *King Lear* by William Shakespeare (d. John
Gielgud), Memorial Theatre, Stratford-upon-Avon

NOVEMBER Viola in *Twelfth Night* by William Shakespeare (d. Hugh
Hunt) Old Vic Theatre

1951

MARCH Electra in *Electra* by Sophocles, trans. J. T. Sheppard (d.
Michel Saint-Denis), Old Vic Theatre

MAY Mistress Page in *The Merry Wives of Windsor* by William
Shakespeare (d. Hugh Hunt), Old Vic Theatre

1952

MARCH Hester Collyer in *The Deep Blue Sea* by Terence Rattigan (d.
Frith Banbury), Duchess Theatre

NOVEMBER Cassius in the Quarrel Scene (with Diana Wynyard) from
Julius Caesar by William Shakespeare, Green Room Rag

1953

MARCH Portia in *The Merchant of Venice* by William Shakespeare (d.
Denis Carey), Memorial Theatre, Stratford-upon-Avon

APRIL Cleopatra in *Antony and Cleopatra* by William Shakespeare
(d. Glen Byam Shaw), Memorial Theatre, Stratford-upon-
Avon

NOVEMBER Cleopatra in *Antony and Cleopatra* by William Shakespeare
(d. Glen Byam Shaw), Prince's Theatre and subsequent
European tour

1954

SEPTEMBER Hedda in *Hedda Gabler* by Henrik Ibsen, adapted by Max
Faber (d. Peter Ashmore), Lyric Theatre, Hammersmith;
later Westminster Theatre, and New Theatre, Oslo

1955

JULY Beatrice in *Much Ado About Nothing* by William Shakespeare (d. John Gielgud), Palace Theatre

1956

APRIL Miss Madrigal in *The Chalk Garden* by Enid Bagnold (d. John Gielgud), Haymarket Theatre

OCTOBER Shen Te/Shui Ta in *The Good Woman of Setzuan* by Bertolt Brecht, trans. Eric Bentley (d. George Devine), Royal Court Theatre

1957

APRIL Rosalind in *As You Like It* by William Shakespeare (d. Glen Byam Shaw), Memorial Theatre, Stratford-upon-Avon

JULY Imogen in *Cymbeline* by William Shakespeare (d. Peter Hall), Memorial Theatre, Stratford-upon-Avon

1958

SEPTEMBER Anthology, *Portraits of Women*, devised by Peggy Ashcroft and Ossian Ellis, Lyceum Theatre, Edinburgh

OCTOBER Julia Rajk in *Shadow of Heroes* by Robert Ardrey (d. Peter Hall)

1959

JANUARY Eva Delaware in *The Coast of Coromandel* by J. M. Sadler (d. John Fernald), on tour

NOVEMBER Rebecca West in *Rosmersholm* by Henrik Ibsen, trans. Ann Jellicoe (d. George Devine), Royal Court Theatre; later Comedy Theatre

1960

JUNE Katharina in *The Taming of the Shrew* by William Shakespeare (d. John Barton), Memorial Theatre, Stratford-upon-Avon

AUGUST Paulina in *The Winter's Tale* by William Shakespeare (d. Peter Wood), Memorial Theatre, Stratford-upon-Avon

DECEMBER The Duchess in *The Duchess of Malfi* by John Webster (d. Donald McWhinnie), Aldwych Theatre

1961

JUNE *The Hollow Crown*, Anthology, devised by John Barton (d. John Barton), Aldwych Theatre; later European tour; revived 1968 Aldwych Theatre, 1986 Swan Theatre, Stratford-upon-Avon

Some Words on Women, and Some Women's Words, Reading, devised by Peggy Ashcroft, Senate House, London; later European tour

OCTOBER Emilia in *Othello* by William Shakespeare (d. Franco Zeffirelli), Royal Shakespeare Company, Stratford-upon-Avon

DECEMBER Madame Ranevsky in *The Cherry Orchard* by Anton Chekhov, adapted by John Gielgud (d. Michel Saint-Denis), RSC Aldwych Theatre

1962

MAY *The Vagaries of Love*, Anthology, devised by John Barton (d. John Barton), Belgrade Theatre, Coventry

1963

JULY Margaret of Anjou in *The Wars of the Roses* (*Henry VI, Edward IV, Richard III*) by William Shakespeare, adapted and edited by John Barton (d. Peter Hall and John Barton), RSC Stratford-upon-Avon; later Aldwych Theatre and revived Stratford 1964

1964

MARCH Madame Arkadina in *The Seagull* by Anton Chekhov, trans. Ann Jellicoe (d. George Devine), Queen's Theatre

1966

JUNE Mother in *Days in the Trees* by Marguerite Duras, trans. Sonia Orwell (d. John Schlesinger), RSC Aldwych Theatre

1967

JUNE Mrs Alving in *Ghosts* by Henrik Ibsen, adapted by Denis Cannan, William Archer (d. Alan Bridges), RSC Aldwych Theatre

1969

JANUARY Agnes in *A Delicate Balance* by Edward Albee (d. Peter Hall), RSC Aldwych Theatre

JULY Beth in *Landscape* by Harold Pinter (d. Peter Hall), RSC Aldwych Theatre

OCTOBER Queen Katherine in *Henry VIII* by William Shakespeare (d. Trevor Nunn) RSC Stratford-upon-Avon

1970

JULY Volumnia in *The Plebeians Rehearse the Uprising* by Günter Grass, trans. Ralph Mannheim (d. David Jones), RSC Aldwych Theatre

1971

JULY Claire Launes in *The Lovers of Viorne* by Marguerite Duras, trans. Barbara Bray (d. Jonathan Hales), Royal Court Theatre

1972

JANUARY The Wife in *All Over* by Edward Albee (d. Peter Hall), RSC Aldwych Theatre

JULY Lady Boothroyd in *Lloyd George Knew My Father* by William Douglas-Home (d. Robin Midgley), Savoy Theatre

1973

OCTOBER Beth in *Landscape* by Harold Pinter (d. Peter Hall), RSC Aldwych Theatre
Flora in *A Slight Ache* by Harold Pinter (d. Peter James), RSC Aldwych Theatre

1975

JANUARY Ella Rentheim in *John Gabriel Borkman* by Henrik Ibsen, trans. Inga-Stina Ewbank and Peter Hall (d. Peter Hall), National Theatre, Old Vic

MARCH Winnie in *Happy Days* by Samuel Beckett (d. Peter Hall), National Theatre, Old Vic

1976

FEBRUARY Lilian Baylis in *Tribute to the Lady* devised by Val May (d. Val May), National Theatre, Old Vic

OCTOBER Lidya in *Old World* by Alexei Arbuzov, trans. Ariadne Nikolaeff (d. Terry Hands), RSC Aldwych Theatre

1977
SEPTEMBER Winnie in *Happy Days* by Samuel Beckett (d. Peter Hall), NT Lyttelton Theatre
Fanny Farrelli in *Watch on the Rhine* by Lillian Hellman (d. Mike Ockrent), NT Lyttelton Theatre

1981
FEBRUARY Voice 2 in *Family Voices* by Harold Pinter (d. Peter Hall), NT platform
NOVEMBER Countess of Rousillon in *All's Well That Ends Well* by William Shakespeare (d. Trevor Nunn), RSC Stratford-upon-Avon; later Barbican Theatre

1986
FEBRUARY Lilian Baylis in *Save the Wells*, devised by Val May (d. Keith Gray and Richard Gregson), Royal Opera House

1991
JUNE Mrs Swan in *In The Native State* by Tom Stoppard (d. John Tydeman), BBC Radio

Films and Television

1933 Ollalla Quintina in *The Wandering Jew* (d. Maurice Elvey)
1935 The Crofter's Wife in *The Thirty-nine Steps* (d. Alfred Hitchcock)
1936 Anna Carpenter in *Rhodes of Africa* (d. Berthold Viertel)
1939 Miranda in *The Tempest* (BBC TV; d. Dallas Bower)
Viola in *Twelfth Night* (BBC TV; d. Michel Saint-Denis)
1940 The Woman in *Channel Incident* (d. Anthony Asquith)
1941 Fleur Lisle in *Quiet Wedding* (d. Anthony Asquith)
1942 ATS Girl in *A New Lot* (d. Carol Reed)
1958 Julia Rajk in *Shadow of Heroes* (BBC TV; d. Peter Hall)
Mother Mathilde in *The Nun's Story* (d. Fred Zinnemann)

1962 Madame Ranevsky in *The Cherry Orchard* (BBC TV; d. Michel Saint-Denis)

1964 Margaret in *The Wars of the Roses* (BBC TV; d. Peter Hall and Robin Midgley)

1965 Rebecca West in *Rosmersholm* (BBC TV; d. Michael Barry)

1966 Mother in *Days in the Trees* (BBC TV; d. Waris Hussein)
Mrs Patrick Campbell in *Dear Liar* (Granada TV; d. Christopher McMaster)

1968 Aunt Hanna in *Secret Ceremony* (d. Joseph Losey)
Olga Knipper in *From Chekhov with Love* (TV Rediffusion; d. Bill Turner)

1971 Belle in *Sunday, Bloody Sunday* (d. John Schlesinger)
Sonia Tolstoy in *The Last Journey* (TV Granada; d. Peter Potter)

1975 Lady Gray in *Der Fussgänger (The Pedestrian)* (d. Maximilian Schell)

1976 Lady Tattle in *Joseph Andrews* (d. Tony Richardson)

1978 Lady Gee in *Hullabaloo over George and Bonnie's Pictures* (d. James Ivory)
Queen Mary in *Edward and Mrs Simpson* (Thames TV; d. Waris Hussein)

1980 Frau Messner in *Caught on a Train* (BBC TV; d. Peter Duffell)
Jean Wilsher in *Cream in My Coffee* (London Weekend TV; d. Gavin Millar)

1982 The Rat Wife in *Little Eyolf* (BBC TV; d. Michael Darlow)

1984 Barbie Batchelor in *The Jewel in the Crown* (Thames TV; d. Christopher Morahan)
Mrs Moore in *A Passage to India* (d. David Lean)

1986 Agatha Christie in *Murder by the Book* (TVS TV; d. Lawrence Gordon Clark)
Miss Dubber in *A Perfect Spy* (BBC TV; d. Peter Smith)

1988 Nettie in *The Heat of the Day* (Granada TV; d. Christopher Morahan)

1989 Lillian in *She's Been Away* (BBC TV; d. Peter Hall)

ACKNOWLEDGEMENTS

I must thank the following for consenting to be interviewed, for sending or collecting information, and for help in one or more of innumerable other ways: Paul Ableman, Lord Annan, William Ashcroft, Frith Banbury, Steven Barry, John Barton, Sally Beauman, Michael Billington, Julian Bream, David Brierley, Richard Brooks, Kevin Brownlow, Alison Carter, Michael Collins, Angela Cheyne, Andy Cornwall, Jackie Cox, R. D. Davies, Tamsin Day-Lewis, Diana Devlin, Margaret Drabble, the late Fabia Drake, Alexandra Erskine, Barbara Everett, Abdel El Kader Farrah, The Rt Hon Michael Foot, James Fox, Sir John Gielgud, Geordie Greig, the late Margaret Harris, Sir Peter Hall, Jocelyn Herbert, Pauline Jameson, Martin Jenkins, Molly Keane, Francis King, Catherine Lambert, John Lancaster, Mark Le Fanu, Lord Longford, Michael Meyer, Christopher Morahan, Trevor Nunn, the late Trekkie Parsons, Blaise Pascal, Harold Pinter, Tim Pigott-Smith, Stephen Poliakoff, Wendy Robinson, Pierre Rouve, John Russell Taylor, Dr George Rylands, the late Suria Saint-Denis, Alexander Schouvalov, Donald Sinden, Yolanda Sonnabend, Lady Spender, the late Sir Stephen Spender, Catherine and Anthony Storr, John Swanzy, Clive Swift, the late Lord Tweedsmuir, Lord Tweedsmuir, Wendy Trewin, John Tydeman, Harriet Walter, John Walsh, Marina Warner, Prue Wilson.

Finally I thank my publisher, Ion Trewin, for all his help; Richard Mangan for advice on illustrations; I have based my chronology partly on that of Richard Findlater, as compiled for his *These Our Actors* (London, 1985); I thank also Jane Birkett for her careful copy-editing, David Bowron for the index, Linda Rowley for her typing and processing various drafts and Cassia Joll and Rachel Leyshon at Weidenfeld & Nicolson for all their work.

The children of Peggy Ashcroft have refused to let me quote from the unpublished letters which the recipients have donated to library collections where they may be read by the public. I must register my sense of confusion at this late action of the heirs, both of whom have lived abroad since the 1960s, for the letters to friends are in some measure an indication of the absence of family, and were originally made available to me by the recipients themselves or their executors. Given the donation of these letters to library collections, and the permission granted to Peggy's previous biographer to quote from those available to him, this restriction seems to me excessive. As a well-respected critic wrote after Peggy's memorial service in Westminster Abbey she had now surrendered to what she had avoided in life and become a truly public person.

G. O'C

ACKNOWLEDGEMENTS

I am grateful to the following organisations for the supply of information, published articles and/or broadcast talks or interviews, on which I have drawn:

BBC Radio (Sound and Written) Archives	*Daily Mail*
	Daily Telegraph
BBC Television	*Era*
The Royal National Theatre	*Evening News*
The Royal Shakespeare Company	*Evening Standard*
Granada Television	*Financial Times*
The British Theatre Museum	*Manchester Guardian* (and *Guardian*)
Imperial War Museum	*New Statesman*
Army Regimental Record Office	*New York Times*
St Catherine's House	*Observer*
Somerset House	*Spectator*
Colindale Newspaper Library	*Stratford-Upon-Avon Herald*
Bodleian Library Oxford	*Sunday Express*
Central Library, Westgate Oxford	*Sunday Times*
Lewes Public Library	*Sunday Telegraph*
King's College Library, Cambridge	*Tatler and Bystander*
Sussex University Library	*The Times*
Birmingham Post	*TV Times*
Daily Express	*Vogue*
Daily Herald	

Few books on the British theatre since the 1930s are without at least a passing reference to Peggy: following is a list of those works on which I have drawn most frequently. (The place of publication is London unless otherwise indicated.)

SELECTED BIBLIOGRAPHY

Paul Ableman, *The Mouth & Oral Sex* (Running Man Press, 1969)

James Agate, *Ego* (9 vols., 1935–48: vol. I, Hamish Hamilton, 1935; vol. 2, Gollancz, 1936; vols. 3–9, Harrap, 1938–48)

——*Brief Chronicles* (Cape, 1943)

——*Red Letter Nights* (Cape, 1944)

Charles Allen (ed.), *Plain Tales from the Raj* (André Deutsch, 1975)

Noël Annan, *Our Age: Portrait of a Generation* (Weidenfeld and Nicolson, 1990)

Enid Bagnold, *Enid Bagnold's Autobiography* (Heinemann, 1969)

Deirdre Bair, *Samuel Beckett* (Cape, 1978)

Sally Beauman, *The Royal Shakespeare Company: A History of Ten Decades* (Oxford, 1982)

Michael Billington, *Peggy Ashcroft, 1907–1991* (Mandarin, 1991)

Denys Blakelock, *Advice to a Player* (Heinemann, 1957)

Peter Brook, *The Empty Space* (MacGibbon and Kee, 1969)

Vincent Brome, *J. B. Priestley* (Hamish Hamilton, 1988)

Ivor Brown, *The Way of My World* (Collins, 1954)

Kevin Brownlow, *Lean* (Richard Cohen, 1995)

William Buchan, *The Rags of Time* (Buchan and Enright, 1990)

Hal Burton (ed.), *Great Acting* (BBC Publications, 1967)

——(ed.), *Acting in the Sixties* (BBC Publications, 1970)

John Casson, *Lewis and Sybil: A Memoir* (Collins, 1974)

Marion Cole, *Fogie: The Life of Elsie Fogerty, 1865–1945* (Peter Davies, 1967)

W. A. Darlington, *6001 Nights: Forty Years a Dramatic Critic* (Harrap, 1960)

Diana Devlin, *A Speaking Part: Lewis Casson* (Hodder and Stoughton, 1982)

Fabia Drake, *Blind Fortune* (Kimber, 1978)

Martin Baulm Duberman, *Paul Robeson* (Bodley Head, 1989)

Richard Findlater, *Michael Redgrave: Actor* (Heinemann, 1956)

——*These Our Actors* (Elm Tree, 1983)

——*Lilian Baylis: The Lady of the Old Vic* (Allen Lane, 1975)

Stephen Fay, *Power Play: The Life and Times of Peter Hall* (Hodder and Stoughton, 1995)

Kate Fleming, *Celia Johnson: A Biography* (Weidenfeld and Nicolson, 1991)

Bryan Forbes, *Ned's Girl* (Elm Tree, 1977)

James Forsyth, *Tyrone Guthrie* (Hamish Hamilton, 1976)

Angela Fox, *Slightly Foxed* (Collins, 1986)

——*Completely Foxed* (Collins, 1989)

John Gielgud, *Early Stages* (Macmillan, 1939)

——*Stage Directions* (Heinemann, 1963)

——*Distinguished Company* (Heinemann Educational, 1972)

——*An Actor and His Times* (Sidgwick and Jackson, 1979)

Val Gielgud, *Years in a Mirror* (Bodley Head, 1965)

Logan Gourlay (ed.), *Olivier* (Weidenfeld and Nicolson, 1973)

Alec Guinness, *Blessings in Disguise* (Hamish Hamilton, 1985)

Tyrone Guthrie, *A Life in the Theatre* (Hamish Hamilton, 1960)

Rupert Hart-Davis, *The Power of Chance: A Memoir* (Sinclair-Stevenson, 1991)

——(ed.) *The Lyttelton Hart-Davis Letters* (3 vols. John Murray, 1978)

Harold Hobson, *Ralph Richardson* (Barrie and Rockliff, 1958)

——*Unfinished Journey* (Weidenfeld and Nicolson, 1978)

——*Theatre in Britain* (Phaidon, 1984)

Anthony Holden, *Laurence Olivier: A Biography* (Weidenfeld and Nicolson, 1988)

Michael Holroyd, *Lytton Strachey: The New Biography* (Chatto and Windus, 1994)

Elizabeth Howe, *The First English Actresses: Women and Drama 1660–1700* (Cambridge, 1992)

Richard Huggett, *Binkie Beaumont, Eminence Gris to the West End Theatre 1933–1973* (Hodder and Stoughton, 1989)

Eric Keown, *Peggy Ashcroft* (Barrie and Rockliff, 1955)

Theodore Komisarjevsky, *Myself and the Theatre* (Heinemann, 1929)

James Lees-Milne, *A Mingled Measure: Diaries 1953–1972* (John Murray, 1994)

Sheridan Morley, *Robert, My Father* (Weidenfeld and Nicolson, 1993)

John Mortimer, *Character Parts* (Viking, 1986)

Laurence Olivier, *Confessions of an Actor* (Weidenfeld and Nicolson, 1982)

——*On Acting* (Weidenfeld and Nicolson, 1986)

David Pannick, *Advocates* (Oxford, 1992)

J. B. Priestley, *Midnight on the Desert* (Heinemann, 1937)

Anthony Quayle, *A Time to Speak* (Century, 1990)

Corin Redgrave, *Michael, My Father* (Richard Cohen, 1995)

Michael Redgrave, *In My Mind's Eye* (Weidenfeld and Nicolson, 1983)

Essie Robeson, *Paul Robeson, Negro* (London, 1930)

Donald Sinden, *A Touch of the Memoirs* (Hodder and Stoughton, 1982)

Robert Speaight, *The Property Basket* (Collins, 1970)

Frederick Spotts (ed.), *Letters of Leonard Woolf* (Weidenfeld and Nicolson, 1980)

J. C. Trewin, *The Theatre Since 1900* (Dakers, 1951)

——*The Birmingham Repertory Theatre, 1913–1963* (Barrie and Rockliff, 1963)

——*Shakespeare on the English Stage 1900–1964* (Barrie and Rockliff, 1964)

——*Edith Evans* (Barrie and Rockliff, 1964)

Kenneth Tynan, *He That Plays the King* (Longman, 1950)

——*Curtains* (Longman, 1961)

Irving Wardle, *The Theatres of George Devine* (Cape, 1978)

E. G. Harcourt Williams, *Old Vic Saga* (Winchester, 1949)

Audrey Williamson, *Old Vic Drama* (Rockliff, 1951)

Sidney Howard White, *Alan Ayckbourn* (New York, 1979)

Billie Whitelaw, *Billie Whitelaw ... Who He?* (John Curtis: Hodder and Stoughton, 1995)

INDEX

Other than in the entry under her name Peggy Ashcroft is referred to as PA.